SO-ADZ-393

DISCARD

AUG 0 6 2003

MAIN

Nearby History

AMERICAN ASSOCIATION FOR STATE AND LOCAL HISTORY
BOOK SERIES

Publications Chair
Ruby Rogers
Cincinnati Museum Center

Editorial Advisory Board
Terry Barnhart, Eastern Illinois University
J. D. Britton, Ohio Historical Society
Carrie Caldwell, Oakland Museum
David Donath, Woodstock Foundation, Inc.
Max J. Evans, Utah State Historical Society
Michael Hammond, Augua Caliente Cultural Museum
Debbie Kmetz, State Historical Society of Wisconsin
Ian Quimby, Historical Society of Pennsylvania
Philip V. Scarpino, Indiana University-Purdue University, Indianapolis
Constance B. Schulz, University of South Carolina
Lawrence J. Sommer, Nebraska State Historical Society
Gretchen Sullivan Sorin, Cooperstown Graduate Program
Bryant F. Tolles Jr., University of Delaware
George L. Vogt, State Historical Society of Wisconsin
Valerie Wheat, Museum Reference Center, Smithsonian Institution

About the Series
The American Association for State and Local History Book Series publishes technical and professional information for those who practice and support history, and addresses issues critical to the field of state and local history. To submit a proposal or manuscript to the series, please request proposal guidelines from AASLH headquarters: AASLH Book Series, 1717 Church St., Nashville, Tennessee 37203. Telephone: (615) 320-3203. Fax: (615) 327-9013. Web site: www.aaslh.org.

Nearby History

Exploring the Past around You

Second Edition

David E. Kyvig and Myron A. Marty

ALTAMIRA
PRESS

A Division of
ROWMAN & LITTLEFIELD PUBLISHERS, INC.
Walnut Creek • Lanham • New York • Oxford

ALTAMIRA PRESS
A Division of Rowman & Littlefield Publishers, Inc.
1630 North Main Street, #367
Walnut Creek, CA 94596
http://www.altamirapress.com

Rowman & Littlefield Publishers, Inc.
4720 Boston Way,
Lanham, MD 20706

12 Hid's Copse Road
Cumnor Hill, Oxford OX2 9JJ, England

Copyright © 2000 by AltaMira Press

"A Worker Reads History" from SELECTED POEMS by Bertolt Brecht, translated by
H. R. Hays, copyright © 1947 by Bertolt Brecht and H. R. Hays and renewed 1975 by
Stefan S. Brecht and H. R. Hays, reprinted by permission of Harcourt, Inc.

All rights reserved. No part of this publication may be reproduced,
stored in a retrieval system, or transmitted in any form or by any
means, electronic, mechanical, photocopying, recording, or otherwise,
without the prior permission of the publisher.

British Library Cataloguing in Publication Information Available

Library of Congress Cataloging-in-Publication Data

Kyvig, David E.
  Nearby history : exploring the past around you / David E. Kyvig and Myron A. Marty.—
2nd ed.
    p. cm.—(American Association for State and Local History book series)
    Includes bibliographical references and index.
    ISBN 0-7425-0270-8 (cloth : alk. paper)—ISBN 0-7425-0271-6 (pbk. : alk. paper)
    1. United States—History, Local. I. Marty, Myron A. II. Title. III. Series.

E180.5.N98   2000
973—dc21   00-026654

Printed in the United States of America

∞™ The paper used in this publication meets the minimum requirements of American
National Standard for Information Sciences—Permanence of Paper for Printed Library
Materials, ANSI/NISO Z39.48-1992.

A Worker Reads History

Who built the seven towers of Thebes?
The books are filled with names of kings.
Was it kings who hauled the craggy blocks of stone?
And Babylon, so many times destroyed,
Who built the city up each time? In which of Lima's houses,
That city glittering with gold, lived those who built it?
In the evening when the Chinese wall was finished
Where did the masons go? Imperial Rome
Is full of arcs of triumph. Who reared them up? Over whom
Did the Caesars triumph? Byzantium lives in song,
Were all her dwellings palaces? And even in Atlantis of the legend
The night the sea rushed in,
The drowning men still bellowed for their slaves.

Young Alexander plundered India.
He alone?
Caesar beat the Gauls.
Was there not even a cook in his army?
Philip of Spain wept as his fleet
Was sunk and destroyed. Were there no other tears?
Frederick the Great triumphed in the Seven Years War. Who
Triumphed with him?

Each page a victory,
At whose expense the victory ball?
Every ten years a great man,
Who paid the piper?

So many particulars.
So many questions.

—Bertolt Brecht

Contents

Appendices

Preface to the Second Edition

Two decades ago we published a small book intended for students in history courses and persons with an independent interest in exploring their own past. We were convinced that students, accustomed to looking at history as a series of national and world events, could benefit from examining a single family. At the same time, we wished to show genealogists concerned with single families that their work could be enriched by viewing their families in a broader context. We sought to demonstrate to everyone that most historical research techniques could be mastered by any literate person. Finally, we particularly wanted to make clear that accurate knowledge of the past, whether gained from one's own efforts or the work of others, could be not only interesting for its own sake but also useful in understanding the present.

Whether *Your Family History: A Handbook for Research and Writing* (Arlington Heights, IL: Harlan Davidson, 1978) met our objectives is for others to decide. Whatever the judgment, interest in the book persuaded us that the goals were worth pursuing further. We therefore decided to enlarge our focus to include the widest possible range of subjects within the realm of ordinary individual, family, and community life. The result was *Nearby History: Exploring the Past around You* (Nashville: American Association for State and Local History, 1982).

Nearby History sought to bring together historical studies of the family, the community, and the built environment. So much unites these fields, we felt, that artificial divisions should not be allowed to persist. Each area influences the others, and all involve everyone's immediate world. We attempted to demonstrate the excitement and value that may be derived from exploring this world. Both to clarify the range of opportunities and to suggest specific possibilities, we offered an extensive list of questions for investigating the family, buildings, neighborhoods, institutions, and communities as a whole. Thereafter, several chapters described methods for using evidence from the nearby world, such as written documents, oral testimony, visual records, material objects, buildings, and landscapes. These chapters could be used independently or in any sequence, depending upon the nature of the topic under study. Next, we offered some ideas for organizing and sharing the results of a personal inquiry into the past. In a final chapter, we described the work of academic historians in the fields of family and community history. By underscoring the fact that academic and nonacademic historians shared interests, we hoped to promote greater communication and cooperation among them.

When we began research for *Nearby History*, we were conscious of the distinctions frequently drawn between amateur and professional historians. The conventional wisdom said that amateurs reworked the local past, while professionals were more concerned with national and world history. The argument continued: the concerns of amateurs were relatively unimportant and frequently too personal to be taken seriously, while professionals worked on important issues with a sense of detachment and clinical skill that deserved respect; amateurs were driven by nostalgia, professionals by a desire to find the truth; amateurs thought in parochial terms, whereas professionals used terms cosmic in character and part of a universal language.

As our work progressed, these distinctions blurred. Many professionals had found value in the detailed consideration of a single community or a local institution, while many amateurs showed sensitivity to the larger picture. Although we were by training academic historians and had spent most of our careers in college and university settings, we had been led by a variety of experiences to see the futility of trying to draw sharp lines between historians of one sort and those of another. These experiences included teaching adult students, participating in the activities of state and local historical associations, doing family history, working in archives, and serving in an agency that supported a full range of activities in history.

As the differences between kinds of historians became less clear, we realized that while there were unquestionably many varieties of interests, there was really only one audience. Some members made their living as historians; others did so in different ways. This was about the only clear-cut distinction between professionals and amateurs.

Consequently, we wrote a book that sought to answer the questions of all historians, no matter how they earned their living. We were conscious that the book merely provided an introduction to the field of nearby history, and almost any of the topics with which it dealt could have been developed in much greater detail and depth. For that reason we provided extensive bibliographies at the end of most chapters. We also recognized the important difference in methods and concerns between historians of the close at hand and historians of the world out there. The former, we believed, tended to focus on the specific. They knew about this person and that place, this building and that organization. The latter were good at identifying, describing, analyzing, and interpreting the universals of history: movements, developments, causes and effects, and so on. One of our principal goals, as the final chapter showed, was to help historians of all kinds find ways to link the particulars with the universals.

Nearby History sought to help increase the effectiveness of research and writing about the history of people and places nearby. To this end we aimed to help our readers understand the nature and purposes of nearby history, realize the importance of caring about it, and know how to research and write or tell about it. At times we informed. At other times we advocated, cautiously and, we hoped, subtly. And at other times we showed step by step the work necessary to accomplish certain goals.

The reception accorded *Nearby History* gratified us enormously. Time and again people wrote or told us that the book helped them with their own historical work and enabled them to see their individual undertaking as part of a larger enterprise. Readers in Arizona, Illinois, Indiana, Iowa, Missouri, Ohio, South Carolina, and Washington, D.C., invited us to meetings, conferences, and workshops at which enthusiasm for exploring the nearby past was as evident as the creativity being brought to it. These experiences, together with the positive reviews the book consistently received, confirmed our initial view that the gap between history within and outside the professional academy could be bridged. The response to the book sustained our belief that there exists a community of persons interested in the close-at-hand past, eager to explore it in a serious, careful fashion, and needing only some guidance in approach in order to pursue satisfying and effective historical inquiries regarding their own immediate circumstances. We were also pleased to learn that teachers of historical research methods who did not focus on nearby subjects also found the book useful. The reception of our efforts has been all that any author could hope for, and we want our readers and reviewers to know that we appreciate the encouragement they have given us to take our work further.

When readers of *Nearby History* told us that the book met a significant need, our first impulse was to provide more detailed and specific guidance to historians interested in particular aspects of the nearby world. We launched a series of volumes addressing selected topics in a manner similar to the approach we had taken to the general topic of nearby history. The first five of those volumes were initially published, as was *Nearby History*, by the American Association for State and Local History. The authors were all specialists in the topic they addressed, talented teachers, and fellow believers in the notion that, with a little straightforward guidance, most people are capable of investigating their own history. Those books, published as the Nearby History Series between 1986 and 1990, and their authors were *Local Schools: Exploring Their History* by Ronald Butchart; *Houses and Homes: Exploring Their History* by Barbara J. Howe, Dolores A. Fleming, Emory L. Kemp, and Ruth Ann Overbeck; *Public Places: Exploring Their History* by Gerald Danzer; *Places of Worship: Exploring Their History* by James P. Wind; and *Local Businesses: Exploring Their History* by K. Austin Kerr, Amos Loveday, and Mansel Blackford. Thereafter we developed a new series with Krieger Publishing Company under the Exploring Community History rubric. Inaugurated in 1994 with *Invisible Networks: Exploring The History of*

Local Utilities and Public Works by Ann Durkin Keating, the series continued with *American Farms: Exploring Their History* by R. Douglas Hurt and *Unlocking City Hall: Exploring the History of Local Government and Politics* by Michael W. Homel. Other volumes on neighborhoods, transportation, and voluntary organizations are currently in preparation, and we anticipate others to follow. The response to these more specialized volumes persuaded us and the new publisher of the Nearby History volumes, AltaMira Press, which took over the book publishing program of the American Association for State and Local History in 1996, that an updated edition of the original *Nearby History* would be useful.

Reviewing and revising *Nearby History* has provided a variety of rewards. One does not often get the opportunity to return to work done twenty years earlier and closely reconsider one's earlier views. In fact, even as historians accustomed to reexamining the past, we did so with a certain trepidation. We were, therefore, enormously reassured to learn that beliefs formed long before still possessed merit. That discovery accounts for the relatively modest revision in this edition of many of the book's chapters, especially those dealing with fundamental principles of historical research. At the same time, we were invigorated by contemplating all that has transpired since we first wrote *Nearby History* to enrich a field that seemed fertile but uncultivated; our observations on new issues and approaches and, in particular, our bibliographies reflect that growth. Finally, we found it stimulating to consider means of pursuing nearby historical investigations that were unavailable when we first addressed the topic. The development of the personal computer, desktop publishing, and, most recently, the Internet, all with implications for historical research and writing, has been particularly thought provoking; some of our most substantial revisions in this edition address the prudent use of these innovations as well as their distinct limitations. Readers need to be mindful that although this book is now sprinkled with Internet addresses and appendix D is devoted entirely to Internet matters, how long these addresses and other information will remain current is uncertain.

Our conviction that investigating nearby history is both justified and within reach has been renewed. We are delighted that the means of exploring the nearby past are more accessible than ever. Above all, we derive satisfaction from the ample evidence that nearby history can be and, in fact, is being done well by people of diverse background and circumstance who possess reasonable degrees of curiosity, judgment, and persistence.

Finally, we wish to thank once again all the people who helped us prepare the first edition of *Nearby History* and add our thanks to the many others who have offered comments, suggestions, and helpful criticism since then. Collectively, they have influenced every page of this new edition. The entire undertaking began and benefited tremendously from time spent at the Family and Community History Center of the Newberry Library of Chicago. The National Endowment for the Humanities funded grants that allowed us to spend an extremely productive summer exploring ideas, exploiting the Newberry's collections, and learning from many of the people drawn together by that extraordinary research center. Richard Jensen, D'Ann Campbell, Janice Reiff, the late Arthur Anderson, David Ruchman, Richard H. Brown, and Mark Friedberger were particularly helpful to us at that time.

Once we had completed a draft of our manuscript, we sent it to a number of people with diverse professional backgrounds, asking for their criticisms and suggestions. Without exception, they read carefully and responded thoughtfully, compelling us to make an extensive revision of the manuscript. For their invaluable assistance we again thank Gerald Danzer, James M. Denny, Thomas Fuller, H. Roger Grant, James K. Huhta, Julie Roy Jeffrey, George Knepper, Jeanette Lauer, Martin Marty, Shirley Marty, Howard S. Miller, John V. Miller, Gayle Olson, Jerrald Pfabe, Charles Piehl, Raymond Pisney, Robert Schnucker, Ingrid Scobie, Alice Shrock, Randall Shrock, John Alexander Williams, and William F. Willingham.

Preparation of this second edition has been assisted by Micah Marty, Kerry McGrath, and Jerome Thompson; also by David Johns and Jason Watson at Drake University as well as by Mitch Allen, Erik Hanson, Pam Lucas, Kathryn Mulkey, and their colleagues at AltaMira Press. We are grateful to the Center for the Humanities at Drake University for a grant that underwrote the cost of acquiring and processing some of the photographs appearing in this book and to Keith Lowman and Media Production-Imaging Services of Northern Illinois University.

There have been no more important influences on our appreciation and understanding of the nearby world than our families—grandparents, parents, siblings, spouses, in-laws, children, grandchildren, and others present in person or memory. We dedicate this edition, as we did its predecessor, to them. Our families, as they have grown and changed, have continued to teach and nurture us as well as inspire and sustain our efforts.

Acknowledgments

For permission to print or reprint the materials listed below and for the courtesy extended by fellow authors and others, as this book was being prepared, the authors and publisher make the following grateful acknowledgments.

The University of Akron, for excerpts on pages 10, 43, 64-65, and 207, from the university's Family History Collection, American Research Center. Reprinted by permission of John V. Miller, University Archivist, the University of Akron.

Pamela Bohlmann, for the excerpt on page 113, from her untitled essay for a family histories project (St. Louis, 1977).

The Henry Francis duPont Winterthur Museum, Inc. for the excerpt on pages 149 and 151 from "Artifact Study: A Proposed Model," by E. McClung Fleming, in *Winterthur Portfolio* 9 (1974): 156. Copyright © 1971; all rights reserved.

Indiana University Northwest, James B. Lane, and Ronald D. Cohen, for excerpts on pages 19-20, from "The Greek Community of East Chicago," by Georgia Kollintzas; and on pages 204-205, from "The Explosion of Standard Oil, August 27, 1955," by Ruthie Williams, in *Steel Shavings*, edited by James B. Lane and Ronald D. Cohen (Gary, IN: Indiana University Northwest, 1976). Reprinted by permission of Ronald D. Cohen.

Guy Johnson, for excerpts on pages 43 and 175 from his manuscript "The Boy on Kiegley's Creek."

The Living History Farms, Des Moines, Iowa, and David Johns, page 159.

Myron A. Marty and Shirley L. Marty, *Frank Lloyd Wright's Taliesin Fellowship* (Kirksville, MO: Truman State University Press, 1999), 105.

Michael Musick for information in the excerpt on page 188.

The Missouri Historical Society, the Western Historical Manuscript Collection of the University of Missouri/St. Louis, and Katharine T. Corbett, for the excerpt on pages 126-27 from "St. Louis Garment Workers: . . . Photographs and Memories," in *Gateway Heritage*, Summer 1981, pp. 22–23. Copyright © 1981 by the Missouri Historical Society.

Mt. San Antonio College and William F. King, for the excerpt on pages 37-38, from *The Vintage Years: Our Valley before 1945*, by William F. King (Walnut, CA: Mt. San Antonio College, Department of Community Services, 1975). Reprinted by permission of William F. King.

The New Republic and Neil Harris for the excerpt on page 168, from "Spaced-Out at the Shopping Center," by Neil Harris, in *The New Republic,* December 13, 1975, p. 23. Copyright © 1975 by *The New Republic.* Reprinted by permission of *The New Republic.*

Paula Presley, for the story and photograph on 110.

Western Pennsylvania Historical Magazine and Josephine McIlvain, for the excerpt on page 94, from "Twelve Blocks: A Study of One Segment of Pittsburgh's South Side, 1880–1915," by Josephine McIlvain, in *Western Pennsylvania Historical Magazine* 60 (October 1977). Reprinted by permission of William F. Trimble Editor, *Western Pennsylvania Historical Magazine.*

1

Why Nearby History?

"History is more or less bunk," declared Henry Ford. Like many other people then and now, he did not believe "history" had any significance for his everyday life; the word referred, he thought, only to the stories of dramatic events, national glory, presidential achievement, and military victory that constituted the bulk of historical literature during his day. "We want to live in the present," he explained, "and the only history that is worth a tinker's dam is the history we make today." It was the experiences, the beliefs and behavior, and the changes in the lives of average people over the generations that interested him. Ford was ignorant, even contemptuous, of traditional "history," but he instinctively knew that what had happened nearby, to himself, his ancestors, his neighbors, and other ordinary people, had shaped their lives. Events and conditions in his family, church, school, workplace, and community had helped form him and his personal world. To Ford, such nearby history was not "bunk"; it was very important.

Ford's inexpensive, mass-produced automobiles profoundly altered twentieth-century life, accounting for everything from the congestion of central cities to the sprawl of suburbia, from the success of fast food restaurants to the inability of parents to keep track of their teenage children, from energy shortages to pollution excesses. Ford realized how rapidly America was changing and how vital the memories of a disappearing society were to an understanding of the changes. So he spent millions of dollars gathering objects, buildings, and other memorabilia from the preautomotive age: a country store, tools, dolls, the house where he was born, wagons, furniture, Thomas Edison's workshop, radios, vacuum cleaners, a blacksmith shop, cigar store Indians, clocks, and a thousand other items. Ford was often sloppy in his efforts. He mistook the phony for the real, removed objects from the setting that gave them meaning, and failed to organize his vast collections so that the process of development over time could be appreciated. He believed that he knew just as much as experts on American history, architecture, and technology about how to collect, display, and interpret the commonplace

1

1.1–1.6   Photographs of communities can only hint at their individual character and the rich diversity of life within them. Think of all that it would be interesting and valuable to know about a metropolis such as Chicago (1.1), a steel town such as Aliquippa, Pennsylvania (1.2), a Vermont farmstead (1.3), a small Iowa town (1.4), an Hispanic American village in New Mexico (1.5), or a California migrant workers' tent city (1.6).

(Photo courtesy of the Library of Congress.)

(Photo courtesy of the Library of Congress.)

(Photo courtesy of the Library of Congress.)

(Photo courtesy of the National Archives and Records Administration.)

(Photo courtesy of the National Archives and Records Administration.)

(Photo courtesy of the National Archives and Records Administration.)

objects in which he was interested. By ignoring professional advice, Ford often fell short of his goals of caring for, learning from, and teaching with his collections. Indeed, some scholars laughed or sneered at Ford's activities. But the millions of visitors who flocked to Dearborn, Michigan, to the Greenfield Village and Henry Ford Museum vindicated Ford's belief in the importance of the commonplace past. An iron sign at the entrance bears his conclusion: "The farther you look back, the farther you can see ahead."

This book is for everyone who shares—or is willing to consider sharing—Ford's concern with the past. We believe that every person's world has a history that is useful, exciting, and possible to explore. Rather than identify this past as "local" or "community" history as some have done and limit it to a concept of *place,* or call it "family history" and restrict it to a concept of *relationship,* or talk about material culture and confine the discussion to *objects,* we have chosen the term "nearby history" in order to include the entire range of possibilities in a person's immediate environment. Since various elements of nearby history—the resources, research methods, questions, and insights—often overlap, we approach the subject in an inclusive fashion. We also wish to employ "nearby history" to distinguish the new approaches that emphasize analysis, comparison, and the examination of change over time from the rather static, narrow, and nonanalytical historical undertakings of past generations.

This book is intended as a guide to help the interested person, with many resources or with few, explore elements of nearby history, including families, houses, farms, schools, churches, civic organizations and facilities, businesses, and communities. By referring to the efforts of other individuals and groups, the book points to possibilities for enjoyment, self-awareness, and intelligent decision making. It assumes that beginners and experienced historians alike need to consider issues and methods in order to learn about the past close at hand. It suggests various questions, approaches, and techniques for studying our immediate environment and for preserving its history. It demonstrates the wide variety of ways in which historians have probed the nearby past. Above all, it actively encourages readers to consider the importance of nearby history and to investigate it for themselves.

THE NEED FOR HISTORY

We all need to know who we are, how we have become what we are, and how to cope with a variety of situations in order to conduct our own lives successfully. We also need to know what to expect from people and institutions around us. Organizations and communities require the same self-understanding in order to function satisfactorily. For individuals and groups alike, experience produces a self-image and a basis for deciding how to behave, manage problems, and plan ahead. We remember—sometimes accurately, sometimes not—what occurred, the causes of certain responses or changes, and our reactions to different circumstances. These memories, positive and negative, help determine our actions. Without memory individuals and groups would be forced to start fresh in analyzing each situation and deciding how to respond. Life would become extremely complicated. Even minor decisions would take much time and effort. Of course, no one has the capacity to store every detail or experience. Too much memory is paralyzing, and so everyone remembers selectively and incompletely. Yet, the more extensive and accurate the memories, the greater the ability to decide whether to follow or depart from past practices. Thus the adult is generally more capable of sensible decision making than the toddler. The ability to observe and recall what has taken place in the nearby world constitutes an essential aspect of human intelligence and well-being.

In the same respect, faulty memory can become an embarrassment or even a crippling hindrance. Not remembering has obvious liabilities; but remembering incorrectly has even more. Distorted memory can be deceptively self-serving and destructively misleading. The more firmly held the flawed recollection, the more it may impede good judgment, making us impervious to other viewpoints or altered conditions. Memory formed quickly, under stress, without access to adequate information, but evolving into a matter of faith immune to doubt, additional evidence, and calm reflection can form a barrier to comprehending past realities.

Social memory serves both society and individuals as personal memory serves the individual alone and possesses all the same values and flaws. Stretching beyond one lifetime and one locale, social memory is a collection of remembrances in a variety of forms and serving a variety of purposes. Historian Arthur Link has noted: "The single most important attribute that enabled man to emerge from his primitive savage state was memory. Collective memory, preserved for long ages at first by oral tradition, enabled primitive man to maintain the practices and customs and to develop the institutions necessary to an ongoing social life."

As human society evolved, distorted memory and current belief repeatedly forged social myths, popular conceptions of past phenomena independent of verification but with strong, sometimes helpful but more often baleful influence. Creation myths, national superiority myths, alligators-in-the-city-sewers myths all reflect the lingering hold of a time of limited knowledge on a later age that should be better informed. Societies have increasingly come to need more reliable means of understanding how they evolved. Social memory and myth might serve to stimulate group pride or dissatisfaction, but it has limited utility for comprehending reality, comparing the experiences of different groups, and setting realistic expectations.

History is an approach to understanding earlier times that diminishes the imperfections of memory and myth. The historical method offers an alternative means of dealing with the past based upon accumulation and critical examination of surviving contemporary evidence, dispassionate assessment of conflicting claims, and perspective built on placing developments in a larger context. As a rational process, it stands in sharp contrast to the casual notion that any treatment of the past constitutes history.

Memory, myth, and history remain in competition as ways of explaining the past. Careful and thorough historical research confronts the challenge of claims that "I was there and I know better!" Conscientious historians seeking to offer improved insights based on newly discovered evidence or fresh perspective face scorn heaped on "historical revisionism" from those more comfortable with familiar views of the past. Perhaps most dispiriting to truth-seekers are the calls that seem to arise most often when the evidence points to an unattractive past, to "Let's only talk about the good times." But as the means of gaining accurate information about the past have expanded, and as recognition has grown that not just the general story but also many of its individual facets deserve realistic appraisal, the value of the historical approach over myth and memory has become more apparent.

THE IMPORTANCE OF THE NEARBY PAST

Just as many distinct, separate, and equally useful recollections contribute to an individual memory, so, too, do many separate elements compose "history." The national and international political, military, and diplomatic developments that Ford dismissed as "more or less bunk" are a part of human history, but no more so than the activities and environments of the ordinary folk whom Ford celebrated. "There is a history in all men's lives," William Shakespeare observed, and that is equally true for plumbers and presidents, printers and prime ministers. The president will no doubt have wider-ranging influence, but the plumber's grandchildren, neighbors, and clients may be more directly affected by him than by the president. An executive order from Washington, D.C., may affect the world, while a decision made in a small town may only affect one neighborhood; but the local event may nevertheless have great and lasting influence on a community, a family, or an individual. A good understanding of the past, whether designated memory or history, needs to take into account nearby as well as national and international developments.

"We may picture the family, the local community, the national state, and the supranational society as a series of concentric circles," wrote H. P. R. Finberg, an English specialist in local history. "Each requires to be studied with constant reference to the one outside it; but the inner rings are not the less perfect circles for being wholly surrounded and enclosed by the outer." The useful image of concentric circles around the individual makes understandable the relationship of one level of history to the others. Obviously, conflict between countries, a national depression, or a community decision on the budget of public schools can affect the family and the individual. Less obviously, personal or family decisions to move,

to bear fewer children, or to buy a foreign automobile, especially if they are repeated by others, can radiate influence to the outer circles. Each of the circles surrounding a person affects the others yet also involves a distinctive past deserving
of separate consideration.

Just because the inner circles involve fewer people or less well-known events
does not mean that they are less important to the person at the center. Indeed, your
own past and that of people closest to you, family and community, have had a
great impact on you. Learning about it enhances your memory and helps you
comprehend influences on your life. Your grandparents' decision to leave Europe
for America, for example, or their cautious spending habits learned in the Great
Depression have affected your parents and you in turn. Similarly, an organization
or a whole community can become aware of why certain practices or patterns developed. The presence of foul-smelling factories in the center of the city at one
time may help explain why the wealthy neighborhoods, pleasant parks, and better schools are all to be found on the upwind side of town, and investigation may
lead to questions about the advisability of permitting such a residential pattern to
continue, now that the factories have moved or changed. Nearby history is thus
worth exploring as it serves important needs of the individuals and communities
directly involved.

The image of concentric circles suggests that nearby history has other values
that we should consider as well. An understanding of national and even international history benefits from increased knowledge of nearby history. The national
and international circles contain not one but many communities, just as each community circle contains many families. When we describe national or international
history, we must usually identify common threads and general patterns in order
for a coherent picture to emerge. The variety and detail of various community and
individual experiences necessarily disappear from view, and, as a result, our sense
of what actually happened to ordinary people is often missing. A history of the
American Revolution or World War II may give an excellent picture of the general issues and overall pattern of the developing conflict without revealing anything about a particular community, family, or individual experience at the time.
Furthermore, the attempt to generalize about a widely shared experience, such as
the Great Depression, may in the end distort the actual, personal situation for
many of those involved. Careful examination of what happened to particular families and communities can clarify and illustrate the broader picture.

During recent decades, historians have begun to appreciate the importance of
family and community history, and growing numbers of them have become involved in "the new social history." Several developments in the 1960s, particularly the civil rights movement, the growth of awareness of the plight of poor people, the rise of feminism, and the realization by the anti-Vietnam War movement
of its political powerlessness, led to calls for the study of America "from the bottom up." The nation's history, it became apparent, could not fully be understood
by looking only at leadership elites and their decisions. The experience of other

social groups, particularly anonymous people who formed the mass of society, needed to be examined. Slavery could not be understood by investigating only Abraham Lincoln; one needed to find out what it meant to the slave. The Great Depression of the 1930s could not be comprehended by analyzing only Franklin D. Roosevelt; one had to consider how the families of unemployed workers lived through it. The Vietnam War could not be appreciated by viewing it only from the perspective of Lyndon Johnson or Richard Nixon; one needed to learn what soldiers, draft evaders, and civilians on the home front thought about it. At first many historians doubted that much could be discovered about obscure people, organizations, and communities who left few of the traces—letters, speeches, diaries, newspaper stories—with which scholars were accustomed to working. But once serious interest arose, scholars began to adapt their traditional methods and develop new techniques to explore past society at the grass roots.

A great stroke of good fortune for the new social history was the development of computers while these new questions were being raised. Before computers, it was difficult if not impossible for a historian to keep track of many facts about all the people in a community. A computer could store endless bits of information about individuals and communities and organize them into meaningful patterns. Large groups could be studied systematically rather than on the basis of haphazard impressions. For example, information from the U.S. Census on the parents, birthplace, previous residence, education, occupation, family relationships, and wealth of each of a community's hundreds or even thousands of residents could be fed into a computer programmed to determine mobility patterns and rates, average family size, amount of education by sex, occupation, and economic status, and many other useful community characteristics that can change from time to time as well as from place to place. Although computers are not needed in researching interesting and useful nearby history, historians have been using computers and quantitative techniques to identify and link economic, social, political, and growth patterns of families and communities, thus developing a much fuller and more accurate picture of American society from the bottom up.

More recently, computer networks such as the Internet and the World Wide Web have come to provide convenient access to some vast catalogs of historical information. In particular, they have become helpful tools for quickly locating historical publications, especially those of recent vintage. At the same time, they cannot now, and possibly never will, provide access to more than a tiny fraction of material available in archives and elsewhere for answering questions about the past. Moreover, the information they do provide is the product of human effort and choice and therefore subject to the same frailties of judgment and execution as other human creations. Computers can be useful to historians, but they are neither all-sufficient nor infallible tools for exploring the past. The notion that "if it matters, it is on the net" is rank foolishness.

Computers are but one research tool available to the historian of the nearby world. Depending on the topic or question involved, a variety of other research

The life of an individual and family intertwines with that of the surrounding community. The history of one illuminates the other. For example, this family's history provides glimpses of community educational and business practices, the impact of changing technology, and social customs regarding death. Additional research would be required, of course, to obtain a full picture of any one of these matters.

When Cyril was fifteen he began to work in the steel mills. His first job was that of messenger. Soon he worked as a tally boy counting and marking the sheets of steel. When he was twenty-one, he quit the steel business and entered mortuary school in Cincinnati. Cyril's father wanted him to be a mortician.

At Cincinnati Cyril went to school for three months, took his state board exam, and passed. Since the required amount of schooling to receive a license was six months, he supervised other class members and taught them the principles of raising veins and arteries. He received his license on October 20, 1917. License requirements and embalming procedures have greatly changed in the past 70 years. Now one year of mortuary school, two years of college, and one year of internship at a funeral home are required before licensing. Embalming fluid has been greatly improved. The chemicals now used to preserve the body do so for a much longer time.

Cyril established his first funeral home at 127 River Avenue in Memphis. A large storeroom for caskets and sleeping quarters was in the back. In the daytime some of the caskets were kept on the bed. Cyril and Mary would lift them off the bed to go to sleep at night.

Funerals in the early 1900s weren't held in funeral homes, but in the homes of the deceased. The embalmer would carry his instruments to the home and embalm the deceased at his home. One of the instruments was called a cooling board. This board was made so that it could be folded up and carried under the arm. The cooling board was unfolded and placed on the bed before the person was embalmed. The average funeral director's salary was twelve dollars a week.

Cyril entered into partnership with Andrew Sherlock under the firm name Medzan and Sherlock. One year later Cyril sold his partnership to Sherlock for one dollar because he was angry with him. Cyril lost the house and all of his equipment.

About the time Cyril and Mary's first child, Tom, was born, Cyril established his own funeral home at 336 South Broad Street. While at this address Cyril purchased an ambulance which he ran with the business.

In 1925 the family moved to 222 East Center Street so that they would be located in the center of the city. Just before the move a second child, Rita, was born. While at Center Street Cyril purchased his first hearse. The "hearse" was a 1927 Ford pick-up with a turtle back. The box was carried in the back of the truck. Funeral directors began to wear special outfits: silk hats, striped pants, frocked coats. The mourners wore black.

As more and more funerals were being held in the chapels rather than the home, Cyril again changed his residence to Davis Street. This funeral home had two chapels, a show room for caskets, two offices, a morgue, and a garage. The family had living quarters above the funeral home. Everyone had their own room, even after Ed was born in 1928. In 1933 while Mary was pregnant with her fourth child, Cyril moved his family once more. Besides another addition to the family, the children were getting too noisy to remain above the chapels.

Source: Family History Collection, American History Research Center, University of Akron, Akron, Ohio.

methods may be more appropriate and less difficult to master. Examining photographs, interviewing people, reconstructing old buildings, sorting out and piecing together a business's financial records, and tracing neighborhood growth patterns from maps and tax records are only a few of the ways in which useful and interesting information about the past can be collected and verified. Research skills developed in doing nearby history can often be applied in other endeavors as well.

HISTORY FOR NOW

Doing nearby history research encourages a way of thinking that can help in dealing with a great variety of current situations. Uncovering what has taken place over the years in a family, an organization, or a community reveals the origins of conditions, the causes of change, and the reasons for present circumstances. It becomes evident that not just one influence but a complex of forces affects most developments. Examining how conditions evolve over a period of time and considering the impact of a wide variety of factors on that process—in other words, thinking historically—provide enlightenment and perspective. Just as searching one's memory for accurate, pertinent recollections can help an individual reach a wiser decision, so, too, can thinking historically be of use to a person, a business, a family, a church organization, a city planner, or a whole community. Sound historical thought can overcome flawed social memory, undermine unfounded myths, and counteract unrealistic images concocted to attract attention, shock, or dramatize. Among other consequences, the use of condensed and unreliable images of the past by social economic, religious, or political advocates to persuade, or by commercial media, to instruct and entertain, almost invariably obscures local variations in larger patterns. Liberation from such influences can be found in historical comprehension.

The value of history beyond its traditional importance in a sound general education seems to be gaining recognition. A most significant development in recent years has been the increase in "public history," a term coined to describe the various types of specialized work that people with historical training and skills can do other than teach. Basically, public history involves two kinds of activities: historical resources management and applied research.

Historical resources management is concerned with saving, caring for, and encouraging the use of materials from the past. Archivists seek to locate historically valuable documents, ensure their preservation and accessibility, and assist anyone with an interest in using them. Museum curators and historic preservationists engage in similar activities with objects, buildings, and landscapes. Saving historic sites and adapting them for new purposes is becoming an increasingly important part of conserving the environment, reviving downtowns and neighborhoods, and holding down construction costs. The federal government gives various types of aid to restoration projects, and experts in the field are in increasing demand. Resources management can also involve directing historical societies, editing print or electronic publications, and other activities that call attention to what remains from the past.

Applied research involves historical investigation to aid in current problem solving or policy planning. Corporations, consulting firms, government agencies, and newspapers are some of the organizations that need to examine past developments in order to function and plan effectively. Whether for marketing and development decisions, public and governmental relations, personnel management, land use planning, assessment of the impact of policies on the physical and social environment, or for other purposes, research of a historical nature, even if not labeled as such, becomes vital. The skills involved in uncovering and analyzing information about particular aspects of the past, comprehending and assessing complex factors that influence directions of growth, and accurately describing processes of development have great utility for public and private institutions alike.

"It is our discipline that asks the question, how did the subject of concern evolve over time into its present condition?" noted historian Robert Kelley. "Other disciplines, as in economics, engineering, political science, and sociology, are concerned with the dynamics of the existing situation. The examples of badly formed policies which would have escaped that condition had some attention been paid to the history of the issue at hand, or of the problem or situation, are endless." Kelley concluded, "Historically grounded policies, in small and large settings, cannot help but be sounder in conception, and they are likely to be more effective, consistent, and, one hopes, more aligned with human reality. In the long run, they should be less costly to administer."

The territory of nearby history is, obviously, both a training ground and a principal workplace for public historians. In exploring the past of subjects close at hand, a person learns to identify, collect, organize, and exhibit historical materials; to analyze complex factors; to examine the relationship of the inner concentric circles of nearby situations to the outer circles of national and international development; and to focus research to answer specific questions of importance to the historian or the client. Practicing public historians are often concerned with helping a planning agency, attorney, filmmaker, museum, advertiser, real estate developer, business, or other public or private body understand a particular community, neighborhood, or local social group's experiences and needs. This emerging field may well offer the greatest opportunities for historical employment for the next generation, and clearly the individual interested in a career as a historian would do well to explore nearby history.

But beyond the serious importance of examining the past of our immediate world to improve memory; dispel myth; understand the contemporary situation; sharpen social, political, and economic generalizations; or facilitate intelligent policy making, nearby history has a further intangible appeal that may be its most notable quality. The emotional rewards of learning about a past that has plainly and directly affected one's own life cannot be duplicated by any other type of historical inquiry. It can be exciting to understand for the first time why your grandparents treated your parents in a certain way, why your community developed certain traditions, why your corporation adopted specific practices, why your civic organization became involved with particular issues. It can be satisfying to feel yourself to be part of something larger and more lasting than the moment, something that stretches both backward and forward in time. Despite his disparaging remarks about "history," Henry Ford instinctively sought that emotional lift. The same feeling can be shared by all who accept the challenge to explore the history of their nearby world.

NOTES AND FURTHER READING

Henry Ford's statement to the *New York Times*, May 20, 1919, is quoted in Keith Sward, *The Legend of Henry Ford* (New York: Holt, Rinehart and Winston, 1948), which discusses the context of the statement, pp. 100–110, as well as the development of Greenfield Village, pp. 259–71.

Henry Ford's historical activities are described in Geoffrey C. Upward, *A Home for Our Heritage* (Dearborn, MI: Henry Ford Museum Press, 1979). The other statements quoted in this chapter were made by Arthur Link at a 1967 conference that produced *The Challenge of Local History* (Albany: New York State Education Department, 1968), p. 71; H. P. R. Finberg, "Local History," in Finberg and V. H. T. Skipp, *Local History: Objective and Pursuit* (Newton Abbott, Eng.: David and Charles, 1967), p. 39; and Robert Kelley, who was quoted in Dianne Martin, "History Goes Public," *History News* 34 (1979): 122–23.

The complex interaction of memory, myth, and history deserves thoughtful contemplation by anyone embarking upon a study of the nearby past. Helpful starting points for such consideration include David Lowenthal, *The Past Is a Foreign Country* (New York: Cambridge University Press, 1985) and *Possessed by the Past: The Heritage Crusade and the Spoils of History* (New York: Free Press, 1996); Peter Novick, *That Noble Dream: The "Objectivity Question" and the American Historical Profession* (New York: Cambridge University Press, 1988); Michael Kammen, *Mystic Chords of Memory: The Transformation of Tradition in American Culture* (New York: Knopf, 1991); John Bodnar, *Remaking America: Public Memory, Commemoration, and Patriotism in the Twentieth Century* (Princeton, NJ: Princeton University Press, 1992); Edward T. Linenthal and Tom Engelhardt, eds., *History Wars: The Enola Gay and Other Battles for the American Past* (New York: Metropolitan Books, 1996); and Mike Wallace, *Mickey Mouse History and Other Essays on American Memory* (Philadelphia: Temple University Press, 1996).

The possibilities of nearby history are examined at greater length and depth as well as from a variety of perspectives in two books by Carol Kammen, *On Doing Local History: Reflections on What Local Historians Do, Why, and What It Means* (Walnut Creek, CA: AltaMira Press, 1986) and *The Pursuit of Local History: Readings on Theory and Practice* (Walnut Creek, CA: AltaMira Press, 1996).

A fascinating and important study of the American public's views of the past and its relevance to their own lives can be found in Roy Rosenzweig and David Thelen, *The Pres-*

ence of the Past: Popular Uses of History in American Life (New York: Columbia University Press, 1998). Also, a lively roundtable discussion of the book appears in the Winter 2000 issue of *The Public Historian*. Nearby historians will find in Rosenzweig and Thelen's book confirmation of the value of their own undertakings, while public history professionals as well as academics will gain from it insights on how better to connect with public audiences.

2

What Can Be Done Nearby?

Exploring nearby history does not first require a long, difficult search for a rare appropriate topic. To the contrary, the initial step involves selecting from a wide range of possibilities. Nearly everyone is surrounded by a vast assortment of people, objects, and institutions, each with a potentially interesting past about which an enormous amount of information exists in one form or another. This chapter seeks to provide help with the all-important task of deciding where to focus one's attention.

FOCUSING

Even if an individual wanted to do so, it would be impossible to cope with every aspect of the nearby past simultaneously. Just as every memory cannot be summoned up and used at the same moment, every facet of local history cannot be investigated at once and expected to fall into place. During close examination of a particular event or circumstance, it is hard to maintain a sharp image of the overall community, and vice versa. Thus it is important to take some time at the outset to define an objective.

As well as determining what he or she wishes to know, every investigator must decide how much depth and detail of knowledge is desirable and what effort is worth expending. Individuals obviously possess varied backgrounds, skills, and interests. A beginner cannot be expected to proceed as fast and far as can an experienced historian. The amount of time and other resources available for the acquisition of techniques and the pursuit of inquiries differs widely. Some people may be prepared to tackle the most complex issues, others not. Nor will everyone be satisfied with the same level of answer. Some historians of the nearby past may want or need to investigate a topic at great length, while others—for equally valid reasons—may decide not to carry it very far. Part of the process of choosing a focus wisely is setting it realistically in terms of one's capacities and interests.

2.1   Group portraits like this one of St. Louis streetcar conductors may contain clues to personalities, relationships, and economic and social circumstances. Note such things as the arrangement of the men in the second row, the different attire of the center person in that row, the positioning of the subjects' hands, and the several men who are smoking cigars despite the "SMOKING STRICTLY PROHIBITED" sign in the background. What might have been the occasion for taking the picture? (Photo courtesy of the Marty family collection and copyright © Myron Marty.)

Only after the purpose and scope of an inquiry into the past are clearly in mind can research plans be formulated. Decisions can then be reached as to what information is worth gathering, examining, and analyzing in order to answer a particular question. Obviously some interesting information will not be pertinent, although were a different question asked, it might have great relevance. Therefore, to determine an approach and judge the value of information, a focus is essential.

Historians find their focus in various ways. Sometimes simple curiosity leads to an interest in a totally new topic or one related to previous investigations. "I want to know something about this strange town to which I have just moved," or "Having read a fascinating history of the rise of the skyscraper in America, I would like to know about the first one built here and its impact on this community." Sometimes a personal need to know sparks interest. "Has this civic organization been sensible and successful over the years in supporting causes I care about, or would I be wasting my time and money by joining?" Ownership of an object or a building can stimulate an inquiry. "I need to find out the background of this house I inherited and the neighborhood in which it is located so that I can determine whether it is worth it to me (or to someone to whom I might give or sell it) to keep and restore to its original condition."

Often the focus of an historical investigation is not chosen but assigned in the course of school, political or civic involvement, or employment. "In this course, students will investigate the history of their family during the twentieth century," or "The company needs to know about this town's past growth patterns in order to make intelligent investment and marketing decisions, and it is your job to find out and prepare a report." Such research assignments are likely to increase as the notion of public history spreads and as private and public agencies realize the value of acquiring accurate information about the past. However it is selected, a focus on a particular topic, whether as narrow as the origins of the antique chest in the attic or as broad as the centennial history of a city, helps determine how to proceed.

Some researchers feel guilty about shifting their focus after they have begun an investigation. There is no reason why they should. Initial choices are necessarily based on limited knowledge and must naturally be considered tentative. As research goes forward, obstacles, better approaches, and more worthwhile topics often reveal themselves, signaling the need to broaden, narrow, or redirect the investigation. Indeed, this refining process is normally a sign of progress. But without an objective to begin with, it becomes difficult to sort through the vast heap of information about the past.

POSSIBILITIES

Whether you already have decided upon a subject or are trying to choose one, it is most helpful to think about the range of possibilities. Considering different topics helps expand awareness of the opportunities, assists in determining where interests lie, and leads to ideas for using resources already at hand. Thinking about the great variety of possible questions helps in deciding exactly what you wish to know. Also, identifying other questions related to yours may make you aware of other ways of looking at a topic, help you recognize useful information, and assist you in finding a more complete, satisfying answer. Explanations are seldom closer to the target than the questions asked. By taking time at the start to consider potential questions, you will bring your undertaking into the sharp focus you seek.

Basically, historical questions seek answers that will help fulfill three purposes: description of the past, measurement of change over time, and analysis of cause and consequence. Often the goal of inquiry is simply an accurate portrayal of an event, personality, set of conditions, or place at some past moment. Such a description may become complex because many interrelated factors are involved. An acute concern with time distinguishes the historian's effort to understand society; the sequence in which various matters unfold and interact is considered crucial to their relationship and individual character. In analyzing causation and effect, the historian must be sensitive to the influence of a wide variety of forces and the impact of timing. If these three fundamental objectives of historical explanation are applied to any topic, appropriate questions for research should suggest themselves.

Keep in mind also that the past is filled with subtle developments as well as obvious ones. Matters that were conspicuous at the moment—the opening of a factory, a local election—may be considered *manifest* events. Slight alterations in unspectacular aspects of life, many of which were largely unnoticed by contemporaries but that over the long term represent significant change—shifts in family size or structure, economic patterns, or assimilation of minorities into the dominant culture, for instance—may be called *latent* events. The relationship between manifest and latent events is a central consideration for historians. For as historian Bernard Bailyn has remarked, "The essence and drama of history lie precisely in the relationship between latent conditions, which set the boundaries of human existence, and the manifest problems with which people consciously struggle." Sensitivity to both manifest and latent developments in pursuing the objectives of description, measurement of change, and analysis of cause and consequence is fundamental to any inquiry and essential to a strategy for devising the questions you wish to ask.

The following lists suggest focuses for inquiry and indicate some possible sorts of questions. A great many other questions can be raised about the nearby past in general or about any individual's particular nearby world. These simply raise some important issues that are common to most communities, usually answerable, and often exciting to explore. Some are straightforward and relatively simple inquiries; others are quite complex and formidable. The list is intended to demonstrate the range of possibilities and to stir thought. It is not meant to suggest that everyone can or ought to tackle each question. You definitely can make additions, deletions, and improvements using your own experiences, imagination, and judgment.

Questions are grouped in institutional or functional categories so that various facets of a general topic can be considered together. This arrangement hints at related issues that may be of interest and divides a potentially enormous catalog into manageable sections. Furthermore, the ordering of various elements of the immediate environment in this fashion allow the dimensions and possibilities of nearby history to be seen more plainly.

THE FAMILY

The family is the most common and for many the most interesting element in the nearby world. Each one has its own definition, identity, and history, the details of which are significant to its members and often to others as well. The following questions suggest the wide range of possible family structures, functions, and experiences.

Research often begins with a summing up of what one knows, believes, or suspects about a topic. Thereafter it is possible to identify the question to be answered, the information to be verified, and the relationships to be examined. A student in East Chicago, Indiana, summing up her view of the ethnic community, touches on a number of issues that could be investigated to discover how conditions developed and changed over the course of time.

The Greek Community of East Chicago, despite its small size of 2,000 people, has made its presence felt in a city of 50,000 inhabitants. There are, for example, at least 8 Greek restaurants there. This business group represents the better established Greek families of East Chicago, the elite in a sense. However, since they are not educated, their style of life does not contrast sharply with that of the community. Yet quite paradoxically, from this pool of wealth springs the inevitable pursuit of the good life: the mod clothes, new cars, socializing with different types of people, in short, Americanizing. This seems to be less true of the parents than their children. Generally speaking, they are a conservative force and speak the language of those who have pulled themselves up by their own bootstraps. There is no such thing as good luck, they insist, one must work and work hard, for "God helps those who help themselves." The Greek immigrants have done their best to demonstrate that God is favoring them. They are employed for the most part, and their incomes provide for a decent living. Exceptions to this generalization are the very recent newcomers from Greece and those who have been beset by costly setbacks. My father, for example, is a restaurant employee, who has been in a precarious economic state ever since his savings were drained by family illnesses for which he was not insured. Fortunately, the majority of Greek immigrants have not experienced such a catastrophe, being employed by the steel mills of Inland and Youngstown which provide them with a family insurance. In terms of work, they are less successful in obtaining good jobs due to the language barrier and their lack of specialized training. After several years in the mills, some manage to get promoted but not before being affected by the heavily polluted air. A substantial number of family acquaintances have been hospitalized, following one or two years of work. The common joke is that since they were never examined by a physician while in Greece, this is a good opportunity for them to receive some medical care.

It would seem from their modest annual wages that little could be put aside for future needs; but the Greek immigrants lead a life of austerity and are able to save. There are cases where the saving power is too unrealistic to be credible, were it not for the simple fact that it is true.

My personal feeling is that the Greek people of East Chicago are not very secure despite their apparent economic progress. Among those who have prospered is my uncle, who did so when he was already past the age of 60. He worked long hours, and the best years of his life were consumed in his striving for success. The surplus money which he now has can do little to brighten his life, for he is old, conditioned, and unable to adapt to a new and better life. His story is that of the Greek immigrants in general, who defer a decent and comfortable present for some undefined future gratification which will never come to pass. . . .

The Greek people socialize among themselves, the women visiting their lady friends, and the men meeting in coffeehouses or other Greek-owned businesses where they play cards. There in some obscure corner they are brought together by a common background to discuss issues ranging from politics to personal problems. They're not a bunch of naive peasants, as one might expect. They read Greek newspapers and are able to follow political developments around the world.

Among themselves they feel a sense of support and freedom derived from their adherences to common values. . . . They ask favors of one another much more readily than do Americans. Friendship is giving, and the Greek people understand that very well. . . . The Church gives identity and cohesion to the group who view themselves not only as Christians but Greek-Orthodox-Christians. The Church is not an organ for spiritual and social reform. . . . The Greek family is patriarchal—based with the husband making the important decisions and the wife running the household and raising children. There are cases where the wife works alongside her husband, and this is the trend among the younger couples. . . . Social mobility between the generations is apparently a reality for most Greeks. The climb upward isn't easy or startling. Some have found a handy formula for social advancement through mixed marriages. . . . This demonstrates that many Greek-Americans find the demand of an ethnic community difficult to accommodate. Some are very blunt about it and declare that they find the Greek Community confining, which it is, and want no part of it.

Source: Georgia Kollintzas, "The Greek Community of East Chicago," in Steel Shavings, *edited by James B. Lane and Ronald D. Cohen (Gary: Indiana University Northwest, 1976), pp. 20–23.*

Family Relationships

- Who was considered to be a member of the family?
- What considerations were involved in the formation of a family unit, whatever form it took?
- How did the people meet who eventually formed a couple?
- What was the relative social and economic status of each member of the couple? What was the effect of any differences?
- How did courtship and the decision to form a family occur?
- If a couple later separated, why and how? What subsequent life course did each one follow? How did the experience affect other family members and, if new relationships were later established, the resulting blended families?
- What were the respective roles of men and women in the family?
- What beliefs, values, customs, superstitions, folk wisdom, prejudices, and legal codes were held, and how did they shape the family?
- How and by whom were decisions made? What were the different areas of responsibility for males and females as well as older and younger family members in decision making?
- How do men and women of different generations within the family compare in age at marriage, age at birth of first child, number of pregnancies and live childbirths, and age at birth of last child?
- Was the birth of children evenly spaced, planned, or unexpected? Where were children born?
- What role, if any, did family members or outsiders—friends, neighbors, professionals—play in childbirth?
- How have child-rearing practices and the roles of mothers and fathers changed over the years?

- How were children regarded and treated before they were old enough to take care of themselves or to work?
- What expectations regarding work and other responsibilities did each generation have for persons of different sexes and ages?
- On what basis and at what age were persons considered to be adults?
- How long did fathers and mothers continue to have authority over their sons and daughters?
- Why and how did relationships between parents and children change as people aged?
- How have separation, divorce, or death affected the family?
- What family crises occurred and how were they handled?
- Has the family had any dominant figures, superstars, outcasts, or embarrassments? What has been the relative esteem for men and women?
- Who cared for sick, aged, disabled, or dependent family members?
- What were the family's customs in the event of a death?
- Where, if anyplace, were family members buried?
- Who inherited what?

Physical Characteristics

- What did family members look like?
- Were there any recurring physical characteristics (stature, complexion, or distinctive features, for example) that made family members similar in appearance?
- What was the general condition of their health?
- Did individuals or the family as a whole suffer from any chronic illnesses, mental problems, disabling injuries, or deformities?
- Did men and women in the family generally live long lives or die young?
- What relationship, if any, did the family maintain with a physician or other health services?
- Were "home remedies" commonly used or passed along through the generations?
- Did superstitions or old wives' tales play an important part in medical diagnosis and treatment?

Location and Movement

- Where has the family lived?
- How and by whom were places of residence determined?
- Who first migrated to the United States or to the community in which the family became more permanently located? Who followed?
- Did the family move from place to place within the community?
- Why were moves undertaken—to change jobs, for health reasons, to escape unsatisfactory conditions, or for other reasons?

- What part did marriage or divorce play in relocation?
- How were moves made?
- What difficulties did moving cause for various members of the family?
- How was the place of origin remembered?
- If friends, boarders, or servants lived with the family, who were they, why were they there, what was expected of them, and how were they treated?
- If married sons or daughters continued to live in their parents' households, what were the circumstances?
- Did elderly persons live in their own homes, with their children, in retirement communities, or in old-age homes?
- If related families lived in the same neighborhood or community, what was the nature of their interaction with one another?
- Did family members who had departed return to the family home for visits or extended residence? What was the response of those to whom they returned or who were otherwise affected?

Family Economics

- How did members of the family earn a living?
- Specifically, what kinds of work did they do as, for example, machine operators, small-business proprietors, clerks, farmers, secretaries, professional people, or executives?
- How did their work change through the years, even though they held the same job?
- How were occupational choices made?
- What part did an individual's sex play in determining occupation, opportunity, family support, and success?
- What were the reasons they changed jobs?
- How did family members help one another obtain jobs or develop farms or businesses?
- What were family members' relations with employers? With unions? With other workers, farmers, or business people?
- If they participated in workforce organizing, informing, slowdowns, speedups, strikes, or strike-breaking, what were the circumstances and results?
- What was the family's general or evolving economic status?
- What expectations prevailed regarding family members sharing all or part of their earnings with the family? Why, if at all, were exceptions made?
- How and by whom were family finances decided and handled?
- To what age and extent were sons and daughters supported financially?
- What was the general outlook on material possessions?
- How did the family cope with hard times?
- If charity or public assistance (welfare) provided part or all of the family's income, how did the family feel about it?
- What did family members feel about their economic status, ambitions for advancement, and "keeping up with the Joneses"?

Daily Living

- What were the daily routines of family members?
- What were the roles and responsibilities of individual family members?
- How was failure to conform to family expectations or values treated?
- How did mothers and fathers decide upon and carry out discipline of sons and daughters?
- How has the family's diet and clothing changed over the years?
- How did changing technology affect the family; that is, when and how did such things as piped water and fuel, electricity, telephones, cars and trucks, radios, vacuum cleaners, refrigerators, televisions, microwave ovens, computers, and so forth come into use, and what impact did they have?
- What kind of family celebrations and reunions were held?
- What holidays and special occasions were observed, and how?
- Did family members use tobacco, alcoholic beverages, or drugs routinely, on festive occasions, seldom, or not at all? Did they cause problems?
- Who were family members' friends: relatives, neighbors, fellow workers, others of the same gender, ethnic group, or religion?
- How were friendships formed and maintained?
- In what kinds of social activities did the family engage?
- To what churches and voluntary organizations did family members belong? What was the extent of their involvement, and what effects did this have?
- How did they participate in the life of the community in which they lived?
- What were their attitudes toward people in the community of other faiths, different ethnic or racial backgrounds, or lower and higher economic status?

Education

- What sort of educational training took place within the family?
- What value did the family place upon formal education?
- How did expectations differ for boys and girls? For children judged unusual or abnormal?
- What level of schooling did family members achieve?
- What schools did they attend, and how did they get there?
- Did they serve apprenticeships, undergo special training in the military, or obtain other nonschool education? If they went to college, how did they finance it and what did they study?
- What do they remember about their teachers?
- What part did initial or subsequent education play in their later vocations and their avocations?
- When education was lacking, what was the effect?
- What unusual skills and abilities did they possess?
- What attitudes did they have about persons less or better educated than themselves?

2.2–2.5   Economic activity can in significant ways define individuals and communities. What can be learned from these photos of an insurance company office (2.2), a printing plant (2.3), a farm (2.4), and a shoe store (2.5)? What can be learned about the physical setting, work practices, equipment, and the workers themselves?

(Photo courtesy of the Library of Congress.)

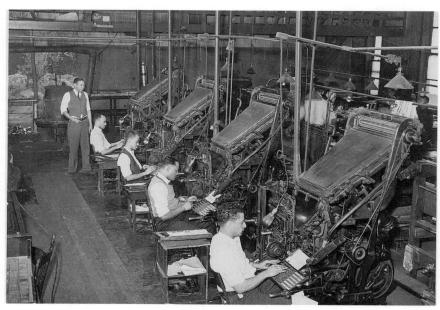

(Photo courtesy of the Library of Congress.)

(Photo courtesy of the National Archives and Records Administration.)

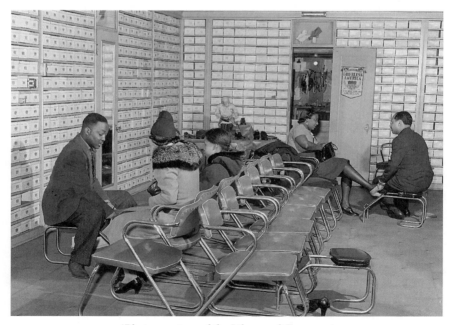

(Photo courtesy of the Library of Congress.)

- What encouragement did they offer to others in the family who sought schooling?
- By what criteria—financial, educational, occupational, or social—did the family measure success?

Military

- What was the nature and extent of military service by family members?
- What were their attitudes about it?
- What did they do during wartime?
- What were their experiences with defense plants, war information and propaganda, rationing and price controls, war bond drives, change in the community?
- How did wars alter their lives?
- What ties with military or service organizations were maintained once active duty ended?
- What use was made of veterans' benefits?
- How did attitudes toward wars and the military change through the years?

Public Affairs

- To what extent were family members involved in community affairs, charitable activities, reform movements, or local government?
- How and why did they or did they not participate? Were some activities considered appropriate for only one sex? Why and to what effect?
- What were their attitudes toward politics, political parties, and prominent local, state, and national political figures?
- What was their political outlook (conservative, moderate, liberal, radical, erratic, indifferent), and how was it shown in their political actions? How did political views and actions differ within the family by age, sex, or other characteristics? What were the consequences of differences?
- How extensive was their participation in party activities? What party?
- How, if at all, did they benefit from being socially or politically active?
- How and why did the pattern of participation change from generation to generation?

PLACES OF RESIDENCE

A house or apartment building can be a part of a family's past, but it can also have a history of its own.

Physical Features

- When was the building built?
- Who designed and constructed the building?

- What was its architectural style?
- What were its dimensions?
- How many rooms (and of what size and nature) did it contain?
- Were bathrooms an original feature, a later addition, or missing? Why?
- Did the building have porches or balconies?
- Was it one of a kind, similar in style to others in the community, identical to others in the neighborhood constructed at the same time?
- Did it ever undergo substantial remodeling or expansion? How? Why?
- How was sleeping, living, and working space arranged?
- How has the use of various rooms, porches, and balconies changed over time?
- How was the building heated, cooled, and illuminated?
- Did the building have fireplaces, indoor plumbing, electricity, or other features?
- How was the house or apartment decorated and furnished?
- How was the kitchen equipped?
- How much property surrounded the building, and how was it used (farm, yard, garden, parking, business)?
- What is the history of other structures on the property?

Ownership and Use

- Who lived in the building?
- Was it owner occupied or rented? A commune, condominium, or co-op?
- Was it used for any purposes other than housing?
- When and how did ownership of the property change?
- Was it purchased outright, with mortgage loans, with government assistance?
- How did the owners maintain the property?
- Did owners and tenants have conflicts?
- Did local government agencies ever inspect or condemn the property?
- Was it ever seized for nonpayment of taxes or mortgages?

NEIGHBORHOOD

A neighborhood can be a cohesive social unit or merely a geographical district. In either case, its history can help explain the presence of particular persons, structures, institutions, and problems; patterns of development; and relationships among those who reside there. The history of each family and residence in the neighborhood can be examined and compared in terms of all the questions already posed. In addition, significant questions may be asked about the neighborhood itself.

Physical Features

- How is the neighborhood defined?
- What, if anything, is its central focus?
- What are its boundaries, and what distinguishes it from the surrounding urban or rural area?
- How and why has the size, shape, and image of the neighborhood changed over the years?
- What sorts of structures and open spaces could be found in the neighborhood at various stages in its history?
- Was it built up over a period of years or developed as one coherent project?
- How is the nature of its development evident?
- How and why have architectural styles varied or remained the same? Has the use to which various structures have been put changed significantly?
- Where did residents go to work, shop, obtain services, worship, and seek entertainment or recreation?
- How did they travel? How easy or difficult was it to move beyond the neighborhood?
- What have been the important institutions in the neighborhood (parks, Grange halls, churches, taverns, libraries, stores, shopping malls, schools, hospitals, others), and what has been their role in the neighborhood's history?

Social Features

- Who has lived in the neighborhood?
- What family or other ties linked various households?
- What ethnic, religious, occupational, social groups, and economic classes have been represented? In what proportions?
- How has this situation changed over time? Has one dominant group been replaced by another?
- Have various groups clashed?
- What caused people to move into and out of the neighborhood?
- How and why have events, activities, or problems brought residents of the neighborhood together, if at all?
- Have there been neighborhood parties, festivals, parades, or other celebrations? If so, what has been their nature?
- How have neighborhood news and rumors traveled?
- Have disapproved activities been conducted in the neighborhood (such as bootlegging, gambling, begging, unauthorized home businesses or room rentals, vandalism, drug dealing, prostitution, organized gangs, loud music and parties)?
- How has the neighborhood reacted?

- Who have been the neighborhood's leading figures (politicians, religious leaders, businesspeople, farmers, cops on the beat, school principals, or others)?
- Why did they acquire influence, and how did they use it?
- In what respects has the neighborhood thought of itself as different from the rest of the community? Why?

ORGANIZATIONS

Institutions and organizations within the communities vary from place to place. They may be educational, religious, cultural, and of a business, voluntary, or other nature. Some are quite common and others quite unusual. Their histories can be worthwhile and interesting and can also form an important part of the past of a neighborhood or an entire community. Some historical questions apply to almost all such bodies, while others relate to particular types.

General Characteristics

- When, how, by whom, and why was this institution or organization formed?
- How and why did its structure, activities, leadership, support, location, funding, and purpose change over the years?
- What were the pivotal events and issues in its past?
- What role has gender played in its evolution, identity, and sense of obligation?
- What has been its influence in the community?
- What have been its relationships with other bodies within and outside the community?
- How have members, supporters, and employees of these bodies regarded themselves in relation to the rest of the community?
- How has the community regarded them?
- How and why have such attitudes changed over time?
- If the institution or organization is no longer part of the community, why, when, and how did it decline, disband, or depart?

Business

- In what sort of activities has this organization engaged throughout its history: agriculture, manufacturing, service, marketing, transportation, finance, or a combination of these?
- Who has owned and managed this business over the years? Were they local people or outsiders?
- How did the business advertise or promote its products or services?
- Were employees hired locally or brought in? If the latter, from where? How have business practices changed or remained constant?

- What has been the business's history of relations with its employees? With unions? With competitors? With government?
- How has the business responded to changes in the economy (periods of prosperity, inflation, stagnation, or depression), technology, or markets?
- How did the business view and act toward the community, and vice versa?

Education

- What educational institutions (public, private, parochial, preschools, schools, colleges and universities, technical institutions, youth associations, and others) have existed in the community?
- Who have been the teachers; and what have been their backgrounds, qualifications, methods, and ideas?
- What has been the nature of the curriculum and extracurricular programs, buildings and other facilities, financial support, and special problems?
- If separate schools and school districts have consolidated, when, why, and to what effect did this occur?
- What special and separate programs and facilities have existed for non-English-speaking students; ethnic, racial, or religious minorities; migrant workers; disabled or gifted persons; the wealthy; and other groups?
- How has the pattern of school attendance varied?
- What has been the history of mandatory attendance requirements or dress codes?
- How have schools been supervised, controlled, and supported?
- What part have school board elections played in addressing educational policies, financing, or other issues?
- What have those elections revealed about community attitudes toward education and the school system?
- If institutions of higher education are located in the community, what have been the "town-gown" relationships?

Culture

- What cultural institutions (museums, libraries, theaters, performance groups, broadcasting stations, publications, and festivals) and styles have attracted local interest and support at various times?
- What sorts of performances, parades, lectures, exhibitions, or other activities have these institutions held over the years?
- How have the efforts of local artists, performers, and writers been regarded in comparison with those outside the community?
- Have creative individuals who grew up in the community tended to stay or leave? Have outsiders been attracted to the place? What seem to have been the reasons?

2.6   *What does the physical appearance of a school suggest about the nature of the educational experience? What does the nature of a posed photograph suggest about matters of importance to those creating the image? (Photo courtesy of the Library of Congress.)*

- How have cultural organizations or activities influenced the rest of the community's life?

Religion

- What religious groups and denominations have been present in the community?
- What have been their beliefs and practices?
- What has been the nature of their leadership, membership, facilities, and other characteristics over the years?
- What splits and mergers have occurred? Why?
- What activities have religious groups engaged in individually and collectively?
- How have they affected the life of the community?
- How have particular religious groups sought community support and endorsement on specific issues, such as charity or civil rights drives, liquor restriction, Sunday business or entertainment bans, abortion, school prayer, or censorship? With what results?
- How has the general community treated various religious groups? By discriminating against them, isolating them, according them leadership roles, or by some other response?

2.7 What does visual evidence suggest about this church and its members? What questions arise that will require other sorts of evidence to answer? (Photo courtesy of the National Archives and Records Administration.)

Voluntary Associations

- What fraternal, civic, patriotic, charitable, professional, recreational, social, political, or similar organizations have existed in the community?
- Who have been members, and how were they selected or admitted?
- Have the stated organizational purposes served primarily as excuses for the group to get together for social companionship, political cooperation, or other unofficial reasons?
- How has the organization felt and acted toward other groups and the community as a whole?
- How has the size, activity, and importance of the group changed over the years?

COMMUNITY

The community may, of course, include any and all of the individual elements already mentioned, but it also incorporates features that are shared by many if not all of its parts.

Physical Characteristics

- When and why was a community established in this location?
- How did it acquire its name?
- How has the location and landscape influenced the nature and direction of community growth?
- How have transportation systems caused or been shaped by patterns of growth?
- What factors have affected the location of commerce; industry; educational, social, and governmental facilities; parks and open space; differing types of neighborhoods; and other community features?
- If the location of various activities shifted, how and why did this occur?
- When did the community obtain electricity, telephones, surfaced roads, parking meters? What changes did this cause?
- What architectural styles have been predominant at various times and why?
- Have old buildings been regarded as treasures or as obstacles to progress?

2.8   The name chosen for a community may reflect the aspirations or identities of its founders, ties to another community, or other considerations. Discovering the reason for that name is a good way to begin an inquiry into the community's history. (Photo courtesy of the Summit County Historical Society.)

Social Characteristics

- What has been the pattern of the community's population growth or decline?
- How has the community regarded the more distant world: with disdain, amusement, fear, or enthusiasm? How have outsiders been treated?
- What have been the major sources of immigration and the destinations of departing residents?
- Has the population been stable or has there been rapid turnover? Has the community had significantly more or fewer children, elderly, singles, males, or females than the national average at the time? To what effect?
- What ethnic, racial, religious, and economic groups have made up the community, and how has the balance altered over the years?
- What conflicts have occurred between groups in the community, and how have these been decided?
- What events have produced displays of community pride or unity?
- Have community-wide patterns of social, religious, cultural, recreational activity existed at any or all times?
- Can community values and standards at various times be seen in low or high rates of out-of-wedlock childbirth, abortion, white-collar or street crime, prostitution, gambling, property neglect, littering, child abuse, or other characteristics?

Economic Characteristics

- What has been the basis of the local economy?
- How and why has this changed?
- If the community has risen (or fallen) as a regional or national economic center, what have been the causes and effects?
- How have individuals and groups, financial institutions, and local government influenced growth, stagnation, or decay?
- What has been the history of labor unions locally?
- How have business development associations, chambers of commerce, and consumer protection organizations arisen?
- What have been their activities and effect in the community?
- What has been the pattern of unemployment, and how has the community responded?

Maintenance of Order

- How has the community established and enforced its standards?
- What has been the nature and rate of prohibited activity?
- How have such illegal or disapproved activities compared with national norms?

- Have changes in patterns of lawbreaking been related to changes in other community social or economic conditions or population shifts?
- When, how, and why was a police force established? How has the ratio of police to population changed?
- Who have been the police?
- What techniques have they employed?
- How well have they met community needs and demands, and in what public esteem have they been held?
- How have police treated juvenile delinquency, prohibition violations, strikes, civil rights and antiwar demonstrations, gambling, prostitution, white-collar crime, or spousal abuse?
- Who have been the criminals?
- How have the courts functioned?
- How have judges been chosen and regarded?
- How have punishment patterns varied depending on the offender and the offense, and how have they changed throughout the years?
- What changes have taken place in penalties and in the nature of penal institutions used by the community?

Health

- What has been the nature of health problems in the community?
- Have there been epidemics or unusual concentrations of particular afflictions?
- What have been the community's standards and institutions of health care?
- When and how were hospitals, nursing homes, hospices, abortion clinics, health maintenance organizations, and other facilities established?
- When did doctors and pharmacists appear to replace home remedies, specialists to replace general practitioners, group practices and HMOs to replace individuals?
- What public health programs developed?
- When and how were water, sewer, and waste treatment systems created?
- How have private groups and government agencies been involved with health issues, such as poor people's clinics, alcoholism and drug programs, birth control information and services, and disability therapies?
- When did psychologists and psychiatrists begin to practice locally?
- How have diagnosis, treatment, and community attitudes toward disabilities, mental illness, and sexually transmitted conditions evolved?

Leadership and Government

- Who have been the community's leaders?
- How have they gained and held their positions?

- In what fashion and to what extent do they exercise leadership?
- How has gender, race, wealth, education, occupation, or some other characteristic entitled individuals or groups to leadership roles or excluded them?
- Is effective community leadership exercised through government, business organizations, the media, ethnic, religious, or labor organizations, or some other device?
- Under what circumstances and to what extent has local government or an alternative become the instrument for meeting community need for public services (police and fire protection, utilities, street construction and cleaning, and so forth); parks and recreation facilities; care for the impoverished, troubled, disabled, aged, or otherwise dependent; and community land use planning and development?
- To what extent have local elections addressed and resolved conflict and reflected community concerns?

FUNCTIONAL CATEGORIES

By dividing the community into many of its component parts and then raising questions about each, we may usefully call attention to many features that have evolved and changed over time. Another way of approaching the study of the community's history involves thinking in terms of functional categories applicable to a wide variety of situations. Doing so will not only suggest additional significant questions but will also help link some of the elements already mentioned.

Environmental Setting

- How has the natural situation, the climate and the terrain, influenced the distribution of space and the design of buildings?
- How have each of these factors influenced family. neighborhood, and community life?
- How have various community elements regarded and shaped the environment?
- What has been the impact on the environment, land use, and architectural styles of technological change, alteration of economic activities and conditions, and shifts in values, knowledge, or political power?

Economic Activity

- At the personal, group, and community levels, what has been involved in the creation or acquisition of wealth?
- How have economic activities served to integrate and divide?

Sudden community growth has causes and consequences, both of which need to be investigated if the development process is to be understood. In William F. King's short history of California's San Gabriel Valley, the introduction of an adequate and dependable water system, the start of a profitable citrus fruit industry, and the completion of a second railroad into the area, turning a monopoly into an intensely competitive situation, were identified as the causes of population influx and land boom in the 1880s.

More than any other east valley city, Pomona embraced the boom spirit and thrived upon it. Of course, the town had a considerable head start on most of its neighbors in the struggle to become worthy of the name "city." Pomonans welcomed the prospect of being a large enough city to have "suburbs" like Lordsburg and Palomares.

Several promotional pamphlets attracted people to Pomona. . . . Attention centered on the climate, agriculture, homes, land prices and the citizenry's quality. The railroad poster exhibited the more outlandish side of boom publicity. It failed to mention that millions of acres of available government land were located in the desert or mountain regions, or that earthquakes had replaced cyclones as a natural hazard.

In the pre-boom days of 1885, Pomona had boasted a population of 2,000. During the peak of the boom, the figure approached 4,000. Some of this later melted away, but real growth in the late eighties topped 80%. Naturally, everything else enlarged to meet the needs of the people. Many years passed before other east valley towns had the capital necessary to form a bank. The Pomona Valley Bank, later the First National, opened in 1886 under the leadership of President Carlton Seaver. The bank erected a small, safe brick building at the corner of Main and Second Streets. One of the first equipment purchases was two sawed-off shotguns. Within a few years the Pomona bank listed deposits of $200,000. There were few phones in the valley then, but Pomona had three of them located in the Palomares Hotel, the bank, and Armour's Drugstore. The company providing the service was the Sunset Telephone and Telegraph Company.

During the first stages of growth Pomona enlarged its two-story Central School and later built three new schools. By the end of the decade, ten churches served the people. The outstanding example of boom-year churches was the remodeled Pomona Methodist Church. Now operated by the Seventh Day Adventist denomination, this splendid building, the core of which was the 1877 building, offers a strong example of the building style of that era.

Along with the normal events accompanying growth, unusual happenings enlivened Pomona's growth. While the town seemingly welcomed all newcomers, certain exceptions existed. In March of 1886 a branch of the Nonpartisan Anti-Chinese League formed under the leadership of William T. (Tooch) Martin. This was a part of the statewide anti-Asian movement. While some spoke out against the movement, calling it anti-Christian, Martin and a large number of citizens persisted. A boycott on Chinese workers, shops, and goods brought the desired result. Finally the Chinese abandoned their homes and businesses and fled the city. A few relocated in nearby Lordsburg and San Dimas. A by-product of this exercise in prejudice was the incorporation of the Pomona Steam Laundry. In order to compete with the Chinese laundry shops in town, Charles I. Lorbeer and J. B. Clump opened the sizeable plant via an open stock sale.

The long term as well as the immediate effects of the 1880s boom were important.

> Although the boom inevitably collapsed, the soundness of the agrarian sector of the local economy prevented a true disaster. In fact, the boom marked the birth pangs of southern California as a population center. A large number of towns trace their origin to this period and the growth momentum generated by this influx of residents, while slowing in the nineties, endured so long it became virtually permanent, a standard par of southern California's folklore in the twentieth century.
>
> *Source: William F. King,* The Vintage Years: Our Valley before 1945 *(Walnut, CA: Mt. San Antonio College, Department of Community Services, 1975), 43, 52–53.*

- What economic ideas have been held, and how have they influenced choices of activity, competition and cooperation, distribution of wealth, decisions on taxation and investment, and other matters?
- How has the economy shaped the social, political, and cultural environment?

Social Relations

- What has been the nature of social relationships among various elements in the community?
- What conditions of wealth, religion, race, ethnicity, gender, education, and occupation gave individuals and groups greater or lesser status and influence?
- Who have been viewed as outsiders, misfits, threats, annoyances, eccentrics, or amusements?
- What social factors have contributed to tension and conflict, harmony and cooperation?
- How stable has the social structure been?
- What has caused change?
- How are social distinctions important in community lifestyles (diet, dress, housing, associations, and activities); religion; values, beliefs, and practices; and political behavior?

Political Affairs

- What political issues and movements have arisen in the community?
- How and why have they aroused, divided, or united individuals, neighborhoods, or groups within the community?
- How and why have various elements in the community responded to reform proposals; local or national appeals from parties and individual candidates; and specific crises such as depressions, wars, communist scares, public school desegregation, revelations of political abuses?
- What have been the patterns of participation and preference in elections?
- How have defeated individuals and groups responded and been treated?

Ideals and Values

- What ideas and values have been highly regarded by individuals, families, neighborhoods, particular elements, and the community as a whole?
- How have beliefs conflicted—and changed—regarding conduct, property, power, and privilege?
- Have the dominant ideas come from local proponents or from outsiders?
- How have creative and unconventional persons been regarded?
- How have those holding various views promoted their ideas and beliefs?
- How have changes in technology, education, or other conditions altered values regarding work, play, religion, society, culture, courtship, sex roles, child rearing, sexual activity, privacy, conformity, or authority?

Armed with a well-chosen focus and specific questions, historians of the nearby world are ready to search for information regarding the past that they seek to understand.

NOTES AND FURTHER READING

Bernard Bailyn is quoted in Michael Kammen, "The Historian's Vocation and the State of the Discipline in the United States," in *The Past before Us: Contemporary Historical Writing in the United States,* edited by Michael Kammen (Ithaca: Cornell University Press, 1980), p. 38.

More extensive and specific questions regarding any area of concern in this chapter can be found in the individual volumes of the Nearby History and Exploring Community History series.

3

Traces and Storytelling

Historians tell stories. The stories may be simple and straightforward or complex, analytical, and interpretive. They may be told in many different ways, but they are stories nonetheless. In this chapter we consider how the stories are created, particularly the kinds that historians of the nearby past seek to tell.

The creation of a story begins with the desire to learn, to discover. Indeed, "history" is rooted in a Greek word meaning "to inquire." Curiosity sends one looking for materials to construct a story and shapes the way they are used. But constructing a story means more than merely relating an episode from the past, more than passing along a tale or an anecdote. It means, among other things, providing descriptions and explanations, ensuring the story's accuracy, conveying its significance, interpreting—or at least suggesting—its meaning, and aiding the understanding of listeners and readers in other ways.

Good storytellers are aware of the meaning and purpose of their stories. A typical purpose might be to teach a lesson. In the story of a church, a teller might show that the church was strong and growing when it was in debt and, in turn, weak and declining when it was solvent. The obvious hazards in defining cause-and-effect relationships in cases like this are good reminders that the lessons of history are not as easy to find as one might think and that, once found, they should not be pushed too far.

Some stories answer questions. What was it like to live in another time or place? Or on a more profound level: How has the meaning of "being human" changed through the years? How does being a part of a particular community affect one's sense of identity? Sometimes stories are a means of leaving a record for future generations or merely a way to satisfy curiosity. Anniversaries or milestones may call for remembrance of past heroes and heroics, and meaning may lie in the spirit and pride such stories arouse. Many stories, to be sure, are told just for the fun of it. Whatever their purpose, good storytellers have a sense of their audience's curiosity and interests.

Sometimes historians find it difficult to find the focus for their inquiry or even to start it. In such instances it helps to have a first question, an opener. The previous chapter suggested many possibilities, but the most natural and intriguing questions concern origins: What conditions gave birth to the town, for example, or who were the founders of the church? Where did the family start in America? When did the community first see itself as a community? Who designed the house? Who began the business? Simple answers to these questions, followed by elaboration, of course, often help storytellers over a formidable barrier—that of putting down the first words. Some people find it useful to start with a question about origins even though they know that both the question and the answer may be drastically reshaped or even discarded as the work progresses. The important thing is to get the story under way.

To keep an inquiry going, you must know where you intend to carry it. If you are writing about an institution, for example, you will want to touch on its high and low points, its developing organizational structure, its leaders, or its unique character. Stories about families or communities invite questions about their distinctive features. If you are writing about a business, you are certain to be interested in its good times and bad. If your subject is a building, you will want to know who occupied it, how it was used, when and why it changed hands, and what was unusual about it.

Some of the questions you raise will deal with people. Some will be concerned with time and place. People, time, and place lie at the heart of all good stories, and they come together in events and reflect ideas. Ordinarily stories reveal issues to be explored and problems to be solved, or they fall together in sequences to be analyzed and interpreted. The good storyteller makes description, explanation, analysis, problem solving, and interpretation integral parts of the story.

FINDING HISTORICAL TRACES

Writers of fiction tell stories, too, but they draw material, in large part, from their imaginations, or at least from experiences and observations treated fancifully. Historians, in contrast, work with real people and with events as they happened, insofar as that is possible. Doing so requires the imaginative use of particular capabilities.

The most important of these capabilities has to do with use of the "traces" people and events have left behind. Traces are everywhere—in the remains, tracks, marks, records, remnants, relics, evidence, and footprints of events. Historians need to know how to find such traces; how to sift and sort them; how to establish their authenticity, credibility, and importance; and how to assemble them as they reconstruct events. In turn, we must know how to treat events in a chronological sequence or some other way, to relate them to people and ideas, and in so doing to build a story that is history.

A story may be passed from one person to another before it is written down, as in the following case. Details can be lost or altered. The careful historian seeks to verify such stories before accepting them but at the same time recognizes that they are rich with traces. The vivid details of this tale, for instance, provide information about a farm family's diet, money, and way of obtaining news. Would the storytellers have had reason to distort such matters?

Uncle Martin and my father liked to tell about how Grandmother sold a loaf of bread for five dollars. They had lived out on the prairie for a number of years. Late one afternoon two rough-looking men on horseback rode into the yard. The boys saw them coming and did not like their looks, so they ran into the hay shed that stood out by the road and hid. They peeked out of a hole in the shed and watched. One man got off his horse and went to the house. When Grandmother opened the door, he asked her if she would sell him a loaf of bread. Grandmother told him, "I have no bread but black, dark bread."

"Nothing wrong with dark bread!" the man said. "Will you sell me a loaf?" Grandmother went and got one of her big loaves of graham flour bread. She had just taken it out of the oven about an hour before. It was still warm. The man felt of it with his finger and asked, "Will you sell it?"

Grandmother put the loaf in a sack and laid it on the table. The man laid down a five dollar bill. Grandmother shook her head and said, "I have no change for money like that."

"Lady," he told her, "nobody will ask you for change," and picked up the bread and walked out. They rode off down the trail towards the southwest. The boys watched them go down across the creek and up and over the hill until they were lost from sight on the prairie.

A few days later three men rode into the yard. One of them got off his horse and came towards the shed. The boys came out. They could see his big bright star on his coat. He said he was a sheriff from Minnesota and he wondered if they had seen two men on horseback go riding along the trail? They told him that they had seen two men going southwest about two days ago. "We're on their trail," the sheriff told his men. They did not seem to be in any hurry and slowly rode down the trail toward the southwest.

The next week when they got their weekly paper it said that Jessie James and his partner had robbed a bank up in Minnesota. A sheriff had chased them all the way across Iowa and then lost their trail down in Missouri.

Source: Guy Johnson, "The Boy on Kiegley's Creek," unpublished manuscript in the possession of the authors.

It is essential, therefore, to examine traces systematically and to apply guidelines for evaluating them. Because everything around us bears marks of the past, the first distinction to be drawn is between historical and nonhistorical traces. There is no absolute or objective distinction between them, for it is the interest of a historian that makes traces from the past historical. Nonhistorical traces are those that historians dismiss as of no use in probing or reconstructing events of the past. What is historical to one person, therefore, may well seem nonhistorical to another, and what is nonhistorical at one time might be regarded as historical at another.

3.1–3.4   These pictures record milestones in the growth and progress of a church. A small group of people began to worship in a real estate tract office in 1931. Three years later, they moved the building (3.1) to a new location and remodeled it (3.2). In 1939 they enlarged the structure (3.3) while planning for the building of a permanent church building. A partial building was opened in 1949 (not shown) and was used while the money was raised to complete it. Completion came in 1955 (3.4). A large wing (not shown) was added to the building in 1962. During these three decades of growth, the congregation was dynamic and distinctive. A historian would seek not only to identify the motivations and to describe the character of the congregation during the growth years, but also to determine what happened to it during the subsequent decades of stability and decline.

(Photo courtesy of and copyright © Unity Lutheran Church, Bel-Nor, Missouri.)

(Photo courtesy of and copyright © Unity Lutheran Church, Bel-Nor, Missouri.)

(Photo courtesy of and copyright © Unity Lutheran Church, Bel-Nor, Missouri.)

(Photo courtesy of and copyright © Unity Lutheran Church, Bel-Nor, Missouri.)

This distinction helps historians confront the need to sift and sort the materials they work with. Without the ability and willingness to draw distinctions and make selections, a would-be historian is paralyzed. If everything is pertinent to a story, it is almost as if nothing is. Selecting historical traces for their authenticity, reliability, accuracy, credibility, and usefulness in relation to the topic under consideration is the most important task one faces after choosing a topic for research. Dismissing nonhistorical traces allows one to proceed with one's work.

Historical traces may be divided into four types: immaterial, material, written, and representational. Immaterial traces consists of intangible but readily apparent remnants from the past, such as institutions, customs, traditions, beliefs, principles, practices, superstitions, legends, and language. The history you study, that is, the past as it has been processed by historians, is itself an immaterial trace. The word "immaterial" carries with it neither positive nor negative implications but simply denotes that you discern the traces rationally rather than through your sensory perceptions alone.

Material traces are easier to grasp. They consist of objects, artifacts of the past, products of human doings, things we can touch. In the sense that artifacts are the culmination of a series of activities—a quilt, for example—they are themselves events. Their sale or exchange is an event that might leave another piece of historical and perhaps even legal evidence, such as a bill of sale or a title. Some material traces are still in use, even though they may be "antiquated." They may range in size from very small—a jewel, perhaps—to very large. Buildings and landscapes are material remains of events and sequences of events. So are such things as tools, machinery, vehicles, paintings, sculpture, clothing, and furniture.

Written traces come in many varieties. Some may be handwritten, such as letters, diaries, journals, and manuscripts. Newspapers, books, magazines, and pamphlets are printed traces. Some may be partly printed and partly handwritten, such as immigration papers, passports, birth and marriage certificates, report cards, and business and financial forms. Sometimes written traces are a part of material goods, such as inscriptions on tombstones, engravings on jewelry, and labels on clothing.

The fourth kind of trace is both a real thing, having tangible, sensory presence, and a representation of something else. For want of a better term, we call this a "representational" trace. The best example is a photograph. It is itself a trace and it captures and preserves other traces. Chapter 7 in this book is devoted to consideration of visual documents as historical traces.

Representational traces are also found in ballads, folksongs, folktales, and stories. These are immaterial in one sense, but they are perceived sensorially, capable of being written down or captured on tape or disc recordings. Like photographs, they convey information, ideas, or sentiments; they are of inherent interest and at the same time they represent something else.

Traces come also in another form that does not lend itself to the notion of a single type, that is, electronic traces conveyed through computers and the Internet. Some traces thus conveyed are written, some representational, and some "virtual," as in museum exhibitions that can be visited through the World Wide Web.

Using such traces is at times efficient, convenient, and rewarding; at other times it can be frustrating and fruitless. Persons searching the World Wide Web for historical traces should bear in mind that there are no widely accepted standards for placing documents and other materials there, so the useful material is surrounded by vast amounts that are at best useless and possibly inaccurate and misleading. Much of what one finds on the Web is there for commercial purposes, some of it as a lure for purchases (as, for example, in genealogical research). Moreover, the sources of information are not always clearly identified and the credentials of those who place them there unknown. Because addresses change and Web sites come and go, the best of directories are of limited value. Only by browsing can you locate some of the sources you seek. That is not necessarily bad, since you will sometimes end up with something better than what you are looking for; just as often you may find dead ends.

Nonetheless, as Jeffrey G. Barlow demonstrates in an essay titled "Historical Research and Electronic Evidence" and as Internet users know very well, electronic delivery makes many primary documents more readily available and research in *some* primary and secondary materials easier. The Internet also facilitates exchange of ideas among persons with common interests, and it makes available new universes of data. Because there are virtually no restrictions as to who can place something on the Web, Barlow calls it a "democratizing agent." (See, for example, resources and connections made possible by H-Net: Humanities and Social Sciences OnLine <www.h-net.msu.edu>.)

With respect to all the types of traces cited so far, users must remember that they can also be categorized in other ways. Some traces are intentional; they are created for the specific purpose of leaving a record. Some people, for example, know that eventually their diaries are likely to be read by someone else, which explains why such documents are sometimes closed and placed in family archives with a stipulation that says something like: "Not to be opened until ten years after my death or March 31, 2021, whichever comes later." But determining the writer's intentions can be tricky, for some people use daily jottings as inexpensive therapy, while others regard them as personal historical records. If papers are found with orders that they must be destroyed at their keeper's death, historians face an ethical problem as well as a methodological one.

Some material traces are clearly unpremeditated. Tools, for example, are made to be used, not to establish a record. Most artifacts are mute, existing first of all for their own sake and unrelated to their later use by historians to establish or reconstruct events. Public records initially serve purposes quite different from those to which historians later put them. A birth certificate, a college diploma, a marriage license, business forms, and a death certificate have specific legal functions. The uses historians make of them—to place persons geographically, to confirm employment records, or to determine turning points in lives—are quite apart from their intended purposes. Presumably, such traces are more reliable factually than are those created to help later historians tell a story. The people who created them had no interest in directing the work of historians or in shaping conclusions.

3.5–3.6   What factual information can be drawn from this legal document? What does the picture on it suggest about marriage ideals at the turn of the century? Descendants of this couple discovered that the family names of both the bride and the groom appear in census data with variant spellings through the years. What might account for the variations?

(Photo courtesy of and copyright © Roy Plunk.)

(Photo courtesy of and copyright © Roy Plunk.)

But the distinction between intentional and unpremeditated traces is often largely artificial. A letter in its original form, especially one that is handwritten, might be regarded as unpremeditated, but if a copy is made and filed, it is intended for later use as the historical evidence of an event. (One wonders, incidentally, whether easy access to photocopiers has made writers more conscious of the possibility that their letters might be preserved, prompting them to write more obviously for the record.) On the other hand, a genealogy may be an intentional transmitter of fact; the compiler may see it as an outline of a family's passage through time. Historians may use it for all kinds of other purposes, such as locating the routes by which a family has moved from place to place, measuring patterns in life spans, or determining the stability of nuclear families and the closeness of extended families. The purpose of a church charter, a public record, is to authorize a congregation to hold property as a legal corporate entity or make tax-exempt status possible. A historian examines such a document for clues to the congregation's beliefs, its sense of order, its relations with the denomination of which it is a member, and its leadership at a given point in time.

So it is better to evaluate traces as both intentional and unpremeditated sources of information than to assume that they are one or the other or that one kind is to be preferred over the other in establishing the truth about events. How to establish the authenticity, reliability, veracity, and usefulness of specific kinds of traces is the concern of other chapters in this book.

USING HISTORICAL TRACES

Still, some general guidelines for the use of traces can be summarized here. First, their relationships to events must be clearly established. The best and most useful records are those nearest in time and place to the event. Thus an account by an eyewitness written the day of an event is ordinarily to be preferred to a recollection years later by someone who received it secondhand. Second, the questions asked of the traces should be ones that they can answer. Do not expect a physical object, for example, to reveal its worth, either at the time of its creation or at any later period. External traces are required to make such determinations. Third, the traces must always relate to events in affirmative and identifiable ways; inferences drawn from the absence of traces are highly questionable. Suppose a family had the tradition of recording its Christmas gatherings with family portraits. Would a gap in the series of portraits indicate that no gathering had occurred? Not necessarily.

Fourth, while traces may be presented in open or unprocessed form, that is, without interpretation, the historian has the responsibility of determining their authenticity and potential usefulness. As historians must be careful that they do not put traces to unwarranted uses, so they must also carefully protect them from improper uses by others. For example, one might want to include in a publication a facsimile of an interesting letter containing choice bits of information. Suppose, though, that the letter is not dated and was written by someone whose identity is not known. The historian must advise readers of these facts and lay out the external traces that lend credence to or challenge the plausibility and usefulness of the information in the letter.

Fifth, because traces do not exist in isolation, they may not be used without regard for their context. Thus, in using an item drawn from the minutes of an organization, a historian must take into account the character and completeness of the minutes, the range of issues with which they deal, the recording practices of the secretary, the circumstances of their preservation, and other matters pertaining to the topic under consideration.

Finally, since it is impossible to reconstruct events in precise form—to provide, so to speak, instant replays—historians' inferences about events must always be expressed as probabilities. Although the aim should be to describe people, places, events, and circumstances in terms that are completely accurate, historians must content themselves with conclusions comparable to those acceptable in a court of law, that is, those that seem plausible "beyond a reasonable doubt." In other words, when absolute and incontrovertible proof is lacking, a verdict may be regarded as highly probable if traces to contradict it do not exist or have been discredited or neutralized. It is appropriate to apply this rule in any consideration of historical traces.

ACQUIRING SKILLS

It is clear by now that those who compile the history of communities, towns, neighborhoods, cities, clubs, churches, houses, landscapes, artifacts, and other things in their own locale must be more than historians in the traditional sense. Besides knowing how to tell a story based on real events, they must know how to gather and make the most of a wide variety of historical evidence. Working with documents, many of which they collect and preserve themselves, demands archival skills. But historians must also pick up fieldwork skills such as those used by cultural anthropologists and folklorists. Concern with terrain, landforms, landscapes, cityscapes, building forms, maps, and measuring devices puts them next to historical and cultural geographers. Locating, extracting (literally and figuratively), analyzing, cataloging, and preserving artifacts requires historians to learn, at least in rudimentary ways, the skills of archaeologists, museologists, and curators. And as historians, they must become conversant in social history, the history of art and architecture, and possibly even psychohistory.

SHARPENING PERCEPTIONS

Before we turn in separate chapters to specific kinds of traces historians look for, let us suggest a first step to be taken by those wishing to become better historians of things nearby. As we noted earlier, historical traces surround us. Yet we may not see them because we are not looking for them. If it is true, as Thoreau remarked, that "you can't say more than you see," it seems useful to suggest ways of expanding the powers of perception—and thus also the evidence-gathering

*3.7–3.8   How many traces of the distinctive characteristics of two different Ohio
communities during the late 1930s can be perceived in these two photographs?*

(Photo courtesy of the Library of Congress.)

(Photo courtesy of the Library of Congress.)

3.9   In studying the traces found in this 1941 photograph of men at their neighborhood club, notice the manner of dress and the artifacts that form part of the world of these recent Greek immigrants. What might a comparable photo show of the world of Greek immigrant women? Another ethnic group? Old-stock Americans? (Photo courtesy of the Library of Congress.)

powers—in the course of daily living. On one level people can simply heighten their awareness of the natural and cultural environments in which they move; on another, actual practice with real or imaginary tools is needed.

We come to know our natural and cultural environments through our senses, as we see, hear, smell, touch, and taste. Psychologists may disagree as to exactly how the sensory processes work, but there seems to be a relationship between perception and our knowledge of the language that describes it. For example, our sense of taste becomes sharper as we learn words for taste. Even the four basic tastes—sweet, sour, salty, and bitter—are apparently learned, since there seem to be no corresponding physiological sensors. The language of taste is actually much larger, including as it does tart, sharp, fruity, tangy, mellow, rich, and bland. When we add texture words such as crisp, fluffy, soggy, light, succulent, dry, crunchy, and gooey, our ability to express and to distinguish is enlarged further. Those who would dispute the relationship between language and taste need only to be asked whether their mouth waters when they hear words describing foods they like.

Perhaps the most important sense that historians use is the visual. Learning the language of seeing and putting it to work while walking or driving or flying is a way of expanding powers of perception and, therefore, a way to improve one's capacity to observe traces effectively. Concentrating on ten terms in the language of vision and looking for places to use them in the environment is a first step: light and shadow; color and texture; lines, shape, and patterns; similarities and contrasts; and movement.

Suppose you set out to use the language of vision in ordinary places to describe things you have never noticed before. You might begin with foundry art—fire hydrants and manhole covers, sturdy sentries of the landscape and guardians of secrets of the underground. Besides noticing their shapes, colors, patterns, and textures, you might also take note of the dates found on them. And as you do this, think about what you might learn from hydrants and manhole covers about patterns of residential growth in your community. Notice the shapes of the numbers in the dates. And then carry this awareness to other places. Take note, too, of differently formed dates chiseled into cornerstones, perhaps, or painted on the side of a delivery truck declaring "since 1921." Look for clues in these numbers to insights regarding the community's past.

While you are looking at numbers you might look at letters as well, not only for the messages they communicate, but for their shapes and the patterns in which they appear. Your eyes will turn to billboards, of course, giving you a chance to do another exercise. Try to imagine how the landscape would appear without them. You might then look at nonverbal signs, particularly arrows. Notice the orders they give as well as the confusing symbols they sometimes are. Do the same with barriers: fences, walls, roadblocks, guardrails, barrels. What were the purposes of those who erected them? What attitudes do they suggest?

Places to study the language of vision are endless. Look at the texture of buildings, streets, and sidewalks, at public sitting places, at the fancywork on houses, at the geometric interplay of shapes on bridges as you move across them, at the recurrence of forms such as circles and squares, at patterns in grillwork. In all of these things, keep in mind the words in the language of vision, consciously trying to increase your sensitivity to them. And then go a step further by observing how your sense of vision is sharpened or otherwise affected by messages from your other senses—perhaps the blowing wind, the roar of the traffic, the pounding of machines, the splash of a fountain, the stench of a smokestack, or the drifting aroma of a barbecue grill.

And take still another step by picking up a camera and looking at the world through a lens. If nothing else, doing this exercise increases your capacity to concentrate on the narrow piece of the environment you are observing. The camera provides a frame, eliminating for a moment extraneous distractions and reducing your subject from three dimensions to two. (If carrying a camera is inconvenient, simply cut a rectangle in the center of a card, perhaps the size of an opening in a 2" x 2" slide, and use it to frame your subject. Increasing or reducing the distance between your eye and the card has some of the same effect as changing the lens on your camera or repositioning yourself in relation to your subject.) Practicing with a camera will have another beneficial effect on your work as a historian, for you will start looking at photographs more intelligently and more critically.

Traces are also found by listening. Being aware of the language of hearing—pitch, volume, and timbre—may be helpful in sharpening your listening skills. More important, though, is the ability to concentrate on the words that reach your ear. An evidence-gathering technique of historians is the oral interview, usually conducted with a tape or video recorder so that the conversation may be reviewed and transcribed later. One can practice interviewing by simulating, perhaps in the privacy of one's automobile, the technique of radio talk-show hosts. The trick is to formulate questions that build on the previous response and at the same time elicit information you would genuinely want to have. Second-guess the interviewer; listen critically to the responses. Not all such practice, we should add, needs to be done in covert ways. The best way to learn the art of interviewing involves a real tape recorder, a live microphone, and another person.

It is also possible to heighten one's sensitivity to written historical traces. One might, for example, take the simple step of creating personal or family archives by pulling together all papers, records, photo albums, certificates, letters, diaries, income tax and other forms, house plans, scrapbooks, and such things. This project may also prompt you to file in your archives photocopies of the most valuable such items and to place the originals in a safe deposit box along with negatives of your photographs.

You might also consider keeping a daily journal of your activities and thoughts or at least filing a copy of letters you write, either in your computer (backed up, of course) or in a hard-copy file. Doing so will not only help you preserve a record but will make you conscious of practical distinctions between intentional and unpremeditated traces as well. It may also help you to realize that while phone calls and the use of e-mail may be convenient, these media leave no traces for the record; as a result, you might even become a better letter writer.

This chapter is a general introduction to traces, events, and storytelling. We believe that historians of the nearby past should begin where their competence and interest are greatest. Consequently, the seven chapters that follow have been written so that they can be used independently or in any sequence that best responds to the user's needs. We will return to the matter of traces gathering and storytelling in chapter 11, where we will use the more formal terms "research" and "writing."

NOTES AND FURTHER READING

The classic volume that develops most effectively the idea of "traces" in the work of historians is G. J. Renier's *History: Its Purpose and Method* (Boston: Beacon Press, 1950;

reprint ed., New York: Harper and Row, 1965). Renier, in turn, noted its use by two French historians, the "wise methodologists Langlois and Seignobos." Occasionally we use other terms, including "evidence," although in today's world this term too frequently suggests legal implications that are not ordinarily applicable in historians' work. John R. Stilgoe's *Outside Lies the Magic: Regaining History and Awareness in Everyday Places* (New York: Walker and Co., 1998) speaks directly and provocatively to the matter of sharpening perceptions as discussed in the final part of this chapter.

A standard guide for research and writing, with several chapters devoted to finding, evaluating, verifying, and using traces is Jacques Barzun and Henry F. Graff, *The Modern Researcher* (New York: Harcourt Brace Jovanovich, 5th ed., 1992). See also Francis Paul Prucha, *Handbook for Research in American History: A Guide to Bibliographies and Other Reference Works* (Lincoln: University of Nebraska Press, 2nd ed., 1992). Allan Lichtman and Valerie French describe and assess current methods in *Historians and the Living Past: The Theory and Practice of Historical Study* (Arlington Heights, IL: AHM, 1978). In *Historians' Fallacies: Toward a Logic of Historical Thought* (New York: Harper and Row, 1970), David Hackett Fischer discusses with wit and insight historians' uses and misuses of traces. Introduction to ways of heightening one's perceptual abilities are found in George Nelson's *How to See: A Guide to Reading Our Manmade Environment* (Boston: Little, Brown, 1977).

History News, the journal of the American Association for State and Local History, is frequently helpful to researchers of nearby history. So is the series of Technical Leaflets the AASLH began publishing in the mid-1960s; almost 100 of the leaflets remain in print, about one-fourth of them having been published in the 1990s. A list is available at <www.aaslh.org>. This Web site also provides information on leaflets published by the National Center for Local Government Records and the AASLH Video Lending Library.

Appendix D provides information about using the World Wide Web in historical research, along with Web addresses that, at the time this is written, are likely to be most useful. See also Dennis A. Trinkle, ed., *Writing, Teaching, and Researching History in the Electronic Age: Historians and Computers* (Armonk, NY: M. E. Sharpe, 1998).

4

Published Documents

A document is recorded information in any form. Whether the information is handwritten, typed or printed on paper, etched on glass or metal, carved on wood or stone, or impressed on film, audiotape, or computer disk, it speaks of its moment of origin. Documents can often be the most direct and reliable link with an earlier day, preserving eyewitness observations, capturing sights and sounds, or tabulating conditions of the time. Indeed, sometimes the only surviving trace of a past event, individual, or circumstance may be recorded in a letter or diary, office memorandum or ledger, newspaper, photograph, map, or cemetery marker, all of which have different uses, values, and limitations as historical evidence that are worthy of consideration.

The utility and reliability of documents vary nearly as much as their form. The circumstances of creation, intended purpose, and preservation all influence historic value. This chapter and the three that follow examine different types of documents. The first type to be considered is produced in multiple copies and is typically found in scattered locations. Chapter 5 will deal with one-of-a-kind documents, individually created, which are usually to be found in private hands, office files, or archives. Chapter 6 will examine records on audio- or videotape or in written transcripts of interviews with participants in (or eyewitnesses to) past events, so-called oral histories or oral documents. Finally, in chapter 7 separate consideration will be given to strictly visual documents—in particular photographs—because of their distinctive values and problems. These four chapters not only indicate the worth of documents in exploring the past but also suggest the sorts of evidence of contemporary life that ought to be preserved for future generations.

Since the act of recording information creates a document, the circumstances in which the act is performed need to be considered first in any evaluation.

- Was it a hasty, spur-of-the-moment act, a routine transaction, or a thoughtful, deliberate process?

- Did the recorder possess firsthand knowledge of whatever was being described or simply report what he or she was told?
- Was the recorder a neutral party or did he or she have interests that could be positively or negatively affected by what was recorded?
- Did the recorder intend the document for his or her own use, for one or more selected individuals, or for a larger audience of one sort or another?
- Was the recorder's intention merely to inform, or was it to persuade the reader?
- Was the information recorded immediately or only after time had passed, causing memories to change or fade?
- Is the present document a replica of an earlier one that in some fashion has altered the original's appearance or meaning, as might be the case with a reprint of the Declaration of Independence, a photocopied letter, a printout of an Internet memo, or a reproduced photograph?

Obviously, one's confidence in what can be learned from any document depends upon the answers to these questions. The circumstances of creation are ultimately much more important than the form of the document, but the form provides clues about the circumstances of creation. The form also determines how easy or difficult it can be to extract desired information, whatever the creator's intent.

Some documents are intended for a wide audience and are therefore prepared and distributed in multiple copies; in other words, they are published. This category includes books, magazines, newspapers, pamphlets, government reports, laws and judicial decisions, catalogs, directories, posters, and maps. The very fact that they would initially have been produced in quantity, for distribution, increases the likelihood that some copies have survived and will be available. Local libraries usually make a practice of gathering published materials regarding the area they serve, but churches, businesses, civic and professional organizations, government agencies, and individuals may have collections as well. Indeed, it may prove easier to find publications pertaining to the nearby past than to evaluate them.

The normal way to locate published materials is to consult library catalogs, union lists (compilations of materials in a group of libraries), and specialized reference guides. Increasingly this can be done electronically, either via the Internet or during a library visit. Most libraries maintain a catalog in which every book in their collection is entered, either on alphabetized cards or in a computer file, by the author's name (last name first), the book's title and, less consistently, the book's major topics. Newspapers, serials or periodicals, and government publications are sometimes listed separately, sometimes included in the main catalog. In addition, better libraries hold bibliographies and other guides to materials not in their own collections but available elsewhere.

More and more libraries have not only replaced or supplemented their card files with computer-based catalogs but also have acquired rights of electronic access to huge research databases. Some libraries permit their catalogs and databases to be searched via the Internet, making it easier than ever to discover the existence of an item, though not always to obtain a copy. The Library of Congress, the largest library in the United States with over 17 million books and nearly 100 million other items (manuscripts, photographs, films, audio and video recordings, prints, and drawings), provides public access to its catalog of holdings at <www.loc.gov>. Other libraries are forming state or regional networks with a common catalog and shared borrowing privileges for member institutions. For instance, over seventy Ohio college and university libraries with combined holdings of over 6 million items belong to OhioLink. Anyone on the Internet can search the catalog at <www.ohiolink.edu> though only member institutions have access to OhioLink's more than sixty databases of article citations, book reviews, biographical data, and other information. Similar networks are being created elsewhere, providing library patrons with shared borrowing privileges and access to databases. Among the largest databases are the Research Libraries Information Network (RLIN), a union catalog of 88 million items from hundreds of libraries, archives, and museums, and the Online Computer Library Catalog (OCLC) with 30 million entries representing material held in over 10,000 libraries worldwide. Such arrangements make it easier than ever before to identify and locate obscure items, either on one's own or with help from a librarian (especially if a computer, an Internet gopher, and precise terminology for a subject search is involved).

Computerized tools for locating material have a major drawback for nearby historians, at least for the time being. Not all library catalogs are computerized, much less networked, and even those that are have not always entered information on older holdings. With a few notable exceptions, databases likewise best reflect information compiled in recent years. While it is fairly easy, and rapidly becoming easier, to find publications and some other materials devoted to local topics through computer searches, it would be a serious mistake to assume that all available material can be identified in this way.

Library subject catalogs and computer databases can simplify and speed a search for information on a particular topic, as can indexes to reference works and other publications, but they vary widely in coverage. Some are extremely thorough and specific; others are limited to proper names, titles, or major topics. Furthermore, catalogers and indexers may have applied different labels to a single topic. "Liquor control" to one person could be "temperance movement" to another and "prohibition" to a third. One city may have been listed in one index as "Richmond, Indiana," and in another as "Indiana-Richmond." It is important to consider all possible listings and alphabetic locations for a topic. If entries do not appear in a catalog or index as expected, it makes sense to browse in the appropriate section of library shelves or to search the table of contents for a promising section of text. Catalogs and indexes are great time savers if they are used with imagination and caution so that material is not overlooked.

BOOKS AND ARTICLES

Nearby history documents that often take the form of books and articles include memoirs, genealogies, travel accounts, biographies, edited letters, speeches, and public records, and histories. An individual's recollections, a traveler's description of things seen and conditions encountered, or a published letter, speech, or official report may reveal many details about the time or topic under investigation. A genealogy, biography, or history may not be as close to the event but may illuminate related matters as well as the object of the inquiry.

There is a natural tendency to assume that information in cold, hard print must be accurate, but such a conclusion must always be resisted until it has been carefully confirmed. What did the author know from personal experience? How did the author acquire and verify other information? Is the information consistent with that provided by other sources? What appears to have been the motivation for publication? Has the work been issued by a publisher with a reputation for care and dependability, or is the firm an unknown quantity? Occasionally documents are published with the intention of deceiving the reader; far more often they contain statements that lack supporting evidence, speculations and opinions passed off as fact, or partial accounts that overlook significant elements. Careful and wary historians of the nearby world will find much help in books and articles.

Of course, no library collects every book ever published. Even the finest local library has probably not obtained every book with useful information about the nearby past. Regrettably, many institutions have not received the steady support they need, and sometimes acquisition of new material has been curtailed or suspended for years at a time. In other instances, certain types of books have been excluded, for instance, genealogies of families who lived in the area. And naturally, if one is interested in a distant community, the local library is likely to have even less to offer.

For all of these reasons, one should search for material in other places. The emergence of computer catalogs and networks has eased the process, but a thorough search still requires attention to nonelectronic finding aids. The Library of Congress has published author-title and subject catalogs of its own vast holdings and union lists of books held by more than 750 American libraries, helpful although far from perfect tools for discovering documents that may exist elsewhere. Also, many specialized bibliographies have been compiled and printed to identify useful publications. (See the references at the end of this chapter for various finding aids.) As more libraries share their catalogs by means of computer networks, it becomes easier to discover not only the title of a relevant book but also the location of a copy. Many libraries participate in interlibrary loan arrangements, so that the desired book may be borrowed from a distant library, usually for a small fee.

Articles in magazines, scholarly journals, or newspapers are harder to locate. Most libraries lack the resources to prepare catalog entries for individual articles, though sometimes they will do so for selected items of local importance. Various reference books and computer databases, however, do list articles under author, title, or subject headings. Still, these guides are not complete by any means. Their greatest weaknesses lie in their lack of coverage of small publications with a primarily local rather than national focus and circulation and, especially for computer databases, the limitation of their coverage to recent years. No one searching for articles on the nearby past should conclude that they do not exist simply because they do not appear in the standard periodical guides or databases. Examining the Library of Congress *Union List of Serials* for the titles of regional, state, local, and topical journals and then looking individually at those not surveyed by guides, indexes, or databases is the only way of ensuring total coverage.

THESES AND DISSERTATIONS

Documents quite similar in many respects to books and articles and yet often overlooked are academic theses and dissertations. The research and writing requirements for advanced degrees in many scholarly fields produce an enormous amount of careful, detailed investigation of local topics. Business conditions, educational practices, architectural styles, agricultural patterns, social habits, political developments, and many other matters are treated either historically or in contemporary surveys. The very fact that the research is so tightly focused on one locale prevents many of these worthwhile pieces of work from becoming books or articles. Even a poorly written thesis sometimes contains arduously collected information available nowhere else that may prove extremely useful. Local colleges and universities keep records of all theses and dissertations done by their own students.

Bell and Howell Information and Learning is the new name for University Microfilms International (<www.umi.com>). Through ProQuest, its on-line information service, this site provides subscription-based access (typically through libraries) to documents in digital or microform, including dissertation abstracts, newspapers, and a wide variety of research collections. The number of M.A. theses greatly exceeds that of Ph.D. dissertations, but unfortunately no general catalog of theses exists. Theses, even more than dissertations, tend to involve topics close at hand, so one can safely assume that if a thesis has been completed on the subject of interest, it is most likely to be found in the collections of local college, university, or public libraries.

NEWSPAPERS

Newspapers, a rich source of information about communities, have been published in America since the early eighteenth century, although they have greatly changed in style and content with the passage of time. Even very small communities have often supported a local paper for at least part of their existence. For instance, Minnesota's first, the *Minnesota Pioneer,* was established in 1849. Before the territory was granted statehood nine years later, seventy-five more newspapers were founded. Virtually every significant settlement in the territory had its own newspaper. Many times communities have been served by newspapers in foreign languages as well as in English. Furthermore, ethnic groups, labor unions, corporations, professional societies, civic associations, and religious, commercial, and neighborhood organizations have frequently produced their own newspapers and newsletters to transmit information of importance within their special community.

The observant historian will find both general and special newspapers useful not only for reports of specific news events but also for many other traces. The relative attention given to international, national, and local news may provide clues to community concerns. In recent decades newspapers, competing with radio and television, have in many cases turned to more extensive coverage of local activities. Social and sports pages may provide insight into community interests and activities. A careful examination of advertisements offers many clues to readers' tastes, styles of dress, entertainment preferences, and other cultural characteristics. Classified ads may provide insights about housing arrangements, occupational shifts (what skills are in demand and surplus), and other matters. Letters to the editor may offer a crude gauge of public opinion on contemporary issues.

Thorough, accurate, and objective coverage of news significant to their readers may be their proclaimed goal, but most papers fall somewhat short of the ideal. Editors and publishers no longer acknowledge their political preferences as openly as they did before the twentieth century, but in many cases their views continue to influence their treatment of stories. Furthermore, the need for haste in turning out each edition can lead to omission, distortion, or error. Caution and skepticism are at least as important in dealing with newspapers as with any other type of document.

Finding what one wants in a newspaper may seem a formidable task. Thousands of separate newspapers have appeared, and the published union lists of titles are incomplete. A survey of Ohio newspapers conducted in the early 1970s, for instance, located more than 5,000 titles, many of which had escaped notice in previous union lists. Not only are better catalogs being developed, but also the number of titles on microfilm is growing rapidly. Local libraries often have collections of local publications or at least have information as to where they may be found and how microfilm copies can be obtained.

Research is further complicated by the fact that very few newspapers have been indexed. The *New York Times* has an excellent index beginning with its first issue in 1851. A number of other newspapers have partial indexes, some of them compiled as Works Progress Administration (WPA) projects during the Great De-

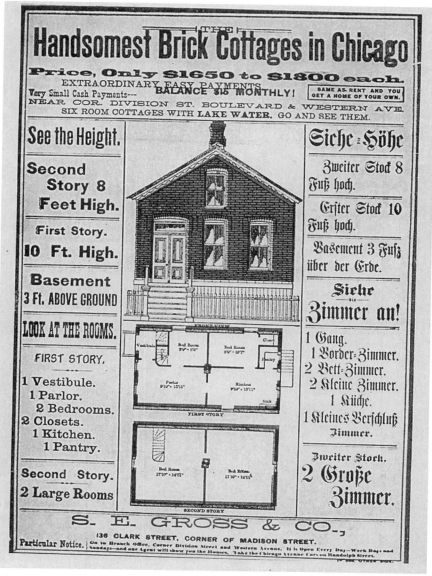

4.1 Ephemera can provide useful and sometimes unexpected information. This Chicago real estate advertising handout not only shows how working-class houses appeared from the street, but also provides floor plans, details about price and financing, and even indications of the developer's appeals to ethnic groups. Such ads often appeared in newspaper classified advertising sections. (Photo courtesy of and copyright © Chicago Historical Society.)

Newspaper obituaries can be very useful sources of information about the lives of individuals and, taken collectively, about patterns of association, social and religious practice, and other matters within a community. It is always wise to check the reliability of obituary data against other sources if possible, since the survivors who provide it may be emotionally upset and their memories of the deceased's earlier life may be uncertain. The style and content of obituaries varies with time, place, and family preference, but generally speaking obituaries from the nineteenth and early twentieth centuries, such as the following, are more detailed than those of more recent years.

The death of Dr. Roswell Rothrock occurred at his home, McClure, Snyder Co., Pa., on Monday, at 5, P.M., March 1, 1897. His death was caused by Bright's disease. He was confined to bed 17 days. During his sickness he suffered great pain. All that medical skill and loving hands could do was done to subdue the pain and stay the ravages of the disease, but all of no avail, the angel of death claimed him and he passed over the River peacefully. The death "taps" have been sounded and he has answered to the last Roll Call of the Great Commander. His remains were interred in the McClure Cemetery on Friday noon, March 5. He was buried, as requested, by the members and ceremonies of Capt. M. Smith's Post, No. 355 G. A. R. and the McClure Lodge I. O. O. F., No. 770. The funeral was very largely attended by loving friends, many of whom came from a distance to pay their last tribute of respect. Rev. W. H. Hilbish and Rev. W. M. Landis officiated at the funeral. Very able and interesting sermons were preached in the English and German language in Christ's Evangelical Lutheran church, from the text, "I have fought a good fight" &c. The deceased attended catechectical lectures held by Rev. Wieand at Samuel's church, was baptized and joined said church in 1873. He afterwards was received into the Christ's Evangelical church at McClure, where he remained a faithful member to date of death.

pression and thus ending by the early 1940s. In recent years, some newspapers have begun creating computer indexes to their current issues. These will grow more valuable as their span of coverage increases, but for the foreseeable future their value to historians is likely to remain quite limited. Indexes, particularly the *New York Times* index, may be of use in searching other papers that have not been indexed. If the indexed paper carried a story on the topic or event under investigation, its index may provide a date that will pinpoint issues to examine in non-indexed papers.

For the most part, research on local topics requires searching all the issues for the time period concerned, keeping in mind that there may be delays of days or even longer before an event is reported and that worthwhile information is not confined to the front page but may be scattered through one or more issues. Careful newspaper research can pay rich rewards for the historian. Detailed biographies may be found in the obituary columns. Business pages provide descriptions of new products, factories, and business activities. Reports of the construction or remodeling of local

He was born at Adamsburg, Snyder Co., Pa., Oct. 14, 1831. He was the oldest son of Dr. Issac Rothrock, deceased, who was elected a member of the House of Representatives in 1866, representing the district composed of Lycoming, Union and Snyder. The deceased was a soldier in the late Civil war. He was enrolled in company C., 78th regiment, Penna., vol., on the 29th day of August, 1861, and was discharged Nov. 27, 1864. He was captured by the Rebels in Shenandoah Valley, Va., and held prisoner in Libby, Belle Isle, and Andersonville, 14 months. He was a faithful member of Capt. Michael Smith's Post No. 355, G. A. R. He served as commander of said Post one term and was surgeon for ten years. He was also a member of the McClure Lodge, No. 770, I. O. O. F., and was R. S. to V. G.

Dr. Rothrock was a successful practitioner of medicine for about 45 years. He first began the practice of medicine with his father at Adamsburg and in 1853 first located at Millville, Clarion county, Pa., where he practiced until 1855. He then located at Beavertown, Snyder county, where he practiced until 1860. He then located at New Bethlehem, Clarion county, where he practiced until Aug. 29, 1861, the date of his entering the war. In 1866 he located at Bannerville, Snyder county, where he practiced until the Spring of 1879, when he removed to Middleburg, where he followed his practice until 1885, when he located at McClure, where he continued the practice of medicine up to the time of his last sickness. He was intermarried with Catherine Mohney, August 4, 1853, at New Bethlehem. This union was blessed with 5 children, 3 sons and 2 daughters. The widow, 5 children, and 13 grand children survive to mourn the loss of a kind and loving husband and father.

> "Can we forget departed friends? Ah, no!
> Within our hearts their memory buried lies,
> The thought that where they are we too may go
> Will cast a light o'er darkest scenes of woe."

Source: Family History Collection, American History Research Center, University of Akron, Akron, Ohio.

buildings, social activities, labor negotiations, school curriculum reforms, and other important local news will come to light elsewhere. Above all, the larger context in which matters of interest occurred should become more evident.

GOVERNMENT DOCUMENTS

Government documents frequently prove to be valuable sources of published information on local conditions and developments, but all too often they are overlooked because the circumstances of authorship and title do not reveal the wealth within. Many federal, state, and local officials and agencies perform activities that involve collecting information, then tabulating and summarizing it in annual reports. A county or municipal planning department in publishing its projection of the community's future may include detailed maps, statistics, photographs, and descriptions of political and economic decisions to account for the area's past growth. At the state or federal level, for instance, an agriculture department concerned with the affairs of farmers might survey each year the types of crops being grown, the acreage planted in each, the prices obtained, the problems of weather or insects encountered county by county as well as statewide. The same report could well have information on the average size of farms, the percentages worked by owners and by tenants, the amount of machinery, the size of families, and the extent of income and indebtedness. Likewise, a treasury department may report on the rate of highway or canal traffic and other economic conditions affecting tax collection, an attorney general's office on the extent and nature of illegal activities being prosecuted, a commerce department on business trends and unemployment levels in various occupations, a department of natural resources on recreational patterns in each of the parks under its jurisdiction. Some of this information may be presented in special reports with clear and descriptive titles, but more often it will appear routinely in agency annual reports. Also, from time to time, city and county councils and state legislative committees conduct hearings or investigations in order to determine whether laws, taxes, or administrative regulations need to be revised; transcripts or reports sometimes contain useful information regarding local conditions.

Libraries often handle government documents differently from other materials, shelving them in a separate section, for instance. More important, ordinary library subject catalogs seldom adequately reflect the range of topics a single government document may cover. Most libraries do not even catalog such reports by individual titles; instead, they simply list the agency title and a general description, such as "Oregon, Department of State, *Annual Reports of the Secretary of State.*" The historian interested in a nearby topic should consider which federal, state, or local agency might have been involved in related activities or information gathering and should then examine its publications. Often one librarian is responsible for government documents and can help in locating government surveys and report concerning local matters.

EPHEMERA

In addition to books, serials, newspapers, and government documents, many libraries try to collect miscellaneous other materials, often labeled "ephemera," that contain valuable information about nearby history. Ephemera, having many origins and purposes, vary widely in nature. Local businesses, agencies, and organizations issue brochures and pamphlets describing their background, activities, and accomplishments. Railroads, airlines, and bus companies print routes and timetables. Annual reports to stockholders are often very useful corporate documents. Businesses and educational institutions publish different sorts of catalogs describing their products and services. For various reasons, many different groups distribute handbills, programs, broadsides, or posters.

Libraries collecting ephemera may try to describe it in their catalogs, but more often they simply keep it in vertical files, folders of assorted materials relating to a topic. Much of this type of material was intended to be thrown away after its immediate use. It is often undated, and its information may be hard to verify. But a library's vertical files often contain surprising treasures and this source should not be overlooked.

It should be evident by this point that published documents concerning the nearby past exist in great volume and variety. It should be equally apparent that even the best library catalogs, published finding aids, and computer search tools cannot always lead historians to the document sought. What should be obvious, but often is not, is that librarians can frequently provide extraordinary assistance. These professionals are familiar with a wide range of reference works, bibliographies, indexes, computer databases, and other tools for locating materials. Furthermore, they often have more information about documents pertaining to the nearby area than even the finest reference works or catalogs. They have assembled the vertical files of ephemera, and they may know of individuals and organizations with private collections. Wise researchers discuss their interests with librarians, ask their advice about sources of information, and pursue their suggestions. No librarian can or should do your research for you, but a good one can often speed and enrich your effort enormously.

A few varieties of published documents deserve particular attention because of their unusual character and exceptional value for nearby history: commercial histories, directories, and maps. Simple and straightforward on their face, these publications have been put to many uses by historians and have revealed far more about a community's past than their creators would have imagined.

COMMERCIAL HISTORIES

Community histories have been written by authors of widely varied background for a great many years, especially in New England and the Midwest, and they continue to appear today. More than 1,000 town and county histories for New England had been published by 1900, and the number increased rapidly thereafter. Similarly, Michigan had close to 200 state, county, and local histories by World War I. Many of these works have been compiled by local people interested in their own community's past. A smaller but growing number have been prepared by scholars. But in addition, a distinctive type of historical publication began to appear frequently in the late nineteenth century and has reemerged in a somewhat more sophisticated form in recent years: the commercial history, sometimes of a town or city, but usually of a county.

Late-nineteenth-century commercial histories were announced in advance by enterprising publishers who would then solicit local residents and businesses to purchase copies of the forthcoming book. Subscribers who paid a certain fee (ten

County histories of the late nineteenth and early twentieth centuries, long on local pride and short on critical observations, nevertheless contain much useful information. Notice how much information is woven into the boasting about developments in towns outside the county's two main population centers.

One of the respects in which Story is an exceptionally good county has to do with its minor towns. It is a very long time since Story County has had all of its interests concentrated in a single place. There are numerous counties in Iowa in which there is one city of considerable consequence and no other town to be considered at all. But such is not the situation in Story. The advancement of Ames by the cross railroad and the college enabled it to become a rival of Nevada, the county seat, and the rivalries of these two towns made easier the development of other towns. Also the fact that other railroads, when they did come, failed to radiate from a common center, but rather crossed the county in parallel lines, had been a condition favorable to the outside towns. Indeed, it was a real blow to Nevada when within two years of each other in the early '80s the Milwaukee railroad was built through the south part of the county and the Iowa Central through the north part. These roads did not touch Nevada nor contribute anything to it. But, on the contrary, they cut off territory, developed some villages and established new towns. Some of these towns, located as they were in good territory and not too convenient to a larger town, have had the opportunity to grow such as is not vouchsafed to outside towns in many other counties. When all of these matters are considered, it would appear that Story County ought to have some good outside towns and that really the inhabitants of such towns have had the responsibility of making good.

Of the outside towns the first place has been fairly won by Story City. It has a population not far from what Nevada and Ames had twenty years ago. But it is much better improved than they were at that time. When the town was laid out, a sentiment of public spirit caused the laying out of exceptionally wide streets; and though the time was when some of these streets were convenient pastures, they are now a conspicuous feature of the town's beauty. Its business district is well built up and its homes give evidence of taste and wealth: it has perhaps the largest department store in the county and it unquestionably has the best public park in the county.

Source: W. O. Payne, History of Story County, Iowa, *2 vols. (Chicago: S. J. Clarke, 1911), 1: 450–51.*

(Photo courtesy of and copyright © David Kyvig.)

to fifty dollars was common) were assured that space would be devoted to their lives and achievements. An additional fee would ensure that the subscriber's picture or that of his home, place of business, or family was included. In community after community, leading citizens and those who aspired to such status rushed to subscribe. The promoter generally accepted the narratives, biographies, dates, and other material that was submitted with little or no checking, eager to assemble information pleasing to as many subscribers as possible. After the completed work had been delivered, the promoter moved on to another profitable locale.

Commercial histories have often been scorned as "mugbooks" by those with a serious interest in knowing what the past was really like. One critic in 1890 saw county history and atlas promoters as swindlers on a level with salesmen of "lightning rods, fruit trees, and patent medicine." Relentlessly cheerful in their descriptions of local conditions and development, silently ignoring people who would or could not pay to be included, commercial histories gave an unbalanced and unreliable view of the local community. Still, they should not be dismissed altogether. These volumes often contain information, drawings, maps, and photographs not otherwise preserved. The biographical sketches give a reasonably good impression of the structure of the local elite as well as of reasons for migration and settlement, dominant tastes, customs, and social conditions, and the community's self-image at the time. No doubt many subscribers felt a responsibility to describe themselves, their families, their businesses, and other matters accurately. Nevertheless, when commercial histories are used, the need to verify information should always be kept in mind, as should the likely underrepresentation of the lower social-economic groups and the neglect of darker moments of the community's past.

DIRECTORIES

City directories also had commercial origins, but of a different nature. These alphabetical listings of residents, together with their occupation, home and work addresses, and occasionally additional data, came into being in an era when businesses found communication with one another as well as with customers difficult because of frequent movement and lack of reliable information about the identity and whereabouts of local inhabitants. The business demand for such directories made their publication a profitable sideline for a printer or newspaper. Boston had one as early as 1790, and by the eve of the Civil War more than three-quarters of America's 6.2 million urban dwellers lived in places covered by directories. Not all of these works were restricted to urban areas; rural counties such as Henry County, Iowa (population 18,701), and Kane County, Illinois (population 30,062), had them by 1860. More specialized business, professional, and social directories generally appeared later.

Directories were often revised annually, and in some cities they even competed. As a result, these volumes often provide frequent reports on individuals

E. O. Zadek Jewelry Co. WATCHES AND DIAMONDS.

GENTS' FURNISHING GOODS at J. LOWENTHAL & CO.

TO FIND A NAME YOU SHOULD KNOW HOW IT IS SPELLED.

MATZENGER'S
MOBILE DIRECTORY
FOR THE YEAR 1892.

ABBREVIATIONS:

agt..	agent	es	east side	res	residence
ave	avenue	ins	insurance	s	south
bds	boards	lab	laborer	se	southeast
bkkpr	bookkeeper	mnfg	manufacturing	sec	secretary
c	colored	mnfr	manufacturer	stbtman	steamboatman
carp	carpenter	n	north	ss	south side
clk	clerk	ne	northeast	sw	southwest
com.mer	commission merch't	ns	north side	up st	up stairs
cor	corner	nw	northwest	w	west
dom	domestic	prop	proprietor	wid	widow
e	east	rd	road	ws	west side

AAR	1	ACA

Aarnes Annie C. wid Hans, res 122 s Royal

Abbot James L. jr. cotton buyer 104 n Commerce, up stairs, res 850 Government

Abbott John H. painter Dure & Chandron, res 355 Lipscomb

Abbey Elizabeth, wid Michael, res 909 Church

Abels Andrew J. c, blacksmith Mobile Coal Co. res 609 south Broad

Abels Benjamin, c, porter Mobile Stationery Co. res 218 north Bayou

Abney Simon, c, lab, res 156 Knox

Abrahams James A. resident student City Hospital, res 925 Government

Abrahams William T. mdse broker 109 n Commerce, up stairs, res 925 Government

Abrams Daniel, vegetable peddler, res 323 Davis ave

Abrams Joseph R. policeman, res 205 Marine

Abrams Walter J. machinist L&NRR shops, res 205 Marine

Academy and Convent of the Visitation, (B. V. M.) Summerville, 3¾ miles, in charge of the Nuns of the Visitation

DON'T PUT IT OFF! BUT GO AT ONCE AND INSURE WITH Hermann & Hynde.

4.3. This page from a Mobile directory begins the alphabetical listing of residents; it follows the street-by-street listing. Blacks were singled out in many northern as well as southern directories. Occupations with commercial significance were more clearly identified than others. (Photo courtesy of the Library of Congress.)

present in a community. On the other hand, editions were hastily assembled and were never absolutely complete or accurate; revisions often merely updated information, leaving misalphabetized names in the same incorrect order from year to year. People who have studied directories carefully and have compared them with census records report that their origins as business tools are reflected in the fact that they very fully and accurately cover middle- and upper-class residents but offer much scantier treatment of lower economic groups. In the 1840 Boston directory, for example, more than 75 percent of heads of white households were listed but only 40 percent of households headed by blacks. Another scholar found that only 7 percent of Boston white-collar workers listed in the 1880 census were missing from the city directory, but 35 percent of unskilled and semiskilled workers were unlisted. The economic bias of directories needs to be kept in mind.

Directories can be very useful for identifying residents and their occupations as well as for judging the local business community (which advertised in the volumes). Street-by-street listings of residents can reveal the character of a block or neighborhood. Comparison of successive volumes may indicate the rate at which people moved into and out of the community and the occupational patterns of stable residents. Other information can be gained indirectly. The absence of occupation in a listing often meant that that person was retired, the omission of home address that the individual resided in a suburb, and no work address that that person's occupation lacked a fixed location (perhaps day labor, perhaps a skilled trade such as carpentry, plumbing, or masonry). Alternative explanations are quite possible, and it is wise not to depend exclusively on directories. Comparison of their information with the much fuller but less frequent descriptions in a census return may provide clarification. Many city directories, as well as business, professional, and other specialized directories, continue to be published to the present day.

MAPS

Maps, whether published or unpublished, can have great value for the historian. As historian G. J. Renier put it, "Geography is indispensable because an event that is not situated in space is as difficult to incorporate in a story as one that is not situated in time." Often remembered in connection with the history of exploration or that of diplomatic and military affairs, maps can also be of considerable use to local historians. Maps visually indicate influential landscape elements and the spatial relationships of natural and artificial features. They provide traces of items that have long since disappeared. Individually and collectively, they also record growth patterns and other historical developments. Fortunately for historians of the nearby past, maps exist in great profusion and variety.

The earliest explorers of every portion of what would become the United States drew maps. By the end of the colonial period, there were thousands of American

4.4–4.5   This township sheet from the 1869 Bennington County, Vermont, atlas (4.4) with the "Clarksville" inset enlarged (4.5) shows quite clearly the physical features, major structures, and resident's names.

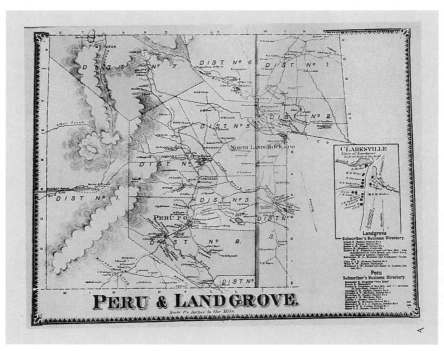

(*Map courtesy of the Library of Congress.*)

maps, ranging from crude sketches based on cursory examination, reports of other travelers, and conjecture to accurate and detailed surveys of limited areas based on careful fieldwork and other research. Individual map sheets of locations, regions, and states were common, but the first American atlases did not appear until almost 1800. Not until the nineteenth century was there systematic standard national mapping. The Congress in 1807 authorized a survey of the nation's coastline to aid navigation and finally in 1879 mandated a topographical survey of publicly owned lands, at first in the far West and eventually nationwide. The U.S. Geological Survey has published large-scale topographic maps for much of the country, with some areas covered more than once, showing landforms, towns, roads, and railroads. The twentieth-century introduction of aerial photography allowed federal agencies to complete an accurate survey of about 85 percent of the national landscape between 1934 and 1943.

Localities have been mapped over the years by a variety of agencies in different formats and for many reasons. Governmental units and land developers produced

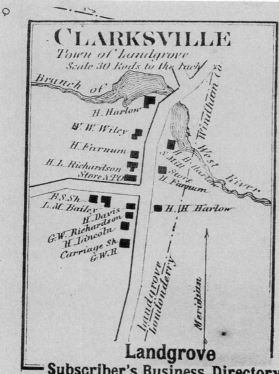

Landgrove
Subscriber's Business Directory.

Abbott E..**Farmer**, District No 2
Abbott J..**Farmer**, District No 1
Bolster J. H..**Farmer**, District No 1
Farnam H..**Merchant**, Clarksville
Harlow H. H..**Proprietor of Grist and Saw Mill. Also manufacturer of Cloth Boards and Chair Stock, and dealer in Lumber, Clarksville**
Richardson H. L..**Merchant and Postmaster**, Clarksville
Utley A. & H..**Farmers**, District No 3
Wiley W. W..**Farmer.** Clarksville
Woodward C. W..**Farmer and dealer in Lumber**, District No 2

Peru
Subscriber's Business Directory.

Batchelder E..**Proprietor "Peru Hotel"**
Bryant R..**Blacksmith**
Burnap E..**Proprietor of Saw Mill, and manufacturer of Chair Stock**, District No 6
Cooledge C. H..**Farmer**, District No 5
Chandler E. P..**Mechanic**, District No 4
Davis Geo. K..**Farmer**, District No 2
Hapgood L. B..**Merchant**, Peru
Lincoln J..**Farmer**, District No 4
Messenger E..**Mechanic**, District No 2
Simonds J. H. & A. J..**Farmers**, District No 2
Simonds W. B..**Farmer**, District No 2
Smith F, B..**Farmer**, District No 5

(Map courtesy of the Library of Congress.)

plats, flat projections, to show land subdivision and record individual property ownership for taxation and sales promotion. Rail and bus companies distributed
sketches of their routes, just as oil companies issued road maps to encourage travel.
Businesses, convention bureaus, parks and recreation departments, churches, and
planning agencies all published specialized maps to serve their own purposes.

Commercial motives led to the creation of a variety of maps very useful for the
nearby historian. County maps and atlases were produced in much the same way
as commercial histories. Subscriptions were solicited, and for a fee a picture of
one's home or business was used as a border illustration. Since this enterprise
proved lucrative to publishers and the space available on a sheet map was limited,
cartographers understandably shifted to the atlas format, which allowed greater
space. County atlases ordinarily had a separate plat for each township and sometimes even for smaller areas. Each plat showed roads, railroads, property lines,
and names of property owners, usually compiled quickly from existing county
maps and records. Subscribers could, for a fee of course, have pictures of their
properties, their families, or themselves and biographies included; these were prepared from a few days sketching in the township and from standard question-
naires. Publishers found atlases inexpensive to prepare and produce by lithography, and they proved quite profitable, especially in heavily populated areas. The
mid-Atlantic and north Atlantic region, especially Pennsylvania and New York,
first attracted county mappers, but the Midwest became their area of greatest activity and success. By the end of the nineteenth century, some Corn Belt counties
had ten atlases, whereas half of all U.S. counties, especially those in the South
and West, had none. Since more than 4,000 county atlases were produced, considerable variety in format and accuracy is to be expected, but for the most part
county atlases are very informative.

A special variety of commercial map, popular from the 1840s to the 1920s, was
the panoramic, or bird's-eye, view of an urban area, a drawing of a city as if seen
at an oblique angle from a height of 2,000 to 3,000 feet. Assembly involved
preparing a street plan in perspective, then having artists walk through town
sketching buildings, trees, and other landscape features. The famous printmakers
Currier and Ives prepared panoramas of a few large cities, but most such maps
were produced by a half-dozen Midwestern artists who concentrated on small
communities of the East and Midwest. Civic pride and promotion spurred the
production of panoramas, which became popular wall hangings. Although permanent features were accurately rendered, they were not always drawn to scale.
Mapmakers catered to local pride by showing streets crowded with people and
carriages, smoke billowing from factories, harbors filled, and railroads busy.
Also, panoramas sometimes showed areas planned for development but not yet
actually built. Nevertheless, used carefully, bird's-eye maps can be extremely
worthwhile, particularly for their depiction of buildings. The largest collection of
American panoramic maps, more than 1,100, is held by the Library of Congress,
which can provide copies of most for purchase.

Other commercial motives led to the development of the even more detailed and far more common fire insurance maps. The maps were developed in the mid-nineteenth century in response to a growing need for information on the potential fire risks of individual commercial, residential, and industrial structures. At first, fire insurance underwriters of rating bureaus inspected buildings, but as the business grew and companies proliferated, this procedure proved neither feasible nor economical, and insurers turned to mapping. By 1900, the Sanborn Map and Publishing Company of New York dominated the business, and by 1924 it had mapped 11,000 towns. Sanborn maps provided great detail for central city areas, showing building materials as well as structural features. Frequently revised, their dating of building construction, alteration, or destruction is fairly precise.

On the other hand, because of their limited purpose, these maps lack information on the use of land without buildings, specific details on homogeneous residential areas, or buildings used for multiple purposes that posed no special fire risks. After World War II, insurance companies became less dependent on maps, and they gradually ceased to be produced. A fairly complete collection, more than 700,000 sheets on more than 12,000 communities produced by Sanborn and others between 1852 and 1961, is available at the Library of Congress, Geography

4.6   This bird's-eye view of the northwest Ohio village of Edgerton in 1881 is typical of panoramic maps. Note the fine detail, the bustling streets, and the two trains steaming into town on a single track. (Photo courtesy of and copyright © Summit County Historical Society.)

*4.7–4.8   This section of an 1886 Sanborn map of Santa Barbara, California (4.7), and
the enlargement of the small inset area (4.8) reflect the detailed and often unexpected
information such maps contained. Two years after this map was issued, the Santa
Barbara Steam Laundry had been renamed the American Laundry, and an added
notation described it as "moderately tidy."*

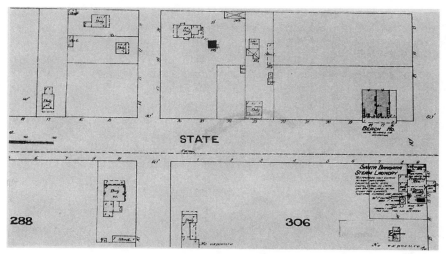

(Photo courtesy of the Library of Congress.)

and Map Division. The entire collection has been microfilmed and is offered for
sale by University Publications of America, 4520 East-West Highway, Bethesda,
MD 20814; film for the immediate area at least may already be available locally
or through interlibrary loan. Sanborn maps may also be obtained directly from the
Sanborn Map Company, 629 Fifth Avenue, Pelham, NY 10803.

Maps must be used carefully, since they vary so widely in purpose, method and
care of construction, and accuracy. They should be checked against accurate
modern maps and reliable noncartographic traces. Establishing their date is crucial and often difficult, because sheets were often reissued with later dates but
without new features on the actual landscape having been added. It is important
to try to determine how complete a map might be and what details might have
been overlooked. Considering the scale and purpose of the map, as well as the
mapmaker's bias, eye for detail, or interest in certain features, is useful.

Singly or in sequence, maps can be very informative about the history of a
community. For example, settlers from different countries initially divided up
land in different ways. The Spanish and Mexican governments granted large
blocks of land to influential developers or groups of settlers. In dry areas, further division was linked to water, with strips of land 100–220 feet wide ex-
tending away from streams for distances of ten to fifteen miles to the next wa-

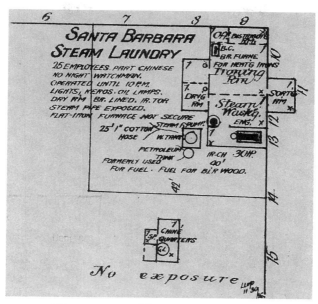

(Photo courtesy of the Library of Congress.)

tershed. In land of marginal quality, gaps or overlaps between grants were considered unimportant. In modern California and the Southwest, large-scale residential development has often been easiest on previously undivided old land grants. The French also laid out long, narrow strips at right angles to waterways, with areas ten times as long as they were wide followed by a second rank of strips. This system was cheap and easy to survey, provided a variety of soil and vegetation on each property, gave easy access to transportation, and allowed residents to live close to neighbors along waterways or inland roads. The French used this system not only in Canada, but wherever they settled, along the Mississippi and elsewhere.

The English, in contrast, preferred to divide land into more regular blocks. Six-mile-square townships granted to groups that then parceled out town and farm lots to members were the norm in New England. Early southern settlement was more irregular, as poor land was often bypassed. The rectangular grid, or checkerboard, system, used by William Penn in planning Philadelphia, was adopted in the development of New York City and was later applied to the Northwest Territory. Land was surveyed along north-south, east-west lines, then systematically divided into townships, one-mile-square sections, and 160-acre quarter sections. This simple, orderly pattern became the standard for most of the American Midwest, determining the course of roads and, some claim, ensuring the isolation of most American farm families.

Towns, too, have been laid out in different patterns. New England towns, not expected to grow very large, were laid out informally around an open space, or common. William Penn's grid for Philadelphia, featuring rectangular blocks, straight streets, right-angle intersections, systematic naming of streets, and a central public square, was widely copied. Its rational and efficient use of space as well as its potential for easy expansion appealed to New Englanders moving west to establish Cleveland, Chicago, and a thousand other towns. Other city plans, such as Savannah's ward modules (each with open squares, sites for community facilities, building lots, and narrow local streets, all surrounded by broad avenues), Washington, D.C.'s spacious symmetry (broad avenues radiating from circles and important public building sites, generous provisions for open space, and considerable distance between principal facilities), and Detroit's reconstruction following a devastating 1805 fire (a triangular street pattern without a focal point, as in Washington, D.C.) not only were seldom copied but were eventually abandoned as these cities grew. An unusual plan raises interesting questions about the ideas of the town's founders.

Maps provide traces of city growth. They reveal whether towns were originally laid out along a river, trail, or railroad or around the site for the county courthouse (if the courthouse square is not at the center of the original town, the county seat may have moved there sometime later, or something else, the railroad depot perhaps, may have been more important to the town fathers). Maps can suggest how the city's development was shaped by geographical features—the waterways and hills of Pittsburgh, Cincinnati, San Francisco, or Seattle, for instance. The names of streets, churches, and schools can indicate original ethnic enclaves, even if the Irish, Chinese, Greeks, or Poles have long since dispersed. Interruptions in regular street patterns, or switches in directions and designs of streets or grids, may show the limits of original settlement, as in Atlanta or in Hays, Kansas, or where two developing communities grew together, as in Milwaukee, Denver, or Indianapolis.

Thoughtful and imaginative consideration of maps can stimulate many ideas and questions about a community's past. Maps are like other documents in that they are usually available in considerable numbers and variety for anyone who cares to search for them. Although they provide much information, they cannot supply all the answers themselves. Those interested in knowing as much as they can about the nearby past should consult and compare a variety of traces, not only the several types of published documents mentioned in this chapter, but also unpublished documents and other sources yet to be discussed.

NOTES AND FURTHER READING

G. J. Renier's comment appears in *History: Its Purpose and Method* (Boston: Beacon Press, 1950; reprint ed., New York: Harper and Row, 1965), p. 116.

An extremely useful introduction to materials for nearby history published before July 1970, is Frank Freidel, ed., *Harvard Guide to American History* (Cambridge, MA: Harvard University Press, 1974). This mammoth compilation lists local histories by state, biographies, books, and articles on many specific topics and many bibliographic tools.

Several specialized bibliographies have particular value for locating older works of the sort least likely to turn up in computerized searches: individual state volumes in Clifford L. Lord, ed., *Localized History Series* (New York: Bureau of Publications, Teachers College, Columbia University, 1964–71); C. S. Peterson, *Bibliography of County Histories of the 3,111 Counties in the Forty-eight States* (Baltimore: Clarence Peterson, 1946); and Marion J. Kaminkow, ed., *United States Local Histories in the Library of Congress,* 5 vols. (Baltimore: Magna Carta, 1975).

Titles of older books relating to specific localities may be discovered in Robert R. Hubach, *Early Midwestern Travel Narratives: An Annotated Bibliography, 1634–1850* (Detroit: Wayne State University Press, 1961); Louis Kaplan, *A Bibliography of American Autobiographies* [to 1945] (Madison: University of Wisconsin Press, 1961); and William Matthews, *American Diaries: Art Annotated Bibliography of Diaries Written Prior to the Year 1861* (Boston: J. S. Conner, 1959). Matthews's later work, *American Diaries in Manuscript, 1580–1954: A Descriptive Bibliography* (Athens: University of Georgia Press, 1974), should not be overlooked.

A starting place for learning more about local publications is G. Thomas Tanselle, *Guide to the Study of United States Imprints* (Cambridge, MA: Harvard University Press, 1971).

Finding articles can be harder than locating books, but several reference works ease the search. The *Reader's Guide to Periodical Literature* surveys many twentieth-century popular magazines, while *Poole's Index to Periodical Literature* does the same for nineteenth-century material. Guides to more scholarly journals, at least for the twentieth century, are the *Social Sciences Index* and the *Humanities Index,* and since 1964 *America: History and Life* has provided unrivaled coverage of state and national historical journals. Various databases are becoming available to aid in locating more recent material.

Locating historical dissertations is made easier by Warren F. Kuehl, ed., *Dissertations in History,* 3 vols. (Lexington: University of Kentucky Press, 1965–72: Santa Barbara, CA: ABC-Clio, 1985), which lists the titles of all works submitted for the Ph.D. in history at American and Canadian universities from 1873 until 1980; it contains a subject index.

Newspaper guides are quite inadequate. *American Newspapers, 1821–1936: A Union List of Files Available in the United States and Canada* (New York: H. W. Wilson, 1937) and *Newspapers in Microform: United States, 1948–1972* (Washington, DC: Library of Congress, 1973) should be regarded only as starting places for a search. One excellent specialized guide is Karl J. R. Arndt and May E. Olson, *German-American Newspapers and Periodicals, 1732–1955,* 2nd ed. (New York: Johnson Reprint, 1965) and their successor volume, *The German Language Press of the Americas* [1732–1968] (Munich: Verlag Dokumentation, 1976).

It is necessary to consult a number of guides in order to cover the great variety of government publications. For federal and state documents, one should look at the United States Government Printing Office, *Checklist of United States Public Documents, 1789–1909* and *Catalogue of Public Documents of the United States, 1893–1940*; William W. Buchanan and Edna A. Kanely, eds., *Cumulative Subject Index to the Monthly Catalog of United States Government Publications, 1900–1971* (Washington, DC: Carrollton Press, 1973); and thereafter the *Monthly Catalog of United States Government Publica-*

tions (Washington, DC: U.S. Government Printing Office). Also see the Congressional Information Service, *U.S. Serial Set Index* (Washington, DC: CIS, 1975–79) for federal publications during the period 1787–1969. For the period since 1970, consult each year's Congressional Information Service, *Annual Index to Congressional Publications and Public Laws.* Federal government publications since 1976 are most easily located on the database MARCIVE.

Individual states often produce similar guides. R. R. Bowker, ed., *State Publications: A Provisional List of the Official Publications of the Several States of the United States from Their Organization* is an incomplete but very useful compilation for the period before 1900, which William S. Jenkins, ed., *Collected Public Documents of the States: A Check List* carries forward to 1947. The Library of Congress produces an ongoing *Monthly Checklist of State Publications,* covering only publications that it receives, which is useful for locating more current material. There are few finding aids for local government publications, the best being J. G. Hodgson, ed., *Official Publications of American Counties: A Union List* (1937) and A. D. Manvel, ed., *Checklist of Basic Municipal Documents* (Washington, DC: U.S. Bureau of the Census, 1948).

Two critical but informative examinations of commercial histories are [Bates Harrington], *How 'Tis Done: A Thorough Ventilation of the Numerous Schemes Conducted by Wandering Canvassers together with the Various Advertising Dodges for the Swindling of the Public* (Syracuse: W. I. Patterson, 1890), and Betty and Raymond Spahn, "Wesley Raymond Brink History Huckster," *Journal of the Illinois State Historical Society* 58 (1965): 117–38. For commercial projects involving maps, see John R. Hebert, "Panoramic Maps of American Cities," *Special Libraries* 63 (1972): 554–62.

The reemergence of commercial histories in recent years has been led by such companies as Continental Heritage Press of Tulsa Oklahoma, which has improved the quality of such volumes by recruiting local scholars as their authors. Local sponsorships, subsidy, and marketing focus still exerts an influence. A new phenomena that began in Cleveland in the 1980s is the urban encyclopedia, usually a cooperative project of a group of academic and nonprofessional historians with institutional and philanthropic support. David D. Van Tassel and John J. Grabowski, eds., *The Encyclopedia of Cleveland History* (Bloomington: Indiana University Press, 1987); David J. Bodenhamer and Robert G. Barrows, eds., *The Encyclopedia of Indianapolis* (Bloomington: Indiana University Press, 1994); and Kenneth T. Jackson, ed., *The Encyclopedia of New York City* (New Haven, CT: Yale University Press, 1995) are early examples of what promises to be a wave of such works.

Helpful guides to early city directories are Dorothea N. Spear, *Bibliography of American Directories through 1860* (Worcester, MA: American Antiquarian Society, 1961) and *City Directories of the United States, 1861–1901: Guide to the Microfilm Collection* (Woodbridge, CT: Research Publications, 1983). All of the directories listed in these publications are available in microform. An excellent discussion of the use of city directories for historical research can be found in an appendix to Peter R. Knights, *The Plain People of Boston, 1830–1860: A Study in City Growth* (New York: Oxford University Press, 1971). Some of the values and defects in later directories as well as other sources are discussed in Stephan Thernstrom, *The Other Bostonians: Poverty and Progress in the American Metropolis, 1880–1970* (Cambridge, MA: Harvard University Press, 1973), pp. 265–88.

Federal topographic and aerial photographic maps are available from the Map Information Office, U.S. Geological Survey, Washington, DC 20242 or at <www.omnimap.com>. Aids for finding other maps include James C. Wheat and Christian F. Brun, *Maps and*

Charts Published in America before 1800: A Bibliography (New Haven, CT: Yale University Press, 1969); Clara E. LeGear, *United States Atlases: A List of National, State, County, City, and Regional Atlases in the Library of Congress,* 2 vols. (Washington, DC: Library of Congress, 1950–53); *Checklist of Printed Maps of the Middle West to 1900,* 11 vols. (Boston: G. K. Hall, 1981); Richard Stephenson, *Land Ownership Maps: A Checklist of Nineteenth-Century United States County Maps in the Library of Congress* (Washington, DC: Library of Congress, 1967); Ralph E. Ehrenberg, *Geographical Exploration and Mapping in the Nineteenth Century: A Survey of the Records in the National Archives,* National Archive Research Information Paper No. 66 (Washington, DC, 1973); John R. Herbert, *Panoramic Maps of Anglo-American Cities: A Checklist of Maps in the Collections of the Library of Congress, Geography and Map Division* (Washington, DC: Library of Congress, 1974); Charles E. Taylor and Richard E. Spurr, *Aerial Photographs in the National Archives,* National Archives Special List No. 25, (Washington, DC, 1973); Norman J. W. Thrower, "The County Atlas of the United States," *Surveying and Mapping* 21 (1961): 365–73; Walter W. Ristow, "U.S. Fire Insurance Maps, 1852–1968," *Surveying and Mapping* 30 (1970): 19–41; *Fire Insurance Maps in the Library of Congress: Plans of North American Cities and Towns Produced by the Sanborn Map Company* (Washington, DC: Library of Congress, 1981); and Douglas R. McManis, *Historical Geography of the United States: A Bibliography-Excluding Alaska and Hawaii* (Ypsilanti: Eastern Michigan University Press, 1965).

An excellent introduction to the use of maps in nearby history can be found in Gerald Danzer, *Public Places: Exploring Their History* (Nashville: American Association for State and Local History, 1987: reprint ed. Walnut Creek, CA: AltaMira Press, 1997). Additional information can be obtained from Grady Clay, *Close-Up: How to Read the American City* (New York: Praeger, 1972); Karl B. Raitz and John Fraser Hart, *Cultural Geography on Topographic Maps* (New York: Wiley, 1975), a series of representative maps with explanations of what can be learned from each; and Thomas J. Schlereth, "Past Cityscapes: Uses of Cartography in Urban History," in *Artifacts and the American Past* (Nashville: American Association for State and Local History, 1980), pp. 66–86.

Many varieties of useful maps are described in Ralph E. Ehrenberg, "Cartographic Records in the National Archives," *National Genealogical Society Quarterly* 64 (1976): 83–111.

David Greenhood, *Mapping* (Chicago: University of Chicago Press, 1964) provides an introduction to the techniques of mapmaking. An excellent general history of American mapmaking can be found in Seymour I. Schwartz and Ralph E. Ehrenberg, *The Mapping of America* (New York: Abrams, 1980).

The influence of geography on history is explored in John Fraser Hart, *The Look of the Land* (Englewood Cliffs, NJ: Prentice-Hall, 1975); Constance Perin, *Everything in Its Place: Social Order and Land Use in America* (Princeton: Princeton University Press, 1977); W. Gordon East, *The Geography behind History* (New York: Norton, 1967); and Norman J. W. Thrower, *Maps and Man: An Examination of Cartography in Relation to Culture and Civilization* (Englewood Cliffs, NJ: Prentice-Hall, 1972).

American historical geography on the local level is discussed and profusely illustrated by John W. Reps, *The Making of Urban America: A History of City Planning in the United States* (Princeton: Princeton University Press, 1965), *Town Planning in Frontier America* (Princeton: Princeton University Press, 1969), and *Cities of the American West* (Princeton: Princeton University Press, 1979). Reps has focused on particular areas in *Panoramas of Promise: Pacific Northwest Cities and Towns on Nineteenth-Century Lithographs* (Pullman: Washington State University Press, 1984) and *Cities of the Mississippi: Nineteenth Century Images of Urban Development* (Columbia: University of Missouri Press, 1994); he has also provided a catalog of town and city lithography produced between 1825 and 1925 in *Views and Viewmakers of Urban America* (Columbia: University of Missouri Press, 1994). Also worthwhile are David Ward, *Cities and Immigrants: A Geography of Change in Nineteenth-Century America* (New York: Oxford University Press, 1971); and Edward T. Price, "The Central Courthouse Square in the American County Seat," *Geographical Review* 58 (1968): 29–60. Examples of efforts to analyze community development in geographical terms can be found in Walter M. Whitehill, *Boston: A Topographical History,* 2nd ed. (Cambridge, MA: Harvard University Press, 1968); Reyner Banham, *Los Angeles: The Architecture of Four Ecologies* (New York: Harper and Row, 1971); Peirce F. Lewis, *New Orleans: The Making of an Urban Landscape* (Cambridge, MA: Ballinger, 1976); Carl Condit, *The Railroad and the City: A Technological and Urbanistic History of Cincinnati* (Columbus: Ohio State University Press, 1977); and Diane L. Oswald, *Fire Insurance Maps: Their History and Application* (College Station, TX: Lacewing Press, 1997).

The names given to towns and other places on the map are often of interest to the historian. Of use in analyzing them is the introduction to George R. Stewart, *American Place-Names: A Concise and Selective Dictionary for the Continental United States of America* (New York: Oxford University Press, 1970), and, by the same author, *Names on the Land: A Historical Account of Place-Naming in the United States,* 2nd ed. (Boston: Houghton Mifflin, 1967).

5

Unpublished Documents

Documents that have not been published but exist instead in single or few copies represent a vast and vital source of traces of the nearby past. Such materials may remain in the hands of their creators or recipients in homes, businesses, schools, community organizations, or government offices, or they may have been moved to an archives or manuscript collection at a library, historical society, or elsewhere. They may even have been microfilmed for preservation or for the convenience of users. Use of unpublished sources poses problems unlike those involved in working with ones that have been published or circulated on the Internet, although each must be evaluated for accuracy and value.

ARCHIVES AND MANUSCRIPT COLLECTIONS

Unpublished documents typically are found in one of two settings. They may exist as part of an ongoing record-keeping system, where the routine maintenance of ledgers, correspondence files, wills, journals, and other sorts of records created or received by an organization or institution is carried out in pursuance of legal obligations or for the effective transaction of business. Such bodies of records, maintained because of their continuing legal, administrative, or historical value after their original purpose has been fulfilled, are considered to be archives. Documents of historical worth that are not part of an archives but have been preserved individually, collected according to a plan, or accumulated by persons or families are referred to as papers or manuscript collections. The difference between archives and manuscript collections is frequently overlooked, especially as both types are often found in the same repository. "Archives" is commonly used as a general label for all unpublished documents. But the distinction is important to keep in mind both in locating pertinent documents and in making judgments about the merits of information obtained.

5.1   The town council of Irwin, Iowa, met in a room that also served as the town's library. Council minutes provide information about a wide variety of local matters, while library records offer insight into community interests and culture. (Photo courtesy of the National Archives and Records Administration.)

Archives are maintained and organized according to a routine by an agency for whom the keeping of records is an aspect of carrying out duties. A county government's archives might contain complaints received, hearings held, contracts approved, and laws adopted. Court records include a wealth of testimony and evidence offered in all manner of cases. Differences of opinion or conflicts of interest in local matters of all sorts have a way of eventually presenting themselves to a judge or jury. A church's archives might contain membership, financial, and social action files, while a business's might have accounts, correspondence, personnel reports, and advertising files. An organization or institution keeps materials to preserve a record of its activities and policies, its customers, clients, or membership, decisions made, problems brought to its attention, and the like on the assumption that the information may be needed later. In any case, the records would have been created shortly after the event or conditions described. The creator of the records normally considers its best interests to be served by maintaining them as completely and accurately as possible so that they may be relied upon subsequently. However, the records creator has a particular purpose in mind and will not bother to gather information unrelated to that purpose, even if it might involve the same person, property, or activity.

An institution's records will be arranged in a form and filing system appropriate to the use their creator has for them. A large organization, for example, will create and maintain files in different offices and departments, according to need, rather than assemble all information on a particular subject in a central location. Information about a church member might be found in the minister's correspondence files, the treasurer's journal of contributions received, the Sunday school committee's minutes, and elsewhere. Several agencies of a county government might maintain records relating to a house or neighborhood, among them the real estate appraiser, the building inspector, the board of health, the public works or street and sewer department, the planning and zoning board, the sheriff, the treasurer or tax collector, and possibly others.

Knowing something about how and why records are kept can be very useful when looking for unpublished information. Traces of the very recent past may be contained in records that are still used for an ongoing government, business, or civic activity and thus remain in office files. Otherwise the records may be in the institution's own archives, or perhaps they have been turned over to a government, university, or private archives. In either of the latter two instances, only the documents thought to have enduring legal, administrative, or historical value are likely to have been preserved, while routine or duplicated material will usually have been discarded. Archivists give considerable thought to the appraisal of records, wishing to use available resources to save only those most likely to have lasting value. Usually less than 5 percent of a business or government agency's files is deemed worth saving. In any case, the documents will most likely still be arranged in the fashion established by the office or department where they were created. Archivists believe that records should be maintained in their original order whenever possible. Rearranging large groups of records not only is very expensive and time consuming but also destroys the picture of how the records-creating agency operated.

Careful thought about who might have kept records having to do with the topic under investigation is the first step in successful archival research. At the same time, thinking about who might have created and preserved a record leads to the question of why and how it would have been kept, which leads in turn to a consideration of how reliable and complete it might be. The county treasurer's tax records may list the names of the owners of a particular house throughout its history, while the real estate appraiser's files may contain less frequent but more detailed descriptions of its value and condition prepared after eyewitness examination. The records of the art museum might indicate who in the community donated money and perhaps even the nature of their tastes and preferences, but information in the museum's files on benefactors' wealth is likely to be secondhand, incomplete, and undependable. Sometimes files are passed from one office to another, and in the process records may be weeded out and even altered. Thus in several respects the provenance of records—the facts of their origin and subsequent custody—is very important to consider in searching for records and then evaluating them.

Manuscripts, or personal papers, as they are sometimes called, can be more difficult to locate and assess as traces of the past simply because their own history can be so much more erratic than that of archives. Whereas archives are accumulated routinely, manuscripts by definition are collected, thus preserved haphazardly, incompletely, and in no particular order. Individuals and families do not exist to record their own activities. One person may keep every letter he or she ever wrote or received, a printout of every e-mail message sent or received, every photograph ever acquired, and a diary for every day of his or her life, while next door someone kept only documents considered important or flattering, and across the street no one kept a scrap. Furthermore, libraries and manuscript repositories have probably collected only a fraction of what may have been created originally, usually the records of the famous, the powerful, the wealthy.

If papers are found, whether in the family attic, the local library, or elsewhere, they are still difficult to judge. In the days before telephones, jet travel, and computers, letters were used to convey ideas and emotions in intimate detail. Now, when technology has made it much easier to communicate face-to-face, orally, or via fax messages and the Internet, letters tend to be written less frequently and contain less information, perhaps only that needed to confirm or distribute a record to a secondary audience. Do papers represent everything a person wrote or knew about some subject, what he or she chose to leave behind so that the matter would be remembered in a particular manner, or merely the fragments found by someone else? Papers may be arranged by a collector rather than by the creator or may be found in no order whatsoever. All the standard questions regarding the origins and dependability of documents apply to manuscripts. Again, any information about provenance can be very enlightening.

FINDING AND USING UNPUBLISHED RECORDS

The search for archives and manuscripts having to do with the nearby past should naturally begin at the source: the family, the business, the civic institution, or government agency directly involved. Families may have kept a variety of records: correspondence from distant relatives, between couples separated because of war, work, or schooling, or from a mother or father to their scattered children; personal and business financial records; diaries; photographs; copies of wills, deeds, credit and job applications; Bibles with information about births, marriages, and deaths written on the flyleaf; school report cards and yearbooks; newspaper clippings; scrapbooks; even trophies, ribbons, or awards in other forms. Within these records may be information covering a long span of years concerning the behavior and motives of individuals, activities, and relationships within families; the nature of family residences and possessions; neighborhood and community institutions and events; and many other topics.

Businesses may have files on customers and employees as well as accounts, inventories, minutes of meetings of the board of directors, correspondence, research and development files, and production, financial, and advertising records. These may show how the company operated, how products were developed and marketed, how workers and labor disputes were treated. Such records may also reveal how local economic circumstances and consumer tastes changed.

Community organizations such as churches, labor unions, political parties, service clubs, and philanthropic or fraternal groups may retain membership lists, minutes of meetings, reports of speeches and activities, and financial records. Such records will reflect the behavior and concerns of particular groups. They may also indicate patterns of social relationships within the neighborhood or community, lines of local authority and decision making, and the identity of the local elite.

County and municipal government records are likely to include legislative minutes; executive reports; highway, engineering, welfare, health, and planning department records; treasurer's accounts and tax lists; election records and voter lists; wills; deeds; school district records; police and court records; and records of poor farms, orphanages, and homes for the elderly and physically or mentally dependent. These records reveal a great deal about individuals, groups, and conditions within the community; the evolution of issues and public policies; the characteristics and uses of buildings and property; the development of transportation systems; and other local phenomena.

Finally, state, regional, and national bodies have records reflecting not only their own activities but also information they have gathered regarding the affairs of local communities. A state or federal census or a corporate marketing survey could provide descriptions of the local population and conditions. The files of a government agency or national association might contain information regarding a project undertaken locally.

A search for unpublished documents sometimes turns up a surprising amount of material. There may be long-forgotten records within a home. Employers, corporations, churches, labor unions, and civic bodies are often very cooperative when the purpose of research is explained clearly and positively, and their files may prove extremely useful. Most local government records are public by law, though polite requests rather than demands usually produce a more cooperative response from clerks and officials.

Records no longer in the possession of the creator may still exist, having been deposited in an archives or manuscript repository. Government agencies, businesses, and other ongoing agencies are usually aware of their own arrangements along these lines and will share this information. In any case, it is wise to inquire about the holdings of nearby libraries, historical societies, universities, and the like.

Various guides to archives and manuscript collections aid researchers in locating the materials they seek. The National Historical Publications and Records Commission (NHPRC) has provided brief summaries of the holdings of more than 4,200 repositories, arranged geographically and including their addresses, telephone numbers, and hours of service in its *Directory of Archives and Manuscript Repositories in the United States* (Phoenix: Oryx Press, 1988). Significant individual collections are described in the Library of Congress's elaborately indexed *National Union Catalog of Manuscript Collections* (NUCMC). Additional volumes of NUCMC ("nukmuk," as it is called) are issued periodically. Both the NHPRC directory and NUCMC have been rendered electronically searchable by the Chadwyck-Healey Company through its ArchivesUSA database, which can be accessed by subscription at <www.chadwyck.com>. These guides do not guarantee complete coverage, since some repositories fail to report their holdings and since small collections are seldom mentioned, but these two volumes are the best general guides available.

A more specialized guide, but one that is national in coverage and may be of particular value is Andrea Hinding, ed., *Women's History Sources: A Guide to Archives and Manuscript Collections in the United States,* 2 vols. (New York: Bowker, 1979). Thousands of collections having to do with women, arranged by city and state, are briefly described and well indexed.

More information about holdings of individual repositories is often available in the guides that they themselves publish to their collections. Significant series of records maintained by various federal agencies, bureaus, and departments are described in the *Guide to Federal Records in the National Archives of the United States* (3 vols.; Washington, DC: National Archives and Records Administration, 1995). This guide, but not the records themselves, can be examined online at <www.nara.gov>. This Web site has a genealogy page that may prove especially useful in tracking down individuals. State and local archives with a geographically confined collection may produce institutional guides, as may denominational church archives and repositories with topical collections, such as the business-oriented Hagley Library of Wilmington, Delaware, and the Immigration History Research Center at the University of Minnesota. News of recently acquired material appears regularly in historical society publications, scholarly journals, and the *American Archivist*. Nevertheless, it is important to keep in mind that few guides or other publications can adequately describe the holdings of an archives or manuscript collection.

The very nature of any archives or large manuscript collection makes its full description in guides or catalogs difficult. Even after unimportant and duplicate items have been eliminated, the remaining documents judged to have enduring value may cover countless topics and may run to several or even several hundred cubic feet (the standard unit by which archivists measure the volume of records). A single cubic foot of archival material may contain three thousand pages of documents. The original National Archives building in Washington, now only one of more than thirty repositories for records of the federal government, alone contains nearly one million cubic feet of records. The National Archives information locator, or NAIL, at <www.nara.gov> demonstrates both the value and limitations of online archives research; it has a searchable list of 350,000 documents as well as 60,000 digitized items for examination (mainly photographs), but this represents only a tiny fraction of the National Archives' holdings of over 4 billion pieces of paper, 14 million still pictures, 9 million aerial photographs, 5 million maps, 300,000 reels of film, and 200,000 sound and video recordings. A researcher makes a great mistake in thinking that an online search exhausts the resources of the National Archives, or any archives for that matter. NAIL and the *Guide to Federal Records* merely point the way to a vast amount of unique material, some of which can be viewed on microfilm available on loan or for purchase but much of which can only be examined by traveling to the repository where it is kept.

It is impossible for archivists to catalog each individual item in a large collection as librarians catalog books. In most cases, archivists must settle for general descriptions of records series, documents, or file units arranged in accordance with a filing system or maintained together because they relate to a particular form, or because of some other relationship arising from their creation, receipt, or use. A typical record series description might be as follows: "Executive secretary's correspondence, 1916–1928, arranged alphabetically by correspondent, 6 cubic feet" or "Annual reports, 1887–1903, 1911, 1915–1954, 2 cubic feet." Knowing which agency, office, or individual might have created or kept records pertaining to the subject in which one is interested comes in handy here.

The archivist responsible for a body of records can be very helpful to a researcher and usually knows far more about them than could possibly be included in a NUCMC entry, a repository guide, or even a finding aid to a body of records, called a register or inventory. The archivist may have acquired the records for the institution, put them in order and written the finding aid, or worked with other researchers using them. The wise researcher, suspecting or hoping that a repository may have relevant materials, goes directly to the archivist, describes the project, and asks what materials might be of use. The archivist can point out the records series that may contain information, sometimes knows what specific files may prove most helpful, and often can suggest other documents in the same repository or elsewhere that may bear examination. Some archivists are willing to identify other researchers who have explored the same records and who might be helpful contacts.

If the repository in which a researcher is interested lies at some distance, it is wise to write in advance of a visit to inquire about records relevant to the project. Generally archivists will respond with a description of what is available. Often they will answer questions or photocopy small amounts of material. Archivists should not be expected to do extensive research, but they can be extremely helpful and should be regarded as partners in historical inquiry, concerned about preserving and expanding knowledge of the past.

In addition to aiding researchers, archivists bear responsibilities for the care and protection of materials in their charge. Donors of manuscripts and organizations transferring archives often set terms for the use of records, usually in order to protect the privacy of living individuals or to maintain the confidentiality of information for a certain length of time. Archivists may sometimes regret such restrictions and at other times may even encourage them to protect a donor's legitimate interests, but in any case they pledge to abide by rules imposed when the records are acquired. Also, archivists have the duty to see that records are not lost or damaged so that they will be available for the use of future generations of researchers. Because of these responsibilities, archivists must impose certain requirements on researchers. These regulations are not intended to inhibit or frustrate research but rather to fulfill important archival obligations to gather and care for historically valuable materials.

In the first place, repositories usually require that a prospective researcher speak with an archivist before using archives or manuscripts. The purpose is for the archivist to determine what materials the researcher wants to see, to find out whether the researcher has enough background knowledge to benefit from being allowed to examine unpublished documents, to indicate any restrictions on the use of particular records (perhaps the researcher may not mention names or quote directly or perhaps may not examine certain materials until some future date), and to explain the institution's research rules. It is normal for the visitor to be required to show personal identification and to sign a research application agreeing to abide by the rules.

Once access has been granted, all archives demand that files of material be left in their original order and that no marks be made upon documents. (Some researchers have the urge to "correct" documents that seem in error, but that must never be done. Passing on the information to the archivist is the appropriate procedure.) Some archives expect researchers to work only with pencils to protect documents from accidental but ineradicable ink marks. Most repositories require researchers to use archival materials in a reading room, not allowing them into storage facilities or permitting them to remove documents from the designated area. As a further security precaution, some institutions do not allow briefcases, purses, or other personal belongings to be brought into the reading room. If photocopying is allowed, it must normally be done under supervision or by a member of the archival staff. Some of these precautions may seem unreasonable, but in a number of cases, unfortunately, valuable records have been damaged or have disappeared. Most archival and manuscript material is unique; once it has been lost it can never be replaced. The minor inconvenience of some repository regulations is a small price to pay to ensure continued access to the vast amount of information that exists in unpublished documents.

The value of archival material for nearby history may perhaps best be demonstrated by a close look at a few types of documents of almost universal availability that contain important information about families and communities. The variety of archival sources is so vast that it is impossible to say what any one researcher may or may not find in a careful search. But some materials are so widespread, have been used so often, and have proved so helpful that they deserve specific mention.

CENSUS RECORDS

The United States Constitution mandated the creation of unquestionably the most widely used unpublished source of nearby history information. The founding fathers stipulated that, to ensure the proper apportionment among the states of seats in the House of Representatives, a federal population census must be conducted every ten years. The first federal census in 1790 and the five following enumerations recorded the names and addresses of heads of families together with the number of free white males and females in broad age categories and the number of slaves in the household. With the 1850 census, eager to gain a fuller picture of the American population, the Census Bureau began to ask more questions. For the first time the name of every person was recorded, together with address, age, sex, color (white, black, or mulatto). It was asked whether the person was deaf and dumb, blind, insane, or idiotic; about the value of real estate owned; the nature of the person's profession, occupation, or trade (for men over fifteen); place of birth; whether the person had been married within the year; whether school had been attended within the year; whether the person was unable to read and write (if over twenty); whether the person was a pauper or convict. Other questions were added in later censuses: in 1860, the value of personal property the person owned; in 1870, whether father and mother were foreign born; in 1880, the person's rela-

5.2 *This typical page from a manuscript census shows how poor handwriting and misspelling could cause census data to be misleading or unusable. (Photo courtesy of the National Archives and Records Administration.)*

tionship to the head of the household; marital status; months for which the person had been unemployed during the year; whether the person had been sick or temporarily disabled and if so how; whether the person was maimed, crippled, or bedridden; and the birthplace of the person's parents. Later even more questions were added. Summaries of the information for cities, counties, and states as well as the nation as a whole were published, but more important, the manuscript census, the sheets on which enumerators recorded information as they went from door to door, was preserved.

The federal census became an effort to take a snapshot of the American people once every decade to determine not only who they were and where they lived, but also the nature of their health, wealth, work, and family background. Numerous colonial or state censuses had been carried out prior to 1790, recording names of household heads and occasionally other information gathered for some special purpose, but these were often incomplete and in several cases actually involved estimates rather than enumerations. The federal census proved so worthwhile that nearly a dozen states and even a few cities conducted their own enumerations, often at mid-decade, asking the same questions (and in some cases even more) of residents.

The federal census expanded to include special enumerations of agriculture and manufacturing, which, like those of the population, improved after 1840. The agricultural census gathered data on farmers and farm workers as well as extensive economic information for each farm, including the amount of land owned, animals raised, and crops grown. The census of manufactures collected statistics about manufacturing establishments, capital invested, nature, quantity, and value of raw materials and products, power sources, machinery, structures, number of persons employed, and labor costs.

The published volumes of the *Federal Census of Population, Agriculture and Manufacturing* provide, especially for 1850 and after, an unparalleled, comprehensive overview of every American community's social and economic characteristics. Beginning with 1910 for cities with populations of more than 500,000 and expanding by 1970 to include all cities of 50,000 or more, census tract data have been tabulated and published. Census tracts are arbitrary divisions of communities into relatively homogeneous areas of a few thousand population that correspond to neighborhoods. Tract data reveal the character of small sections of a city.

The manuscript records, for the years they are available, allow even closer examination of individual families, neighborhoods, farms, and businesses. Since the census takers usually covered their district systematically, house by house, street by street, and always listed addresses, it is possible to compile a picture of a block or neighborhood. Ethnic, racial, occupation, and wealth patterns can be identified. High concentrations of blacks or foreign born, young or old, and male or female residents can be clues to the special character of a neighborhood, as can the presence of unusual numbers of lodgers or households with the same family name.

No census was ever absolutely complete or accurate. Enumerators were under oath to do their best, but the people they interviewed sometime withheld or misreported information because of suspicion, embarrassment, fear of taxation, or simple lack of knowledge. People either did not remember or would not admit their exact ages, as shown by the phenomenon of "age heaping," the clustering of reported ages around years ending in 5 and 0 rather than a more even spread. When residents could not be found at home, enumerators turned to neighbors and accepted secondhand information. Additional errors could be introduced as a result of differing definitions of occupations or economic value, the census taker's bad handwriting, or personal ideas about how to spell particular sounds. Various enumerators might spell a family name in different ways; for instance, in the 1790 census there were at least 100 persons with each of the following names: Burns, Bearn, Bearnes, Bern, Berns, Berhans, Burn, Burne, Burnes, Byrn, Byrnes, and Byrns.

Inevitably the census would miss people, most frequently minorities and the very poor. But since enumerators were sometimes paid by the number of entries, there might also be overreporting. Censuses were usually supposed to be taken as of June 1, but they could be delayed by weeks or even months; with people constantly moving, individuals could easily be missed and totals distorted. Historian Sam Bass Warner has concluded on the basis of careful studies of Boston that census totals cannot be depended upon to be more accurate than ±6 percent, while Eric E. Lampard believes that economic statistics may have errors of ±10 percent. Individual entries may, of course contain even greater errors or be missing altogether. The researcher who approaches every document with care and attempts to check information against other sources will discover incorrect and missing information in census records but will also find much of value.

The federal census is readily accessible up to a point. Guidance on locating information about individuals is available from the Census Bureau <www.census.gov>, and through a fee-for-search database from <Ancestry.com/census>. The published compilations for states, counties, towns, and census tracts are widely available. The manuscript returns, arranged by state and county, have been microfilmed for each census through 1920 (with the unfortunate exception of 1890, for which almost all of the returns were destroyed by fire in 1921). The search for individual names in the manuscript returns is made much easier by soundex indexes, state-by-state alphabetical lists of names by phonetic spelling of the surname, followed by the given names of heads of households. Many local libraries and historical or genealogical societies have copies of the census microfilm for at least the local area, and it is all available for purchase from the National Archives, Washington, DC 20408. Currently the manuscript census is kept closed for seventy-two years after an enumeration from regard for the privacy of people listed therein. Information on individuals from the 1930 and later manuscript censuses can be obtained only by the person described, the next of kin, or an authorized legal representative. (See appendix A for forms.) State censuses, where available often extend into the 1920s and have no restrictions on their use.

Census records can help the historian begin to develop a picture of a community or a neighborhood at some point in the past, as this description of a south-side Pittsburgh neighborhood in 1880 demonstrates.

[The neighborhood] lies between Eighteenth and Twentieth streets, from the Monongahela River to East Carson Street. A curve of the river broadens the valley here, at the site of East Birmingham, and Carson, Sidney, and Wharton streets were widened accordingly, with narrow alleys added between them. Small, neat houses lined both streets and alleys, fronting squarely on the sidewalk; they were rectangular, two-story boxes exhibiting to the public eye a door and two long, narrow front windows. The 1880 census referred to such structures as examples of good housing for workers. Behind those doors lived generations of glassblowers, puddlers, laborers, and their wives, widows, and children. Nearby were the factories and stores in which they worked, and the churches and taverns where they spent leisure time.

The first and most detailed picture of the area appears in the 1880 manuscript schedule census. Jarrett, Duvall, and Plank, enumerators, recorded the inhabitants of each dwelling, their ages, places of birth, literacy, and employment or lack of it. In the 286 houses of these twelve blocks lived 1,777 people—902 men and women and 875 children. Forty-four percent of the adults but less than 3 percent of their children were foreign born, indicating that these immigrants were well settled by 1880. Almost 60 percent of them had come from some part of the German Empire, although German immigrants made up only one-third of the total population of Pittsburgh at this time. In this part of the Twenty-sixth Ward were 238 Germans, 64 Irish, 69 English, Welsh, and Scotch, and a few French and Swiss. One-fourth of the first-generation Americans were of German descent, making this area one of the predominantly German sections of the city.

The neighborhood was near the center of the city's glass industry, and the census information regarding individual's employment provided clues to the nature of the industry:

Of the 583 working men, women, and boys in the area in 1880, the largest single group, 169, were glassworkers. . . . Fifty-one of the area glassworkers were between eleven and seventeen years of age. Only three boys in this age group were listed by the census as apprentices, but all hoped to learn the skills which might enable them to earn good wages as adults. Most boys performed indispensable small jobs such as "carrying-in" and "cleaning-off," earning between fifty and sixty cents a day. High unemployment rates, even among the more skilled workers, indicated that the glasshouse boys must have been doing more than their share of the family breadwinning. Of working boys seventeen and under, 11 percent were out of work between one and three months; 15 percent between four and six months. But young men between the ages of eighteen and twenty-nine were laid off at the rate of 14 percent for one to three months, 30 percent for four to six months, and 7 percent for more than six months. By comparison, workers over thirty reported an even higher rate of unemployment, with 30 percent not working between one and three months and 28 percent out of work between four and six months. Only six glassworkers in the area were over fifty years old. As one employer stated in his census return, "when a man reaches 55 years of age he seems to lose his skill as a workman and has to take a subordinate place."

Source: Josephine McIlvain, "Twelve Blocks: A Study of One Segment of Pittsburgh's South Side, 1880–1915," Western Pennsylvania Historical Magazine *60 (October 1977): 352–53, 356–57.*

FEDERAL RECORDS

Lesser known and more specialized federal records can also be quite valuable sources of community and family information. The federal postal system, for example, necessarily took note of the creation and growth of every American town. The Records of Appointments of Postmasters, 1815–1929 contain information on the dates when post offices were established or discontinued as well as changes in town names and significant events in community affairs. Reports of Site Locations, 1867–1946, submitted by postmasters, contain geographical information on communities, including rivers, railroads, and landmarks; they may be especially useful for people investigating small towns. The National Archives, Washington, DC 20408, will reply to inquiries about these and other records.

During World War I, all resident males between eighteen and forty-five years of age were required to register for the military draft. Some 24 million registrants, almost every male born between 1873 and 1900, gave information on their birth date, race, citizenship, occupation, employer, nearest relative, and physical characteristics. These draft registration cards are stored at the Federal Records Center, East Point, GA 30344, and have been microfilmed. Staff archivists will search for an individual registration card if given a name, birth date, and location (at least the county and preferably a street address, especially for larger cities); if the card is found, a modest bill will be sent, and on receipt of payment, a photocopy of the card will be mailed. Since the cards are arranged and filmed by draft board, county, and state, they can be used to study the population of a community as well as to learn about individuals. Although these records contain only the names of males of a certain age, they represent the largest unrestricted body of nationwide information on individuals for the years after 1910.

Other federal records can be useful in research on individuals, if not communities. For military volunteers, 1775–1902, the National Archives holds records that show the person's term of service, rank, and unit, and often his age, birthplace, and place of enlistment. A search will be conducted for an individual record if the person's full name, the war in which he served, and the state from which he enlisted can be provided. If the record is found, copies will be provided and the inquirer billed. Applications for military pensions and service records of those in the regular army may contain even more information. Access to these and other military records is discussed in the pamphlet *Military Service Records* in the National Archives of the United States, available on request from the National Archives, Washington, DC 20408. A form for requesting military records can be found in appendix A.

The National Archives also has passenger lists and indexes from the Customs Bureau and its successor, the Immigration and Naturalization Service, for most ships arriving at Atlantic and Gulf Coast ports since 1820. Similar West Coast lists were destroyed by fire. These lists normally contain the name, age, and occupation of each passenger, the country from which he or she came and to which

5.3   Every World War I draft registrant provided current personal information. Many later changed residence and occupation, of course, although few gained the notoriety and fortune that this young man achieved by doing so. (Photo courtesy of the National Archives and Records Administration.)

he or she was going, and in later years information on literacy, U.S. relatives, and the name of the person who paid for the passage. Archivists will search the customs and immigration lists more than fifty years old if the name of the passenger, the port of embarkation or entry, the name of the ship, and the date of arrival can be provided. (A request form is included in appendix A.) With any part of this information, one may be able to determine the rest from the *Morton Allan Directory of European Passenger Steamship Arrivals* (New York, 1931) for New York arrivals, 1890–1930, and Philadelphia, Baltimore, and Boston arrivals, 1904–1926. The Immigration and Naturalization Service also has records of people naturalized as citizens after September 25, 1906, including date and place of arrival in the United States and names of spouses and children.

Not every difficult-to-solve historical question involves a time centuries past. The Social Security Administration, established in 1935 in the midst of the New Deal, is not a particularly old federal agency. It has yet to turn over its records to the National Archives. Social Security files contain information as to where enrolled persons worked and what income they received year by year. On request (the form is in appendix A), the Social Security Administration will provide this information. Privacy laws require, however, that the request must be signed by the individual involved or by a legal representative. Although this stricture limits access to Social Security records, they may be a useful means of documenting a personal history or buttressing the slipping memory of a cooperative relative or acquaintance.

LOCAL RECORDS

State and local archives, as mentioned earlier, can be rich sources of information on communities and the people within them. For instance, in some areas the city or county assessor's files not only provide valuable economic data but also list names, addresses, and occupations of residents, arranged by streets. Thus, such records may be used to obtain a picture of occupational and wealth patterns of neighborhoods, even for periods much earlier than federal census returns would allow. Municipal and state courts as well as federal district courts held naturalization proceedings prior to September 26, 1906, and their records can provide information on community immigration patterns as well as on individuals.

Vital records—birth, death, marriage, and divorce records—are among the most useful documents kept by state or local governments. They can provide names, birth dates, and places, names and birthplaces of parents, length of residence in the United States, and other information, and for death certificates, time, place, and cause of death, and burial site. Prior to the early twentieth century, many states did not centralize vital records, and they may have been kept by a county or city official, usually the clerk of courts. The U.S. Superintendent of Documents publishes a booklet, *Where to Write for Vital Records*, which can help in locating birth, death, marriage, and divorce records in individual states. It can be obtained for $2.25 from the Consumer Information Center, Pueblo, CO 81009 or free online at <www.pueblo.gsa.gov>. It is important to remember, however, that even vital records contain errors. Birth, marriage, and death certificates all ask for parents' names, but that information is more likely to be correct when a baby's parents are in a position to give their own names than when an elderly person with long-

5.4   In addition to documenting the names, life dates, and family relationships of local residents, the tombstones in this Landaff, New Hampshire, cemetery suggest by their design the economic status and cultural values of members of the community. (Photo courtesy of the National Archives and Records Administration.)

deceased parents dies. Death certificates are filled out during times of stress and often by persons not in a good position to know such information. Vital records deserve the same skepticism one brings to any other untested document.

Cemeteries can supplement vital records as well as substitute for them during periods before the latter were kept. It may be difficult to think of a cemetery as an archives or a tombstone as a document, but the marker may have information carved on it that appears nowhere else. Not only the inscriptions showing name and birth and death date but also epitaphs, symbolic carvings, and the size and style of a headstone may be instructive. Adjacent headstones may mark relatives. In addition, many cemeteries keep written records, copies of obituaries, and interment maps and indexes. A family, church, or community cemetery may reveal details about its sponsoring group. Of course, many people could not afford cemetery markers, and wood and even stone do wear away. Some groups have systematically copied cemetery inscriptions to preserve their information. Such copies can sometimes be found with the local historical or genealogical society or in a nearby library.

Deeds and other property records kept by county officials can be extremely useful for identifying patterns of land division and urban growth, tracing property ownership, and describing changes in the use of real estate. Building and zoning

Wills provide a public record of a deceased person's intentions for the distribution of his or her property. As such they can provide a view of economic status, personal tastes, and lifestyle. In addition, wills can offer clues about an individual's relationships with family and friends, as in this brief will made in Tennessee in 1822.

In the name of God, amen, I, John Cox, in the County of Carroll, and State of Tennessee, being weak in body, but of perfect mind and memory, knowing the uncertainty of this life, do make and ordain this my last will and testament. First, I recommend my soul to Almighty God who gave it, and my body to the grave, to be interred in Christianlike manner. As to my worldly estate, which it has pleased God to bless me with, I do will in manner and form as follows, vis; I will that my beloved wife, Purity Cox, have all my estate, during all of her natural life. I do also will that my executors do sell my wagon, hindgear, rifle, gun and ball, horse and grey mare, and with the profits arising from the sale of the above and the money I have on hand, I will that they purchase land for the benefit of my beloved wife, Purity Cox, during all her natural life, at her death the said land to be equally divided between my beloved sons, William and James Cox.

I do also will that my beloved daughter, Sally Cox, have one good bed, one cow and calf, one side saddle and one flax wheel. I also will my beloved daughter, Rhoda Barnhart, have twenty-five dollars. I also will that my son-in-law, Peter Culp, have ONE DOLLAR. I also will that at the death of my beloved wife, Purity Cox, that my negro girl Mary, and all the balance of my property not here to fore willed, be equally divided between my daughter, Sally Cox and Sally Culp, and Nancy McMackin, my niece. I do here by make and ordain this my last will and testament revoking all others by me made as witness my hand and seal this fourth day of February in the year of our Lord, One thousand eight hundred and twenty-two.

Source: Family History Collection, American History Research Center, University of Akron, Akron, Ohio.

codes, which became widespread in the 1920s, provide further information on land use. They may also provide clues as to the status and treatment of various ethnic and economic groups or businesses within the community.

Wills and related probate records can prove to be very rich sources of information. Even people who die without a will sometimes leave property that a court must administer. Probate records inventory, often with detailed descriptions, a person's property and indicate to whom it is left. Heirs usually include relatives who might appear in other records and sometimes friends and favored organizations otherwise hard to identify. Estate inventories can provide clues to a family's lifestyle and economic situation and, considered cumulatively, a neighborhood or community pattern. Historians can easily obtain access to probate records, since they are open to public inspection so that all potential heirs can see that they are receiving their rightful shares of an estate. Laws vary from state to state, but a probate court or some similar county office maintains and indexes such records.

State and local public records might ordinarily be found only in the files of the creating agency or its archives. However, the Genealogical Society of Utah, an agency of the Church of Jesus Christ of Latter-day Saints, has made such records much more accessible. Since Mormons feel a religious obligation to identify their ancestors, they have sponsored an enormous effort to microfilm and collect documents that may be of use in genealogical research. The Genealogical Society has collected land, immigration, naturalization, probate, vital, and other public records; church and cemetery records; and many other types of records from foreign countries as well as the entire United States. Millions of rolls of microfilm are available for use at the society's Family History Library in Salt Lake City or through several hundred family history centers connected with local LDS churches. Information about a vast array of resources is available at the LDS home page <www.lds.org>. Some of these resources may now be accessed directly at a site opened in the summer of 1999: <www.familysearch.org>. For more information about LDS resources see *Wired,* July 1999, 134–41, 183–84.

Many private as well as public unpublished documents are worthwhile for nearby history. One set that can be useful for many communities is found in the Baker Library of the Graduate School of Business Administration at Harvard University, Boston, MA 02163: the 2,580 volumes of R. G. Dun and Company credit reports for the years before 1890. Beginning in 1841, the Mercantile Agency, which became R. G. Dun and Company in 1851 and later Dun and Bradstreet, collected information on American businesses in order to rate their suitability for credit. Because the Dun agency wished to continue selling credit reports, it worked hard to provide accurate data. The 2,000 or more local correspondents of the company would file reports at least once a year on the activities, financial improvement or decline, and other noteworthy features of area businesspeople. Many reports included information on former residences, marital status, family and ethnic background, business experience and prospects, and personal characteristics, supposedly all factors useful in judging credit worthiness. Although bigger and wealthier businesses were more likely to apply for credit and were therefore more likely to be investigated, self-employed artisans and owners of small retail and service shops, seldom treated in the federal census of manufacturers, may be found in the records of R. G. Dun. The credit reports can help supply the details of nineteenth-century individual or community business history.

This brief survey can only suggest a little of the contents of archives and manuscript collections. The possibilities are as numerous as the creators of records. During the Great Depression of the 1930s, the Works Progress Administration (WPA) conducted surveys of local, state, and private records that turned in thousands of series of records in county courthouses and elsewhere. The WPA records surveys can still be helpful in identifying and locating materials for use in nearby history. Since that time universities, social agencies, and other organizations as well as government offices have collected more and more data about individual communities. Keep in mind that if the records first regarded as a source prove to be nonexistent, inadequate, or of doubtful accuracy, there may well be other archives or manuscripts that contain part or all of the information desired. Regional branches of the National Archives and addresses of state archives, historical societies, and preservation offices can be located through Web sites listed in appendix D. These agencies provide starting points for a search. Determined historians of the nearby world, whatever their topics, will pay careful attention to a wide range of unpublished documents.

Finding the particular unpublished material needed in one's research can present a much greater challenge than locating widely duplicated materials. Even when a collection of letters or official files has been brought to light, uncovering desired information therein remains a larger task than examining a book, newspaper, published report, or computer file. At the same time, the rewards of the search can include the wonderful excitement of discovering something unique that unlocks a mystery about the past. Knowing about archives and manuscript collections in general and a few special types of records in particular can help stir appreciation for the worth of unpublished documents for nearby history.

NOTES AND FURTHER READING

Philip C. Brooks, *Research in Archives: The Use of Unpublished Primary Sources* (Chicago: University of Chicago Press, 1969) remains a clear and helpful introduction, but see as well Frank G. Burke, *Research and the Manuscript Tradition* (Lanham, MD: Scarecrow Press, 1997). Also useful are O. Lawrence Burnette, Jr., *Beneath the Footnote: A Guide to the Use and Preservation of American Historical Sources* (Madison: State Historical Society of Wisconsin, 1969); Kenneth W. Duckett, *Modern Manuscripts: A Practical Guide for their Management, Care, and Use* (Nashville: American Association for State and Local History, 1975); and H. G. Jones, *Local Government Records: An Introduction to Their Management, Preservation, and Use* (Nashville: American Association for State and Local History, 1980).

Several guides written to assist genealogists contain information on archival and manuscript materials that can be of value to any nearby historian. Raymond S. Wright, *The Genealogist's Handbook: Modern Methods for Researching Family History* (Chicago: American Library Association, 1995) is the most up-to-date. Excellent specialized guides are Charles L. Blockson, *Black Genealogy* (Englewood Cliffs, NJ: Prentice-Hall, 1977); Dan Rottenberg, *Finding Our Fathers: A Guidebook to Jewish Genealogy* (New York: Random House, 1977); Arthur Kurzweil, *From Generation to Generation: How to Trace Your Jewish Genealogy and Personal History* (New York: Morrow, 1980); John Grenham, *Tracing Your Irish Ancestors* (Baltimore: Genealogical Publishing, 1993); Angus Baxter, *In Search of Your European Roots* (Baltimore: Genealogical Publishing, 1994); Rosemary A. Chorzempa, *Polish Roots* (Baltimore: Genealogical Publishing, 1993); George Ryskamp, *Finding Your Hispanic Roots* (Baltimore: Genealogical Publishing, 1997); and Sharon DeBartolo Carmack, *Italian-American Family History* (Baltimore: Genealogical Publishing, 1997).

Among the many Web sites devoted to assisting genealogical researchers, connecting them to Web sites of records-holding institutions and providing other useful information, one of the best can be found at <www.cyndislist.com>. Its creator, Cyndi Howells, has also written a useful guide: *Netting Your Ancestors: Genealogical Research on the Internet* (Baltimore: Genealogical Publishing, 1997).

For a comprehensive listing of genealogy-related Web sites, see Thomas J. Kemp, *Virtual Roots: A Guide to Genealogy and Local History on the World Wide Web* (Wilmington, DE: Scholarly Resources, Inc., 1997). Readers should be mindful, however, that many Internet addresses are ephemeral in nature and that even for more stable sites the addresses change.

A book that relates individual family research to questions and approaches of broader applicability is David E. Kyvig and Myron A. Marty, *Your Family History: A Handbook for Research and Writing* (Arlington Heights, IL: Harlan Davidson, 1978).

Many ideas on how federal records can be used in local research appear in Jerome Finster, ed., *The National Archives and Urban Research* (Athens: Ohio University Press, 1974), and Timothy Walch, ed., *Our Family, Our Town: Essays on Family and Local History Sources in the National Archives* (Washington, DC: National Archives and Records Administration, 1987).

The use of census records for community history is discussed in Sam Bass Warner, Jr., "A Local Historian's Guide to Social Statistics," in *Streetcar Suburbs: The Process of Growth in Boston, 1870–1900* (Cambridge, MA: Harvard University Press, 1962), pp. 169–78. More on the subject can be found in Edward K. Muller, "Town Populations in the Early United States Censuses: An Aid to Research," *Historical Methods Newsletter* 4 (1971): 2–8; Robert G. Barrows, "The Manuscript Federal Census: Source for a 'New' Local History," *Indiana Magazine of History* 69 (1973): 181–92; and Lutz Berkner, "The Use and Misuse of Census Data for the Historical Analysis of Family Structure," *Journal of Interdisciplinary History* 4 (1975): 721–38. On the census of manufacturers, see Margaret Walsh, "The Census as an Accurate Source of Information: The Value of Mid-Nineteenth Century Manufacturing Returns," *Historical Methods Newsletter* 3 (1970): 3–13, and "The Value of Mid-Nineteenth Century Manufacturing Returns: The Printed Census and the Manuscript Compilations Compared," *Historical Methods Newsletter* 4 (1971): 43–51. Anyone employing federal census records can profit from Margo J. Anderson, *The American Census: A Social History* (New Haven: Yale University Press, 1988).

Guides to state and territorial censuses are Henry J. Dubester, *State Censuses: An Annotated Bibliography* (1944; reprint ed., Westport, CT: Greenwood, 1976), and Ann S. Leinhart, *State Census Records* (Baltimore: Genealogical Publishing, 1992).

Discussions of more specialized records include James H. Madison, "The Credit Report of R. G. Dun and Co. as Historical Sources," *Historical Methods Newsletter* 8 (1975): 128–31; Richard K. Lieberman, "A Measure for the Quality of Life: Housing," *Historical Methods Newsletter* 11 (1978): 129–34; and Larry R. Gerlach and Michael L. Nicholls, "The Mormon Genealogical Society and Research Opportunities in Early American History," *William and Mary Quarterly* 32 (1976): 625–29.

Historians faced with masses of material culled from census returns, local archives, and other sources may wish to learn how to assess it quantitatively and perhaps how to store, retrieve, manipulate, and analyze it using a computer. These are sophisticated techniques, but they are not beyond the capacity of most individuals willing to invest a little time to acquire basic statistical and computer skills. It is of course helpful to have access to a computer through one's school, business, or agency, but many useful statistical analyses do not require a computer. To gain a sense of what is involved and how to begin, consult Hubert M. Blalock, Jr., *Social Statistics*, 2nd ed. (New York: McGraw-Hill, 1972); Charles M. Dollar and Richard J. Jensen, *Historian's Guide to Statistics: Quantitative Analysis and Historical Research* (New York: Holt, Rinehart and Winston, 1971); Edward Shorter, *The Historian and the Computer: A Practical Guide* (Englewood Cliffs, NJ: Prentice-Hall, 1971); and Roderick Floud, *An Introduction to Quantitative Methods for Historians* (Princeton: Princeton University Press, 1973). For examples of the application of these techniques to nearby history, refer to the many recent works cited in chapter 12 in this book, especially those having to do with mobility and assimilation.

6

Oral Documents

Referring to something as an "oral document" may seem unusual, but only until one recalls that "document" derives from the Latin *docere,* "to teach." Not everything that teaches by words is written down, at least not in its original form. With this in mind, we turn our attention to traces of another kind, those carried in the memories of participants in and eyewitnesses to events of the past. If the information and insights in those memories can be retrieved, they are potentially of immeasurable historical value.

Tapping into human memories to extract recollections and reminiscences is particularly important for historians of communities, institutions, and families, for the history they are dealing with was most likely made by men and women who had neither the time nor the inclination to leave an extensive written record of their doings. Nearby historians can be practitioners of "the new social history," that is, the history of the nonelite, of men and women in ordinary walks of life. Some individuals among them stood out from others, of course, and they should receive the attention they deserve, but local historians should not ignore the opportunity to draw composite sketches of the anonymous folks who through the years have played important but unheralded and so far unrecorded parts in the communities, institutions, and families to which they belonged.

Sometimes participants and eyewitnesses to history can be induced to write down the information and insights in which historians are interested. Persons asking for written responses to questions should observe two very important rules. First, the questions should be as specific as possible. Avoid asking questions like: What was Uncle Bill like? Ask rather: What did he do for a living? How did he prefer to spend his free time? What was the nature of his relationship with his parents?

Second, do not ask questions requiring lengthy and involved answers. Make responding to your questions as simple as possible. Leave space after your questions for the answers to be written in. Include a stamped return envelope. Courtesy and appreciation must always be shown. People are more likely to supply information if they are assured that they are providing genuine assistance. Tell them why the information is being sought.

A better way to reach into the memories of history's participants and eyewitnesses is to ask them questions person to person. Conversations made up of questions by an interviewer and responses by the person being interviewed are the essence of what is called oral history. Ideally these exchanges are recorded on tape and themselves become durable traces of the past. It is possible, of course, but less satisfactory to record interviews over the phone, but the interviewer must tell the responding person that the conversation is being taped.

Devoting an entire chapter to practices involved in capturing recollections and reminiscences is meant neither to enshroud oral history in mystery nor to elevate it to a place of superiority among research methods. Oral history is simply a way of gathering and preserving information gained from persons who have firsthand knowledge of historical events, thus adding to the sum total of knowledge about these events and the people involved in them. The quest for new knowledge, incidentally, distinguishes oral historians from producers of broadcast documentaries. By interviewing, historians seek to elicit previously unrecorded evidence from the past and to convert it into a form—aural to begin with, but possibly also written—that will make it useful to themselves and other historians.

Oral history is neither a new nor a rarely used research tool. Historians have relied for centuries on eyewitness and participant accounts that they and others have created by asking questions and writing down the answers. But the method was institutionalized with the founding by Allan Nevins of the Columbia Oral History Project in 1940. It took its first big step toward popular use in 1948 when the wire recorder was introduced, making possible verbatim transcripts of interviews. Audiotape recorders, especially cassette recorders, which came into use in the 1960s, helped sustain an oral history movement, and more recently videocassette recorders have given it a new dimension. It should be noted, however, that interviews do not always have to be tape recorded. Interviewers can simply take notes by hand, as reporters for newspapers often do, as was done in the Federal Writers Project in which former slaves were interviewed during the 1930s, and may have been done by Herodotus and Thucydides in ancient Greece.

USING ORAL HISTORY EFFECTIVELY

How can oral history be used most effectively? Some manuals on oral history create the impression that it is a complicated technique, and indeed it can be. But reduced to its basics, oral history is nothing more than the application of common sense to the pursuit of information. Common sense, however, is often lacking, as for example, when interviewers:

In 1932, Frank Lloyd Wright and his wife Olgivanna established the Taliesin Fellowship and invited young men and women wishing to become architects to work with him as apprentices in his studio. Through the years many came, as they do yet today, forty years after Wright's death. One who joined the Fellowship in 1953 is Tony Puttnam. In an interview, he described how his interest in architecture led him to Taliesin.

I had for years and years as a young person thought that I wanted to be an architect, and then after the war, in Chicago, Mies van der Rohe was the great rage of architectural circles. Finally, a few new buildings were built, which was a very big, big thing. After five years of war and ten years of depression there were very few new buildings built. Any new one was an enormous novelty. But when they finally were built, they were very disappointing and not inspiring. They just didn't have very much adventure to them.

Coming to Taliesin was like walking into a place and hearing music for the first time. Here was overwhelming experience about architecture and space, and the whole atmosphere to begin with was overwhelming: all the new things that you found in those buildings that you did not find in other buildings that I had experienced. It's still very difficult to describe or deal with in any kind of objective way. There are a lot of buildings that have space in them, but Taliesin was like having space as a kind of energetic force moving through the building and relating to various parts of the building in various ways. The materials that this pier or this wall or that window, the materials that you found in the building influenced the dynamics of that space . . . and that configuration speeded it up or made it rhythmical, or other things.

So, it was a big revelation about what the possibilities were. And the works of art there which all related to this in a sort of mysterious fashion—Japanese prints and screens and ceramics and sculptures and all that sort of thing. The ensemble of the place was also quite overwhelming, along with the landscape and the whole way that the building managed to be both an expression of the landscape and be forceful enough almost to make the landscape an expression of it.

I decided, on the basis of that weekend that I went to Taliesin, that this was the place for me. And whether or not I would ever really be any good at design, I didn't feel like this was something I was going to deal with easily or ever become proficient with. The whole thing in total was the first experience I had ever had with someone who had made the world whole. It was the world that was as put together, as whole in one piece in any place, that I think it could have been.

With a great piece of synchronicity, I received a small inheritance totally unexpected from someone I had never heard of before. I didn't realize that I had a relative of that nature. And so I went to Mr. Wright and asked him if I could stay. He was not markedly enthusiastic about this, but I told him my Mies van der Rohe story, and that pleased him a good deal, and so I guess he figured that at least I knew the difference between this and that.

Source: *Myron A. Marty and Shirley L. Marty,* Frank Lloyd Wright's Taliesin Fellowship *(Kirksville, MO: Thomas Jefferson University Press, 1999), pp. 34–35.*

- appear unannounced for an interview at the doorstep of someone about whom they know practically nothing;
- bring to the interview equipment they do not know how to operate or that they have not tested before coming;

- begin an interview without setting the narrator* at ease and with no idea of what they want to accomplish;
- ask poorly framed questions;
- allow the interview to drift or, quite the opposite, force it to fit into a preconceived format;
- fail to listen to answers to questions;
- interrupt the narrator's comments and dominate the conversation;
- try to interview two or three people simultaneously;
- try to conduct the interview with the television or radio blaring in the background;
- keep the interview going until the narrator drifts away from exhaustion or loses interest;
- fail to take notes during the interview, recording dates, names, especially how to spell them, and other matters that might need clarification later;
- fail to seek the narrator's permission to use the information produced in the interview;
- fail to identify on the tape and in writing the narrator, the interviewer, the date and location, and the subject of the interview;
- fail to thank the narrator after the interview;
- use the information gained without verifying it for accuracy.

Still, mistakes of the kind that no one would expect to make do occur, and anyone who has worked in oral history could no doubt add to the above list. Fortunately, as we know from experience, it is possible to learn from practice how to avoid these simple mistakes and produce good results.

Before we consider specific suggestions for doing oral history properly and effectively, two general comments may be helpful. First, circumstances alter practices. Persons working alone—say, on a family history—will approach interviewing of persons with whom they are acquainted in a manner quite different from that used by teams of interviewers working collaboratively in projects with clear and specifically defined purposes. In the former instance, the interviewers probably aim to collect reminiscences and to evoke interpretations of facts that may be already known. Knowing that new information may turn up when interviews roam off course, such interviewers are not particularly intent upon keeping to preestablished sets of questions.

In group projects—for instance, a neighborhood history—in which a cadre of interviewers is sent out to elicit information from persons they have never before met and may never meet again, it is desirable to give each interviewer precisely worded questions arranged in a specific order and instructions to use the questions as provided. In such circumstances the interview is part of a larger survey, and questions left unanswered by some of the population surveyed will diminish the value of the entire project.

Circumstances also alter the type and extent of training given to interviewers. Personable and engaging conversationalists working on their own projects can probably do an effective job of interviewing without too much training. A quick reading of the suggestions in this chapter should be sufficient to start them off. They will learn quickly from experience, and the price paid for mistakes will not be too high. On the other hand, interviewing does not come naturally to some people, and training and practice are helpful to them. Again, when interviewing is done as part of a project—one, say, that is attempting to determine migration patterns or to record the experiences of persons who participated in a specific event—systematic training is almost always necessary. Whether the interviewers are volunteers or paid workers makes little difference. The nature of the project and the personality of the interviewer determine the extent of training required.

The second general comment is that oral history is only a means to an end, not an end in itself. It is but one part of a process aimed at gathering, assimilating, and interpreting information. Some of the most enthusiastic advocates and practitioners in the oral history movement occasionally give the impression that the interview itself is of paramount importance. This is understandable, since it can be exciting *and* fun. Furthermore, because the persons interviewed are often elderly, interviewers develop a sense that time is running out. Libraries and archives will always be there, but people die. Someone has said that doing oral history is like climbing *up* a down escalator—there is no time to rest. Enthusiasm for oral history is fine, but what really counts is the potential of oral history for accomplishment, for a contribution to the historical record.

GUIDELINES FOR INTERVIEWING

Whether working alone or in a larger project, historians will want to make their interviews as good as possible. These guidelines will be helpful.

Before the Interview

1. Call or write the narrator well before the time you would like to conduct the interview. Explain your plans and purposes, solicit the person's interest in your project, and set a time for an interview. Keep notes on your first conversation. In a larger project it may be desirable to follow the initial contact with a letter describing how the individual interviews fit as parts into the whole and listing four or five major topics to be covered. Your advance contacts will probably set the narrator to thinking about your interests, and you are likely to secure a better interview. More than courtesy is involved in laying the groundwork for interviews.
2. Gather as much background information about the narrator as you can and familiarize yourself thoroughly with the relationship between the narrator and the project you are working on.
3. Outline the main points of interest for your interview. To avoid being trapped in a rigid format, it is best not to write out specific questions but

6.1 In an interview, what questions might this picture prompt? Examples: What are the ages of the sisters appearing in it? Why were they posed as they were? Why was one wearing a fur coat and the other a dress? What does the setting suggest about the economic circumstances of the sisters' family? (Photo courtesy of the Marty family collection and copyright © Shirley Marty.)

to jot down short phrases around which you can readily build questions. This use of notes will give the conversation a touch of spontaneity and will help set both the interviewer and the narrator at ease. If you choose to write out questions, be prepared to abandon them if the interview takes unexpected but productive turns (except in group projects, as noted above).

4. If you plan to use a tape recorder, become thoroughly acquainted with its operation, especially the microphone, volume controls, and tape-changing procedures. Practice with someone before going to the interview. If you feel comfortable in the presence of a microphone, so will the person being interviewed. Also practice control of the tape so that you are adept at reserving a minute or so of blank tape before the recording of the interview starts; you may want to use this reserved portion of the tape to record information about the interview. Prepare a kit of materials that you will want to take with you to the interview: your notes and interview outline, pens and pencils, a notebook, an extension cord, and extra tapes. It makes sense to use the best equipment you can afford.

5. Where possible, power the recorder with a line from an electrical outlet. If you rely on battery power, be sure to have extra batteries with you. For very important interviews it makes sense to use two recorders.

Starting the Interview

1. Situate yourself and the narrator in comfortable positions. The recorder should be placed within your reach but where the narrator will not be too conscious of it. Try to avoid distractions, interruptions, and background noises from radios, television sets, or traffic.
2. Let the recorder run for a few minutes as you chat about matters not directly related to the interview. Listen to a minute or two of what you have recorded. This should relax both you and the narrator while you make sure that the recording is at the proper level. You might be surprised to discover that the narrator may be hearing his or her voice for the first time, and you may have to offer assurance that there is nothing unpleasant or unnatural about the sound.
3. If you can do so without making your narrator nervous, begin the interview with identifying information: name the interviewer, the narrator, the date, the place, and the subject of the interview. A conversational style will provide a nice transition between the informal conversation and the interview that follows, establishing the basis for an easy flow between questions and responses.
4. Be sure to check the time and to know the length of your tape so that you will not have to look constantly to see how much tape remains. Interviews should not normally be scheduled to last more than an hour or at most ninety minutes.

During the Interview

1. Remind yourself that the interview is not intended to show off your knowledge—though you must appear knowledgeable to the narrator—but to elicit from the narrator clear responses to your questions. Above all, do not dominate the conversation with displays of knowledge.
2. Avoid asking questions that can be answered with a simple Yes or No. Useful leads include: "What led up to . . . ?" "Tell me about . . ." "What did you feel when . . . ?" and "I would like to hear about . . ."
3. Ask only one question at a time; in other words, avoid running questions together or protracting them so that the narrator is confused regarding which one to answer.
4. Keep your questions brief and to the point.
5. Start with noncontroversial matters, saving more delicate ones until good rapport has been established.
6. Listen.
7. Do not let periods of silence fluster you; the narrator needs time to think.
8. Do not worry excessively about a question that seems to be clumsily worded. A little fumbling by the interviewer may help to put the narrator at ease.

The Wonder Bread Reunion

This photograph, found in a family collection, prompted Paula Presley, now of Kirksville, Missouri, to recall the circumstances in which it was taken. (Used by permission.)

The time was most likely August 1945. The older couple in the photo are my grand-parents, Joe Jones and Martha (Daniel) Jones. I'm the eight-year-old in the new dress with the appliquéd bow on the bodice (in the front row, I seem to recall).

Joe and Mattie, as she was called, lived in Arkansas, about three miles from town. They farmed 40 acres of cotton. Joe and Mattie had five children—two daughters and three sons. Clara (my mother), their second child, married a carpenter, Herbert, and moved to Detroit in 1936.

Then WWII began. All three of Joe and Mattie's sons served during the war; Mattie kept a flag with three stars hanging in her window while they were away. Before the war, Joe would not allow a radio in his house ("the Bible says that Satan is the Prince and Power of the Air—and the radio uses 'the air waves' . . . "). But after his sons went to war, Joe purchased a radio so they could listen to President Roosevelt.

The family was happy to have their sons return home safely after the war. The photo was taken after all the family was back together again at "the old homeplace." A lot of cousins, aunts and uncles were there that day, too, but this is a photo of Joe and Mattie, their five children, their spouses and their grandchildren.

The table is a hayrack with a large tablecloth or sheet on it that Joe and the boys had moved to the "front yard." In the back, a fish-fry was going on. Folks had caught catfish in the bayou nearby and were frying them in lard in Mattie's big black washtub. Having Wonder Bread ("light bread") was really something! Everybody usually served biscuits or cornbread for meals, but this was a special occasion.

6.2   (Photo courtesy of and copyright © Paula Presley.)

9. Do not interrupt a good story simply because another question has occurred to you or because the narrator has wandered from the planned framework of questions. If you do, valuable remembrances might escape. Try to find gentle ways and the appropriate time for pulling the conversation back on the track.

10. To help the narrator describe persons, ask about their appearance, then about their personality, character, and activities.

11. Remember that persons being interviewed are likely to give more interesting and more vigorous responses to questions or statements that imply uncertainty on your part than to ones that suggest you are merely seeking agreement. A phrase like "I'm not sure I understand" or "This can be confusing to someone who wasn't there" may elicit useful information.

12. Try to establish where the narrator was at the time of the events being described as well as his or her role in them. Determine whether the narrator was a participant or a passive witness.

13. Use the interview to verify information gained from other sources. Do not take issue with accounts given by the narrator even if you believe another version to be more accurate. Be content to elicit as much information as possible, possibly by offering alternative versions: "Some people say . . ." or "I have heard . . ." You can decide later which version of a story is accurate.

14. Try to avoid off-the-record comments; instead persuade the narrator to speak in terms that permit the statement to be part of the record. Sensitive material can be protected by closing the tape for an agreed-upon period of years, that is, by sealing it so that researchers will not have access to it until the material in question is less sensitive. It is better to have such material recorded and waiting for later use than to let it escape entirely.

15. Do not interrupt the narrator unless the story strays too far from its course. Interruptions, when necessary, should begin with phrases like "Let's go back to where you . . ." or "A moment ago you were telling me about . . ."

16. Avoid turning the tape recorder off and on unless the narrator becomes unduly agitated or uncommunicative. Having some irrelevant material on the tape is better than losing the flow of the conversation by switching the recorder off and on again.

17. Be alert to points in the interview when special factual information is brought out. Take note of this information by writing it down. Asking the narrator to spell names is not at all inappropriate. Accuracy is more important than an uninterrupted interview.

18. Use photographs, clippings, or other documents to encourage the narrator to talk about persons or events that are of particular interest to you and about which his or her memory might need some jostling. Asking narrators to dig out photographs and other memory-prompting materials before the interview is a way of inviting them to think about the topics you want

to discuss. If possible, make copies of these documents and include them
with the tape when you deposit it in the archives.

19. At the end of the interview, repeat the identifying information: the inter-
    viewer, the narrator, the date, the place, and the subject of the interview.

After the Interview

1. Secure the written permission of the narrator to use the tape and transcription.
2. Record the identifying information in writing on a card to be placed in an
   interview file. On the same card list a summary of the major topics discussed, along with the point in the interview when discussion of these topics begins. This index, which requires the use of a tape-footage indicator
   or a stopwatch, makes the tape useful to researchers before a typed transcript becomes available. Such an index is important even when the researcher is also the interviewer.
3. Make a duplicate copy of the tape and store both copies in places where
   they can be preserved without damage, which means low humidity and
   temperature that avoids extremes of heat and cold. At the same time, take
   precautions against the tapes being erased.
4. Place a note with the tape indicating the date when it was recorded and requesting that it be played and rewound periodically, noting that the life of
   an unplayed tape may be less than twenty years, if that. In hot and dry conditions the tapes become brittle and crack, or they stick together, or a
   "print-through" or "voice-over" occurs, causing an echo on the tapes.

THEN WHAT?

Experts in oral history are not all of one mind about a number of questions, some
of which are discussed briefly here.

How important is it for tapes to be transcribed? Some contend that a tape
recording that is not transcribed is not oral history. Transcriptions are without
question the best means for making the contents of tapes available and useful
to researchers, but the labor involved is time consuming and therefore costly.
It takes as much as five hours, and possibly even longer, to transcribe a one-
hour interview. The consensus among experts is that transcriptions should be
made if at all possible, but that it is better to continue interviewing than to
spend most of one's time and money on transcriptions. The topic index described above serves as a good interim device for making the tapes useful. Despite this consensus, however, we strongly urge beginners in oral history to
transcribe diligently in order to hear and understand the interview. This exercise will make novices conscious of things they missed and the reasons for the
omissions. Transcriptions are self-training exercises. Almost always they
prompt the interviewer to return for a second interview, which is likely to be
much more informative than the first.

This brief excerpt from a family history shows how a picture used to elicit information during research can be incorporated into a finished product.

This is a family portrait with all six sons, around 1941. The ages of the sons are paired in groups of two from three years to seventeen years. This was not a coincidence or some sort of family planning. Hermena wanted a daughter and had been told that if you had a son and then got pregnant soon after that birth, the next baby would be a girl. She tried this three times without success.

The car in the background was a neighbor's Buick; however, the family now had a 1932 Chevy. Papa had rebuilt their 1916 Model T continuously until it would not run, even with a miracle. They eventually bought a 1932 used Chevy with the money Papa had managed to save in the three–four years while working for WPA and hiring himself out for farm work.

The family was still living on a rented farm, but their clothes are not tattered or patched as they had been three–four years earlier. They had electricity via a "wind charger," a propeller-driven generator, which charged the battery and could light one bulb, taking the place of the kerosene lamp, and run their newly acquired radio. Their diet had improved, with meat much more frequent. The crops had improved and the profits were small but more steady. About a year after the picture Pap gave up farming and moved to the city to work as a carpenter full time, less risky "business."

Source: Pamela Bohlmann, untitled essay for a family histories project (St. Louis, 1977).

6.3 *A 1941 family portrait. (Photo courtesy of and copyright © Pamela Bohlmann.)*

Should transcriptions be literal, or is editing permitted? Answering this question requires an explanation of the successive stages in the transcription process as they are generally accepted by authorities in oral history. In the first stage, the transcriber's task is to put on paper (or the screen) a verbatim transcription of the inter-

One of the New Deal's many programs to put people to work during the 1930s depression was the WPA Federal Writers' Project. Among its other activities, the project sent historians, sociologists, journalists, and others to interview people throughout the country about their lives and customs. In that era, before the time of the tape recorder, responses to interview questions had to be written up from notes or from memory by the interviewer. Many of these early oral histories were then placed in the Library of Congress, where they remain. Best known among the interviews with ordinary people who had been largely overlooked by historians were many with aged blacks old enough to remember slave life, but other ethnic minorities were also represented. For instance, a series of interviews with the Italians and Cubans of Ybor City, Florida, provided much information about that community's past and present.

I was born in the town of Santo Stefano di Quisquina, Sicily, on May 12th, 1860, and am now 75 years of age. My father was a farm peasant working the soil for a land owner. Since my early years I toiled at the farm with father.

I was married at the age of 22 years, and then leased a tract of land which I worked planting wheat, horse feed, potatoes and vegetables. After we had been married a year, my wife gave birth to a child, a baby boy, who died when he was a year old. In the year 1885 my wife again gave birth to another son who died soon after.

In this same year I decided to come to New Orleans where many Italians were living at that time. The trip was long and tedious, lasting 30 days. I was afterwards introduced to Mr. Vaccaro who was the owner of the steamship line in which I had sailed to America with my wife. We soon became fast friends, and he proposed to me that I work for him at his Produce Company in New Orleans. He handled bananas chiefly which he brought from Honduras. There I was employed as foreman, which position I held for some two years.

Several friends described Tampa to me with such glowing colors that soon I became enthused, and decided to come here and try my fortune. Accordingly, in 1887, leaving my wife in New Orleans, I took the train to Mobile. At Mobile I took the boat that brought me here. We disembarked at the Lafayette Street bridge. I was then 27 years of age.

I had expected to see a flourishing city, but my expectations were too high, for what I saw before me almost brought me to tears. There was nothing; what one may truthfully say, nothing. Franklin was a long sandy street. There were very few houses, and these were far apart with tall pine trees surrounding them. The Hillsborough County Court House was a small wooden building. Some men were just beginning to work on the foundation of the Tampa Bay Hotel.

Ybor City was not connected to Tampa as it is today. There was a wilderness between the two cities, and a distance of more than one mile between the two places. All of Ybor City was not worth one cent to me. In different places of Ybor City a tall species of grass grew, proper of swampy places. This grass grew from 5 to 6 feet high. I was completely disillusioned with what I saw. There was a stagnant water hole where the society of the Centro Espanol (Spanish Club) is today located. A small wooden bridge spanned this pond. I remember that I was afraid to cross that bridge, and especially so at night, because of the alligators that lived there. They would often crawl into the bridge and bask there in the sun all day long.

The factory of Martinez Ybor had some twenty cigar-makers; Sanchez y Haya had some fifteen; while Pendas had about ten. I worked for a time at the factory of Modesto Monet as stripper [a stripper removes the center stem from the tobacco leaf], and made

35¢ for my first day's work. Of course, I was then only learning the cigar business, and could not expect to make more. When I became more skilled in my work as a stripper, I would make from $1.00 to $1.25 a day.

While still at this work, I gradually began learning the cigar-makers' trade as I saw that they were making a much more comfortable income. When I had become somewhat proficient as a cigar-maker, I was earning from $14.00 to $15.00 a week.

When I had been in Tampa some two or three years I sent for my wife who was still living in New Orleans. When she arrived in Tampa she burst out crying at what she saw: wilderness, swamps, alligators, mosquitoes, and open closets. The only thing she would say when she arrived was: "Why have you brought me to such a place?"

Here we had two more sons, and one died. We had in all four children, of whom three died. We only had one child left whom we were able to raise.

At about this time Mr. Martinez Ybor (the cigar manufacturer) was offering homes for sale at a very low price. I, therefore, went to him and purchased a home at the corner of 18th Street and 8th Avenue for the price of $725. I still have this house, although considerably remodeled. I paid $100 cash, and the balance I paid off in monthly terms. I was able to do this with the help of my wife, who worked also at the cigar factory. We worked in several factories, sometimes in West Tampa, and sometimes in Ybor City, wherever working conditions were better. . . .

There is not much hope in Ybor City. The cigar factories are on a continuous decline. The factory of Corral & Wodiska had 1500 persons working, today it has only some 150 or 200 persons. . . . The Trust has also purchased many factories here and have removed them to the Northern cities. The people of Ybor City are orphans, not only of father and mother, but of everything in life. They cannot find work at the cigar factories because of the machines. . . .

Under present conditions the people of Ybor City have no other alternative but to leave for New York City. Here they get only 50¢ a week for the maintenance of a whole family, and the single person is not given any relief whatever. In New York City they are given a home, groceries, coal to warm themselves in winter, and electric lights.

Source: Federal Writers' Project Records, Library of Congress Manuscripts Division, Washington, D.C.

view. Next comes a review or audit of the recording, as the transcriber or interviewer listens to it while reading the transcription, making corrections as necessary. Transcribers frequently remark that words and expressions that seemed indecipherable in the first stage become clear in the second. In the third stage, the transcriber may be permitted to delete verbal clutter, such as "you know" and "uh-huh," and brief comments of the interviewer that are designed merely to keep the narrator talking. More extensive editing is frowned upon by many oral historians and is not tolerated at all by some. As a practical matter, the extent of editing is dictated by the nature and quality of the narrator's account.

Should transcriptions be shown to narrators, giving them a chance to change what they said on the tape? Most oral historians agree that if the interviews are likely to be published or quoted extensively, or if they form an integral part of a published work, narrators must be accorded the privilege of reviewing and even revising the transcripts so that they show not merely what people said but what they wanted to say. Giving the narrators this prerogative discourages some oral historians from making transcriptions. In their writing, they quote directly from the tape.

What are the circumstances in which further editing of the transcripts is permitted, after they have been checked by the persons interviewed? In preparing the transcripts, or portions of them, for publication, editing practices generally encourage, or at least permit, elimination of redundancies, confusing digressions, crutch expressions, false starts, and some of the narrators' contractions. It is permissible also to clarify the text by bringing consistency to matters of tense and number and making certain that the identity of persons referred to by pronouns is clear. Such editing may be done, however, only when the complete, literal transcripts as edited by the persons interviewed are placed in accessible archives, along with the audio recordings of the interviews, in accordance with the terms of deposit agreements between the persons interviewed, the archives, and the interviewer.

Should the tapes be kept after transcriptions have been made? Practices here are often dictated by economic considerations. Oral history on a large scale is expensive, and reuse of the tapes is occasionally necessary. In such unfortunate instances, representative portions, at least, should be preserved so that the researchers can hear the voices of the narrators and discern the tone of the conversation. Portions dealing with critical issues should also be preserved.

What are the advantages and disadvantages of videotaping oral history? As Donald Ritchie has written, "Memories are recounted with more than words. Transcripts can indicate laughter, sobs, finger pointing, or fist shaking. But some expressions are too complex or subtle to reduce to words." Videotapes add important visual dimensions to interviews. It helps to see the narrator's smiles, gestures, frowns, or expressions of certainty or uncertainty. Videotapes, particularly if they are done in the homes of the persons interviewed, add color and context to the spoken words. The medium, as one observer has remarked, definitely affects the message. For interviewing groups of people, videotapes offer decisive advantages over audiotapes, since they make it easy to identify the individual narrators.

But there are also disadvantages: The recording equipment is more expensive and cumbersome, although this is less true than it was just a few years ago. The availability of small, hand-held camcorders that function well in conditions where lighting is inadequate make videotaping more feasible, and improvements in video technology will no doubt continue. Still, videotaped interviews are more complicated because they typically require two persons to conduct them. Transcribing the interviews is also more difficult, since it is ordinarily necessary to make an audio recording of the videotape so that the transcriber can use standard transcription equipment. Leaving them untranscribed is a disservice to researchers, since it is a rare researcher who has the time or patience to view an entire tape or use the fast-forward and reverse features of the equipment to find the recorded lines of greatest interest to her or him. Finally, the archival life of video-tapes is shorter than that of audiotapes and the attention and care they require is significantly greater.

Some oral historians recommend recording a portion of an interview on videotape, to preserve the visual image of the respondent, and continuing it with audiotape.

How should ethical and legal issues relating to use be handled? Persons using oral history must be mindful that they are working with a research method that sometimes raises ethical and legal questions, which include, perhaps most important, those dealing with the right to privacy. At stake are not only the rights of the person being interviewed, who may not wish to reveal certain things, but those of third parties as well. Every precaution must be taken to guard against violation of privacy. While release forms such as the sample in appendix B can be used as a way of preparing for possible questions and the potential consequences of misuse of the interviews, they are no substitute for sensitivity and good judgment. Release forms attempt to ensure only that tapes and transcripts may be used in specified ways by qualified researchers, not that the documents will necessarily be open to all who might be curious about their contents. Legal questions may arise, even for nonprofessional historians of the nearby past, if they ignore the federal copyright law. This law grants copyright protection automatically to persons whose words are recorded in any tangible form. This protection lasts until fifty years after that person's death, even without registration with the Copyright Office. Use of the interviews or excerpts from them beyond the very small number of words allowed by "fair use" without a deed or contract permitting such use makes the user vulnerable to a lawsuit for copyright infringement.

A statement by the Oral History Association and the American Historical Association addresses another legal issue facing oral historians, that is, protecting the interests of the persons interviewed and gaining their "informed consent." This involves being certain that they are not taken advantage of, that they understand the process, and that they know what a signature on a consent form means. The statement reads: "Certain interview research may be governed by the Federal Policy for the Protection of Human Subjects (codified at 45 CFR 46). Such research may require prospective review by an Institutional Review Board (IRB) as well as written informed consent by the interviewee. Additionally, institutions engaged in biomedical and behavioral research are likely to have internal policies that also pertain to interview research. Historians should be cognizant of and comply with all laws, regulations, and institutional policies applicable to their research activities." (See the Oral History Association's Web site: <omega.dickinson.edu/organizations/oha/>.) Although this statement apparently applies only to interviewing done through or for an institution, it makes sense for individuals engaged in oral history projects to conduct themselves in a manner consistent with the statement's requirements.

ORAL HISTORY AND FOLKLORE

Local history is "naturally and inescapably linked with the study of folklore," as the preeminent folklorist Richard Dorson asserted, and one of the great attractions of research in local history is "the opportunity to record folk traditions and employ them for the enrichment of the historical narrative." Oral folk history is an adaptation of oral history as described above to the circumstances in which it is used.

The folklorist, Dorson points out, does not *interview;* he *collects* folklore from informants (the folk variant of narrator) in ways that are least disruptive to the situation in which the folk share their lore. And folklorists are interested in much more than lore. They collect, as one guide points out, tales (jokes, tall tales, tales of supernatural, legends, marvelous, or fairytales), songs, (ballads, lyrics, ditties, spirituals), instrumental music, dances, play (drama, games, verbal games), riddles, speech (proverbial, vocabulary, grammar), beliefs (regarding human life, plants, animals, and weather, medicine, and witchcraft), customs (daily, occasional, seasonal, annual, or relating to the life cycle), and material culture (art, craft, cookery, and architecture). This collectors' list amounts to a functional description of folklore, which is perhaps the best kind to give, since practitioners are at odds on formal definitions. The *Funk and Wagnall's Standard Dictionary of Folklore, Mythology, and Legend* shows the differences of opinion by supplying twenty-one brief definitions.

The authors of this collectors' guide, MacEdward Leach and Henry Glassie, define folklore further by distinguishing between folklore and popular lore, between folk traditions and "the ephemeral products of mass culture." Folklore, they say, "has internal strengths and beauties given it by generations of carriers and molders," qualities that "distinguish it from comparable materials found at other levels of culture." Although folk things are traditional, old-fashioned, and local in character, the best sign that something is really "folk" is evidence that it may be found at different times and in different places. Variations of folk things, folklorists point out, indicate a long life in the oral tradition.

Historians of the nearby past who use oral history as a research tool do not become folklorists merely by collecting rather than interviewing or by paying attention to folksy aspects of the people with whom they work. Yet, being mindful of the concerns of folklorists may help historians do a better job of gathering material for the story they want to tell.

Nor, for that matter, does reading a chapter on oral history make one an oral historian. As with most kinds of historical research, there is only one way to learn oral history, and that is by doing it.

NOTES AND FURTHER READING

Quotations in this chapter can be found in: Richard M. Dorson, *American Folklore and the Historian* (Chicago: University of Chicago Press, 1971), p. 146; Dorson, "The Oral

Historian and the Folklorist," *Proceedings of the Sixth National Colloquium on Oral History,* Bloomington, Indiana, October 8–10, 1971, p. 42; MacEdward Leach and Henry Glassie, *A Guide for Collectors of Oral Tradition and Folk Cultural Material in Pennsylvania* (Harrisburg Pennsylvania Historical and Museum Commission, 1968), pp. 7–8; Donald A. Ritchie, *Doing Oral History* (New York: Twayne Publishers, 1995), and at the Oral History Association's Web site (see next paragraph).

The Oral History Association <omega.dickinson.edu/organizations/oha/> is a valuable resource for practitioners of oral history. Its address is: Dickinson College, P.O. Box 1773, Carlisle, PA 17013. The OHA's journal the *Oral History Review* is published by the University of California Press, which also manages its membership database; see <www.ucpress.edu/journals/ohr>. The OHA also publishes the *Oral History Newsletter* (since 1967) and a pamphlet series. The Web site of the OHA includes the "Oral History Evaluation Guidelines," 2nd edition, 1991. This publication has been adopted by the National Endowment for the Humanities as the standard for conducting oral history. It is available free on the Internet and for $5.00 in published form. As this book is being completed, the OHA is in the process of revising the Guidelines; a copy of what has been approved so far is available on the Internet. It also includes information about the OHA's pamphlet series, which includes Barry A. Lanman and George L. Mehaffy, *Oral History in the Secondary School Classroom* (1988); Laurie Mercier and Madeline Buckendorf, *Using Oral History in Community History Projects* (1992); and John A. Neuenschwander, *Oral History and the Law* (1993). The Baylor Institute for Oral History provides a valuable "workshop on the Web": <www.baylor.edu/~Oral_History/Workshop_welcome.html>.

Guides to the practice of oral history are numerous; the best of them are: Donald A. Ritchie, *Doing Oral History* (New York: Twayne Publishers, 1995); and Willa K. Baum, *Oral History for the Local Historical Society* (Nashville: American Association for State and Local History, 1987); also by Baum is *Transcribing and Editing Oral History* (Nashville: American Association for State and Local History, 1991).

Other works include: Barbara Allen and Lynwood Montell, *From Memory to History: Using Oral History in Local Historical Research* (Jackson: University of Mississippi Press, 1981); Cullom Davis, Kathryn Back, and Kay MacLean, *Oral History: From Tape to Type* (Chicago: American Library Association, 1977), which pays more attention to preparation of transcripts from the recording than most others; William P. Fletcher, *Recording Your Family History: A Guide to Preserving Oral History with Videotape, Audiotape, Suggested Topics and Questions, Interview Techniques* (New York: Dodd, Mead, 1986); Ramon I. Harris, Joseph H. Cash, Herbert T. Hoover, and Stephen R. Ward, *The Practice of Oral History: A Handbook* (Glen Rock, NJ: Microfilming Corporation of America, 1975); James Hoopes, *Oral History: An Introduction for Students* (Chapel Hill: University of North Carolina Press, 1979); Edward D. Ives, *The Tape-Recorded Interview: A Manual for Workers in Folklore and Oral History* (Knoxville: University of Tennessee Press, 1980); John A. Neuenschwander, *Oral History as a Teaching Approach* (Washington, DC: National Education Association, 1976); Brad Jolly, *Videotaping Local History* (Nashville: American Association for State and Local History, 1982); Elizabeth Bryant Merrill, *Oral History Guide: A Handbook for Amateurs, Students, Teachers and Institutions* (Salem, WI: Sheffield Publishing Company, 1985); Robert Perks, *Oral History: Talking About the Past* (London: The Historical Association, in association with the Oral History Society, 1992); and Herbert J. Rubin and Irene S. Rubin, *Qualitative Interviewing: The Art of Hearing Data* (Thousand Oaks, CA: Sage Publications, 1995).

William W. Moss, *Oral History Program Manual* (New York: Praeger, 1974), deals with practical, ethical, and legal questions in oral history programs. The best discussion of oral history as history is found in Paul Thompson's *The Voice of the Past: Oral History* (Oxford: Oxford University Press, 1988). Other works dealing with issues relating to oral history include: David K. Dunaway and Willa K. Baum, *Oral History: An Interdisciplinary Anthology* (Walnut Creek, CA: AltaMira Press, 1996); Michael Frisch, *A Shared Authority: Essays on the Craft and Meaning of Oral and Public History* (Albany: State University of New York Press, 1990); Trevor Lummis, *Listening to History: The Authenticity of Oral Evidence* (Totowa, NJ: Barnes and Noble, 1988); Eva M. McMahon and Kim Lacy Rogers, eds., *Interactive Oral History Interviewing* (Hillsdale, NJ: Lawrence Erlbaum Associates, 1994); David Stricklen and Rebecca Sharpless, eds., *The Past Meets the Present: Essays on Oral History* (Lanham, MD: University Press of America, 1988); and Valerie Raleigh Yow, *Recording Oral History: A Practical Guide for Social Scientists* (Walnut Creek, CA: AltaMira Press, 1994). On legal questions in oral history, see John Neuenschwander, *Oral History and the Law* (Denton, TX: Oral History Association, 1985).

These articles present useful perspectives on oral history: Jacob J. Climo, "Transmitting Ethnic Identity Through Oral Narratives," *Ethnic Groups* 8, no. 3 (1990): 163–79 (focuses on Jewish narratives); Julie Cruikshank, "Oral Tradition and Oral History: Reviewing Some Issues," *Canadian Historical Review* 75, no. 3 (September 1994): 403–18; Joan Finnigan, "Say, That Reminds Me of Another Story," *Canadian Literature* no. 108 (Spring 1986): 82–90; Shirley Brice Heath, "Oral and Literate Traditions," *International Social Science Journal* 36, no. 1, (1984): 41–57; and Peter Martin, Gunshild G. Hagestad, and Patricia Diedrick, "Family Stories: Events (temporarily) Remembered," *Journal of Marriage and the Family* 50, no. 2 (May 1988): 533–41. Since 1986, the September issues of the *Journal of American History* have included articles on theory, method, historiography, and other subjects relating to oral history. The 1990 issue (Vol. 77, no. 2) included the American Historical Association's "Statement on Historical Documentation," which had appeared originally in the AHA's *Perspectives* (October 1989): 8. The September 1998 issue (Vol. 85, no. 2) includes three articles in a roundtable on "The Uses of Memory," a review essay on "Taping History," as well as the usual section of articles on oral history.

The possibilities for effective though widely different uses of oral history as a research method have been demonstrated in such works as Haruko Taya Cook and Theodore F. Cook, *Japan at War: An Oral History* (New York: New Press, 1992); Peter Friedlander, *The Emergence of a UAW Local, 1936–1939: A Study in Class and Culture* (Pittsburgh: University of Pittsburgh Press, 1978); Heather J. Frazer, *We Have Just Begun to Not Fight: An Oral History of Conscientious Objectors in Civilian Public Service During World War II* (New York: Twayne Publishers, 1996); Dorothy Gallagher, *Hannah's Daughters: Six Generations of an American Family* (New York: Crowell, 1976); Kathy Kahn, *Hillbilly Women* (New York: Avon, 1972); Harry Hampton and Steve Fayer, with Sarah Flynn, *Voices of Freedom: An Oral History of the Civil Rights Movement from the 1950s through the 1980s* (New York: Bantam Books, 1990); Tamara Hareven and Randolph Langenbach, *Amoskeag: Life and Work in an American Factory-City* (New York: Pantheon, 1978); Alice Hoffmann, *Archives of Memory: A Soldier Recalls World War II* (Lexington: University Press of Kentucky, 1990); Myron A. Marty and Shirley L. Marty, *Frank Lloyd Wright's Taliesin Fellowship* (Kirksville, MO: Thomas Jefferson University Press, 1999); Joan Morrison and Charlotte Fox Zabuskey, eds., *American Mosaic: The Immigrant Experience in the Words of Those Who Lived It* (New York: Dutton, 1980); Theodore Rosengarten, *All*

God's Dangers: The Life of Nate Shaw (New York: Knopf, 1974); Laurel Shackelford and Bill Weinberg, eds., *Our Appalachia: An Oral History* (New York: Hill and Wang, 1979); Studs Terkel, *Hard Times: An Oral History of the Great Depression* (New York: Pantheon, 1970); also by Terkel, among others: *The "Good War": An Oral History of World War II* (New York: Pantheon, 1984) and *The Great Divide: Second Thoughts on the American Dream* (New York: Pantheon, 1988); Tom E. Terrill and Jerrold Hirsch, eds., *Such as Us: Southern Voices of the Thirties* (New York: Norton, 1979); Tom Tiede, *American Tapestry* (New York: Pharos books, 1988); and T. Harry Williams, *Huey Long* (New York: Knopf, 1969). Ann Banks, ed., *First-Person America* (New York: Knopf, 1980), a collection of interviews conducted in the Federal Writers Project of the 1930s and 1940s, shows that oral history has been in use for a long time. Ira Berlin, Marc Favreau, and Steven F. Miller used materials from this project in *Remembering Slavery: African Americans Talk About Their Personal Experiences of Slavery and Emancipation,* a book-and-audiotape package (New York: New Press, 1998).

The number of books available on American folklore is considerable. Guides for using oral history in folklore research include Jan Harold Brunvand, *The Study of American Folklore: An Introduction* (New York: Norton, 1968) and *Folklore: A Study and Research Guide* (New York: St. Martin's, 1976). Also Kenneth S. Goldstein, *A Guide for Field Workers in Folklore* (Detroit: Gale Research Company, 1964, reprinted 1974); Elaine S. Katz, *Folklore for the Time of Your Life* (Birmingham, AL: Oxmoor House, 1978); MacEdward Leach and Henry Glassie, *A Guide for Collectors of Oral Traditions and Folk Cultural Material in Pennsylvania* (Harrisburg: Pennsylvania Historical and Museum Commission, 1968); and Warren E. Roberts, "Fieldwork: Recording Material Culture," in Richard M. Dorson, ed., *Folklore and Folklife: An Introduction* (Chicago: University of Chicago Press, 1972).

A good general introduction to folklore is found in Richard M. Dorson, *American Folklore* (Chicago: University of Chicago Press, 1959). Another is a collection of essays edited by Alan Dundes, *The Study of Folklore* (Englewood Cliffs, NJ: Prentice-Hall, 1965). More closely related to the concerns of this chapter are Richard M. Dorson, *American Folklore and the Historian* (Chicago: University of Chicago Press, 1971), and "The Oral Historian and the Folklorist," *Proceedings* of the Sixth National Colloquia on Oral History, Indiana University, October 8–10, 1971; and Henry Glassie, *Pattern in the Material Folk Culture of the Eastern United States* (Philadelphia: University of Pennsylvania Press, 1968). Three works that show the wide range of folklore concerns are Kenneth L. Ames, *Beyond Necessity: Art in the Folk Tradition* (Wilmington, DE: Winterthur Museum, Norton, 1977); William Lynwood Montell, *The Saga of Coe Ridge: A Study in Oral History* (Knoxville: University of Tennessee Press, 1970); and Michael Owen Jones, *The Handmade Object and Its Maker* (Berkeley: University of California Press, 1975).

*The terms "narrator," "subject," "respondent," and "interviewee" are used interchangeably by oral historians, according to personal preferences.

7

Visual Documents

Images of the past abound. There are snapshots in family albums, for example, and portraits and candid shots in school yearbooks, photographs in museum files, pictures in mass media publications, or transmitted through the Internet or on CD-ROMs, drawings, advertisements, paintings, videocassettes, movies, and maps.

Images offer good testaments to changes through the years—in the skyline, the landscape, or the texture of a neighborhood, for example, or in the appearance of individuals and the composition of groups. They reveal customs, preferences, and styles. They permit viewers to observe celebrations of past holidays and special occasions; to watch people at work, at play, and at home; to see how they courted, married, raised children and saw them through the rites of passage, and coped with stress, disruption, hardship, and the changing seasons of their lives. Images reveal communities discovering, building, and maturing; institutions forming and growing; agencies serving and struggling; businesses prospering and declining; and people at war and in peace. They give one a sense of what it was like to have been there.

Images from the past provide raw material for constructing stories. Their considerable possibilities as "visual documents" make it essential that they be used well. This requires a clear understanding of what they are and how and why their creators made them. Once they are made, they become independent documents, existing on their own. Just as images representing the same subject but produced by different creators are quite distinct, so a single one may be seen differently by the persons who look at it. Meaning also depends, in part, on how the image is presented for viewing.

For the sake of clarity and example, the discussion here concentrates on the form of visual documents likely to be used most extensively by historians of the nearby past, that is, photography. Statements that apply to photographs may be adapted to other visual documents as well. So references to "photograph" and "photographer" also pertain to "painting" and "painter" (or to any other visual art form and its creator). Remember, though, that a photograph is not "like" a painting, and attempts to compare them should be made cautiously.

STILL PHOTOGRAPHS: MEDIATED DOCUMENTS

Photographs are useful in constructing and telling stories because they provide evidence of events. They may reveal who was present at specific events, what people wore, and the settings in which the events occurred. A picture showing a family occasion, such as a wedding, depicts a social rite, but the taking of a picture is, in such instances, a ritual itself. Sometimes the decision to take a picture confers importance on an event that would otherwise be lacking. While a photograph may appear to be a thin slice of a moment in history, a real piece of the past, it may also create a feeling of unreality as one studies it. The commonplace becomes the mystifying.

Some photographs are works of art—not only those of renowned photographers like Eugene Atget, Alfred Stieglitz, Edward Steichen, Edward Weston, and Henri Cartier-Bresson, but also of unpublished and unexhibited photographers whose work may be awaiting discovery. Photographs may be artistic bearers of messages, like the work of Walker Evans, Dorothea Lange, and others, depicting the hardship brought by the Great Depression of the 1930s. They may be attempts to capture one art form through another, as in the picture of a piece of sculpture; in such an instance the photograph might simply be an illustration. Advertisers use photographs to entice, realtors to display, archaeologists to record, journalists to report, and reformers to prod social consciences. Whatever the initial use of photographs, historians learn from them.

Cameras and films are tools in the hands of the photographer, the media they use to create images. This means that a photograph, whatever else it might be, is a mediated document. The relationship between the media and the user is a unique one, for the media function to a large extent mechanically or electronically. The camera is thus both something more and something less to the photographer than the brush to the painter. The film is something more and something less than clay to the sculptor. Cameras can be used in ways that do not even require the presence of the photographer at the instant when pictures are taken, and photographs sometimes reveal things that the photographer did not see when taking the picture. Indeed, professional as well as amateur photographers are eager to have their exposed film processed so that they can "see what they got." Awareness of this makes the study and use of photographs all the more intriguing.

READING PHOTOGRAPHS

Looking at a photograph and reading a photograph are two different things. Looking comes first. By looking, giving no thought to the photographer, people take from the picture an impression. If you pass up the chance for an impression, it may never come your way again.

Reading a photograph ordinarily means putting words with it. A few photographers help their readers find words by providing captions. Others, like Henri Cartier-Bresson, fiercely resist captioning or explaining photographs. They argue that pictures should stand on their own, without words. We maintain that reading photographs, giving them "verbal scrutiny," as novelist-photographer Wright Morris calls it, gives them their image, and it is the image that has meaning for the reader.

Reading photographs is done best by systematically addressing questions about them. A good way to begin is to attempt to form a *consciousness of the photographer.* What did the photographer see when she took the picture? What is in the photograph that she possibly did not see? What were her purposes? What were her biases? Why did she pose people as she did? Why did she shoot from the vantage point the picture indicates? How did the circumstances in which the picture was taken limit the photographer's choices?

Then a look at the *frame* of the picture might follow. The eye would have seen the subject of the picture differently, for it could not have drawn an arbitrary boundary around a section of the field of vision. What was omitted from the picture that the eye would have seen? What effect does the framing have on one's

7.1 *What do pictures of the family home reveal about economic circumstances, other residents, the surrounding neighborhood, or other matters? What do you make of the curious arrangement and poses in this picture? What do you suppose was the photographer's intent when he took it? (Photo courtesy of and copyright © Summit County Historical Society.)*

Two St. Louis historians faced the task of verifying the sparse documentation that arrived with a photograph collection deposited in an archives where one of them worked as a cataloger. The photographs depicted incidents that occurred during a strike by the International Ladies Garment Workers in 1933–1935—a strike involving more than two thousand women dressmakers in forty-eight shops in the St. Louis garment district. One of the historians describes the way they approached their task:

Writer and photographer Susan Sontag suggests that the use of a photograph may help make it possible to get to the complexity of an event, because it records an event that is different for the photographer, subject and viewer. But, she argues, a photograph is only a fragment, "and with the passage of time, its moorings become unstuck."

What we attempted to do in this project was to stick some old photographs back into their moorings by showing photographs of a dramatic event to some of the people who had taken part in it, stirring their memories of the occasion. The results were startling. When retired St. Louis garment workers, all over the age of sixty, saw for the first time scenes of labor activity in which they had engaged as young women, they recalled not only those events, but how they felt about them at the time. By connecting the years between past and present, the photographs helped the women re-experience their half-remembered emotions of fear and conflict, excitement and satisfaction.

7.2   *(Photo courtesy of and copyright © Western Historical Manuscripts Collection, University of Missouri, St. Louis.)*

Bertha Lichtenburg looked at [one] of the Preisler photographs and chided us for not recognizing a scab who was somewhat the worse off for trying to cross the picket lines. "Six of us would get around her," Lichtenburg remembered, as she looked at the strikebreaker, "and she wouldn't go nowhere with us pushing her. And we'd get [her] around the corner of the building, and we'd get her up against the wall and tell her she should join the union!"

Jessie Sulkowski looked at another Preisler photograph and exclaimed, "That's me and my sister in that picture!" Jessie told of how she walked the picket lines and of being blackballed by the industry for her strike activities. Then she brought out studio-made photographs of herself in the chorus line of the local ILGWU pageant, Pins and Needles, which had been in her scrapbook for forty years.

Source: Katharine T. Corbett, "St. Louis Garment Workers: . . . Photograph and Memories," Gateway Heritage *(summer 1981): 22–23.*

7.3 *(Photo courtesy of and copyright © Western Historical Manuscripts Collection, University of Missouri, St. Louis.)*

sense of having been there? How would one's reaction to the picture change if the picture were to be cropped—that is, to have its frame reduced further?

Paying heed to the effects of framing leads naturally to a look at the *place* of the photograph. Was it taken indoors? If so, what effect did the indoor setting have on the picture? Was it contrived or artificial? What clues does the picture provide to the cultural landscape? To the natural landscape? If the camera could have caught sounds and odors, how would the image it captured have been enhanced?

By freezing the scene for the instant that the camera's shutter is open, the photograph directs the reader's attention to *questions of time.* How does the photograph reveal the time of the day or year? What preceded the taking of the picture? What followed it? How does the picture reveal the stopping of time? What is caught in motion? What does the picture reveal of the times in which it was taken?

It is helpful also to pay special attention to the *details* of the picture and the artifacts in it—the lace on a dress, for example, or the bric-a-brac on the mantel. What do the parts contribute to the whole? How does the picture enable you to interpret the details in it? How do the details help in drawing conclusions about the time and place of the event portrayed in the picture? What is revealed about the occupations, social class, tastes, beliefs, or values of the persons shown? What conclusions can be drawn about the culture of which the setting in the picture is a part?

A little practice enables one to notice the *technical aspects* of a picture. Snapshot cameras and those used for most group photos have typically been fitted with wide-angle lenses that allow fitting a wider field into the frame and minimize difficulties in precise focusing. Wide-angled lenses affect perspective by exaggerating the distance between near and distant objects and may cause distortion of shapes (including bodies and faces), especially those near the camera and toward the edges of the photograph. An opposite effect, flattening of perspective, occurs when photographers use long focal-length ("telephoto") lenses. (The focal length of a camera is the distance from the center of the lens to the film.) The more extreme the wide-angle or the telephoto lenses, the more extreme are the perspectives evident in photographs. Extremes produced either way increase the difficulty of distinguishing accurately the spacing between background, subject, and foreground. (It must be noted that the explanation provided here refers to the 35mm cameras that have been popular for several decades. With APS [Advanced Photo System] cameras now gaining in popularity the focal lengths are shorter.)

Cameras, lenses, and lighting accessories affect the appearance of photographs in other ways. Blurred parts of a picture indicate that the subject was moving too quickly to be "frozen" by the shutter speed. Because older cameras and film required more light—by means of a larger aperture or a longer exposure—the shutter speeds were often too slow to stop motion. As a result, photographs made decades ago are more likely to show blurring than are modern photographs. This helps to explain why persons in old photographs look so somber and serious: They had to settle on an expression they could maintain during a time of exposure of many seconds or even minutes.

If the primary subject of a photograph is clearly focused but the background or foreground, or both, are "soft," the photographer probably used a longer focal-length lens or a wider aperture setting, or both, either to draw attention to the primary subject or to cope with low light levels. Understanding the "look" produced by different focal lengths and focus techniques can help viewers of photographs to determine the distance between the photographer and the subject; this in turn may suggest the degree to which the photographer encroached on the setting.

Any photographic setting, in any era, is encroached on when the photographer supplements the natural light in a room. Artificial light, including flash, tends to give an artificial look to photographs, and the proficiency of the photographer, as well as the equipment used, reveals itself in the obviousness of supplementary lighting in the final print. Lighting is an area in which newer photographs are not necessarily better than older ones. Back when photographers held their supplemental lighting, often a flashbulb, away from the camera, the light struck the subject at an angle, revealing contours naturally. Modern compact cameras often mount the flash adjacent to the lens, so the light is reflected straight back at the camera and the features of the subject are flattened and thus more difficult to discern.

Similarly, despite huge advances in camera and lens technology, older photographs are often sharper than modern ones. In earlier times, photographs were usually "contact printed," with the negative or plate laid directly on the photographic paper to create a positive image. Thus the print was never larger nor less sharp than the negative. Eventually it became possible to project a small negative onto a much larger piece of paper, with the result that everything on the negative, including grain and imperfections, is enlarged as well.

Considering the changes in photographic technology outlined briefly here, and those yet to come, attention must be paid to *historical* considerations surrounding a photograph. A daguerreotype, for example, has a distinctly different look than does a wet-plate contact print, Kodak snapshot, or a modern digital photograph (the worst of which have clearly visible pixels). Through experience in working with photographs one develops an eye for the various distinctions.

One should also read the *artistic aspects* of photographs, even of snapshots—those innocent snips from the past that are often characterized by haphazard

7.4   Snapshot portraits like this one of a Nebraska farmer and his wife offer insights into their circumstances and character, as well as a glimpse of their seldom-used parlor. In what respects do the people and the place fit together? What does the picture lead one to want to know about the subjects? (Photo courtesy of the Marty family collection and copyright © Myron Marty.)

arrangement of the subject matter and amputation of heads and feet of the persons in them. Look for expressions of the language of vision referred to in chapter 3: light and shadow; color and texture; lines, shape, and pattern; similarities and contrasts; and movement. Look also for the things that photographer Andreas Feininger (in *Photographic Seeing*) lists as photogenic qualities: simplicity; order, and clarity; outlines that are hard, sharp, and concise; surface textures; subject coloration; live subjects and objects in motion; spontaneity; the unusual; and repetition of similar or identical forms. A soft-focus pictorialist, by the way, would undoubtedly have a different set of photogenic interests, so it is essential to keep the photographer's intention in mind when assessing a photograph.

Pay attention also to the *unphotogenic qualities and techniques* Feininger lists: insipidity and lack of subject interest; too great a distance between the camera and the subject; overabundance of subject matter; a cluttered or meaningless background or foreground; too much subject contrast; wrongly placed or harsh shadows; overlighting; and posing and faking.

This listing of photogenic and unphotogenic qualities opens the way for a look specifically at the *people* in photographs. It may not be wise to attempt to base psychoanalysis of individuals or groups on photographs, but observations of the kind a psychoanalyst might make are useful for historians. Pay attention, for example, to the manner in which the subjects present themselves in their poses and facial expressions—and then ask who chose the pose or the expression, the subject or the photographer. Notice, too, whether people in a picture are touching one another or how they have arranged themselves in relation to others in the picture or in a series of pictures of the same group taken through the years. Consider also the kinds of emotions projected by persons in the picture, perhaps matching what you see against a list of terms a psychoanalyst compiled in his photoanalyses: shy, compliant, aloof, proud, fearful, mad, suspicious, introspective, superior, confused, happy, anxious, angry, weak, pained, suffering, bright, curious, sexy, distant, blank, bored, rigid, arrogant, content, lonely, trusting, strong, crazy, involved, frustrated, attractive, docile, bemused, correct, friendly, hurt, spontaneous, satisfied, depressed. Your analysis of the people in a picture will lead you to ask such things as whether a group mood is apparent or if there is a dominant figure apparent in the group.

A historian reading a photograph must ask questions that determine whether the photograph is good for historical purposes, and if so, why. Does it present an accurate record? Does it say something significant about the subject or the photographer? Does it provide knowledge and insight into the culture of which it is a trace? Are the time and place of the photograph clear?

It should be noted that reading photographs in the manner suggested here may become too rational a process, that the parts of the picture should not be emphasized to the exclusion of the whole, and that these reading suggestions should be used with discretion.

7.5   *A family portrait, whether of adults or children, permits the viewer to ask what it conceals about the subjects as well as what it reveals. Does knowing from other traces that there was a fourth child in this family put this posed photograph in a different light? (Photo courtesy of and copyright © David Kyvig.)*

7.6   *Close study of photographs often yields surprises. In this one, a reflection on the window behind the subjects shows photographer Ben Shahn shooting a picture while the subjects watch. While his wife poses in the street as a decoy, he is using a right-angle finder on his camera to take the picture you see. (Photo courtesy of the Library of Congress.)*

PHOTOGRAPHS IN HISTORICAL RESEARCH

Photographs are useful to historians in two forms: first, as evidence representing events from the past and as artifacts in their own right, and second, as records of information gathered in fieldwork. The line between the two forms is neither clear nor inevitable, but it is helpful to be aware that an old picture of an old house differs from a contemporary picture of the same house taken for comparison. A variation in the latter form is created when one takes a picture of an old picture to ensure its preservation or for some other purpose.

Whatever the form of the photograph, certain principles apply to its use in historical research. First, photographs must be treated according to the same standards, particularly where accuracy is concerned, that are applied to other documents or artifacts when they are identified, authenticated, described, evaluated, and interpreted. Second, because there are definite limits to the extent to which photographs can speak for themselves, extrinsic data must be used with them. Notes on the backs of the pictures or in albums in which they are mounted often provide some such information, but unfortunately it is sometimes misleading or just plain wrong, and it must always be verified before it is relied upon. Conversations with persons shown in the pictures provide more information (using photographs as points of reference in oral interviews was discussed in the preceding chapter). Third, pictures should not be included in a story merely because they are nice or interesting. They must relate to the story being told, offering some evidence that completes or clarifies it. Fourth, photographs used in telling the story must be captioned, but neither too extensively nor too skimpily. Wright Morris notes, "It is better that the photograph have no commentary at all than that it appear to be necessary to the picture," but he adds, "Words can be as intrusive in their absence as in their presence." And fifth, the technical reproduction of the photographs used in a published or filmed history should be the very best possible. Just as care is given to honing sentences into precise form and to fitting them neatly into purposeful paragraphs, so care should also be given to the presentation of photographs.

CHANGES IN PHOTOGRAPHY AND LIMITS OF PHOTOGRAPHS

While capitalizing on the rich possibilities photographs offer, historians cannot ignore the limitations, some of which become apparent in a review of the medium's history. Although photography goes back to the 1830s, the earliest daguerreotype pictures, for all their beautiful details, were always mirror images and could be produced only one time on a metal plate. Furthermore, because exposures had to be lengthy, subjects had to pose rigidly to avoid creating a blur by moving. Although photography achieved almost instant popularity, with thousands of persons acquiring cameras, picture taking remained beyond the reach of amateurs.

By the 1850s, the wet-plate process had replaced daguerreotypes, making possible unlimited numbers of prints from glass-plate negatives. But because enlargements from the plates were impossible, the only way to create large pictures was to use large plates, which made photographic equipment cumbersome. Furthermore, wet-plate negatives could not accurately represent distinctions between colors, nor could they distinguish between clouds and the sky, which meant that weather conditions could not be portrayed adequately. The need for bright light coupled with the fixed shutter speed of cameras made pictures in dark places and of things in motion impossible.

George Eastman's success in simplifying the technology of photography in the 1880s allowed for a dramatic increase in the number of persons who could take pictures. The Kodak, with its preloaded flexible film, made possible the snapshot, the amateur photographer's work of art and the symbol of popularized photography. Further advances in technology—the single-lens reflex 35mm camera, for example, and the more recent fully automatic compact cameras—made photography increasingly a hobby of the masses. For both the sharpness of the images they produce and their convenience, the 35mm camera has been a technological wonder.

7.7 Saloons have often been neighborhood gathering places. At times, they have served as social centers, welfare agencies, and political headquarters. Saloon histories, often neglected, deserve the attention often given to churches, schools, and businesses. (Photo courtesy of the Library of Congress.)

*7.8–7.9   Pictures were often changed long before digital alterations became possible. On
the reverse side of the picture at left (7.8) are instructions to an artist: "Take arm off coat
on back of neck   Press pants   Run over shadow by the side of arm   Remove quilt." The
result is a tinted portrait in an oval frame (7.9) that now adorns a family room wall.*

(Photos courtesy of the Chapman family and copyright © Shirley Marty.)

    As digital photography makes further advances, as it promises to do in the next
several years, the impending changes in photography will be more dramatic. At
the moment, the limiting factor is cost, but that is likely to come down as digital
technology in photography becomes more popular. Already the pictures in many
catalogs and books and on most posters are shot digitally, and many more publications (including this one) make use of digital scanning. The implications of the
transition to digital photography are enormous, in part because of the manipula-
tion possibilities. Future historians will not be able to discern, even under micro-
scopic scrutiny, what is authentic in a digital photograph and what was added
later. Once an image is digitized, any and all parts of it may be changed, deleted,
or inserted into another photograph without detection, since no unaltered original
will remain. Contributing further to changes in photographic practices is the potential for producing high quality images using archival-quality paper and ink
with computers and printers. At this time, however, the stability and durability of
such paper and ink is unproven.

7.10   *Finding this picture in a family collection makes one wonder whether physically or mentally impaired persons get their share of space in such places. On the reverse side, this picture is dated April 18, 1892. In a different handwriting is this statement: "A boy your great-grandmother took care of in an institution." But because the owner of the picture cannot determine when this notation was written, although it is in her mother-in-law's handwriting, and because she cannot verify the statement, the accuracy is questionable. (Photo courtesy of and copyright © Peggy Creed.)*

Whatever the medium by which photographic images are produced, limitations in their use continue to exist. One is imposed by the fact that the images never represent more than a small part of larger scenes. Because they deal in single rather than repeated moments, it is impossible for them to convey a sense of the ongoing routines that are so much a part of life. And because crucial moments ordinarily elude photographers' instant attention, they are often re-created strictly for the benefit of the camera. Depending on the skill of the photographer, the contrived character of such moments is often apparent in the photographs that record them. Until the development of flash photography, scenes set indoors could not be recorded by a camera in the hands of an amateur photographer, and only with special equipment by a professional.

The use of photographs by historians is further complicated by a number of seemingly contradictory circumstances. On the one hand, there is an overwhelming abundance of photographs available—whether in family archives, corporate archives, public archives, or institutional archives. Historians must make hard choices in selecting the right ones in their research. On the other hand, this abundance of material is collected unsystematically, preserved indifferently, and identified and cataloged scarcely at all. While there is an abundance in quantity, not as many significant photographs of good quality have been preserved and filed as historians would like or could use. The majority of family albums are all but useless for want of identification of the persons in the pictures. Moreover, many of the photographs in family collections have deteriorated because they are made of low-grade paper and were stored improperly.

One more limit to the uses of photography in historical research is now being experienced painfully and with dismay. The pain and dismay will surely increase when more and more people who would like to use the color photographs taken in the past several decades discover that the prints and slides before them have lost their original colors, if they retain any images at all. The rather sudden transition from black-and-white to color photography that occurred in the 1960s was encouraged by the popular appeal of beautiful pictures—for now. The materials and processes used, however, have left the colors unstable. Although technological changes have improved color stability, those who wish to ensure the leaving of a record or the preservation of visual remembrances of events should observe the recommendations provided in the next section. Particular attention should be given to color photographs, especially those that are a decade or more old.

CARE AND PRESERVATION OF PHOTOGRAPHS

Historians have a responsibility to provide for the care and preservation of photographs that come to their attention or into their possession, as well as those taken in the course of their work. It is perhaps unnecessary to comment here on the use of photographs already housed in established archives, where proper conditions are maintained for their care and preservation, and there are rules governing such things as access and reproduction rights. Yet researchers sometimes find that photographs are not as well cared for as they might be, and a properly placed suggestion to the curator may make a difference in what is available to later researchers.

Persons doing their own photography or having direct responsibility for the care and preservation of photographs find themselves confronting many difficult tasks. These tasks are too complex and far ranging to consider in detail here, and those who are deeply committed to photography as a tool of research and story-telling will seek specialized information on what to do and how to do it. Persons who do not have the time or desire to immerse themselves in the ins and outs of photography are well advised to defer as much as possible to professionals who offer services of the sort they need. These comments are intended to help you deal knowledgeably with such professionals.

Photographs are vulnerable to destruction by fungi, moisture, residual chemicals, molds, fumes, insects, and human mishandling—to say nothing of the inherent capacity of paper and dye for natural deterioration. The most important thing one must do, therefore, when finding an old photograph is to prevent further deterioration.

Some basic steps can be taken to ensure the preservation of photographs as valuable historical resources. In outlining these steps, bear in mind that in recent years it has become possible to distinguish between preserving a *photograph* and preserving an *image*. As far as preserving an image is concerned, everything is changing with the advent of digital processes. Pictures taken with digital cameras are preserved electronically, and those taken by conventional cameras—slides, prints, negatives, and photocopies—can be scanned and preserved in electronic files. While digitally stored images can deteriorate over long periods of time (and the technology is too new to ensure the accuracy of projections), the files holding them can simply be copied and stored again. The discussion that follows focuses on preserving actual photographs, but some of the principles involved apply also to preserving digital images.

A first step in addressing preservation questions is deciding whether a given photograph is worth preserving. This requires identification and assessment of its historical significance, as determined through the reading process discussed earlier. Once it is concluded that the photograph should be preserved, the identification must be recorded in writing and stored with it, or at least the photograph should be coded so that it can readily be associated with the written identification. If each photograph is properly stored in a separate acid-free envelope, the identifying information might be written on the envelope. Care must then be taken to ensure that the photograph and the envelope are not separated or mixed up with other photographs and envelopes.

Photocopying machines are able to make relatively clear plain-paper copies of photographs. Writing information directly on the photocopies serves two purposes: the information is readily accessible for use with the originals, and the photocopies may also be used independently, thus preventing wear and tear on the historically valuable photographs until they are needed for specific purposes.

One rule of identification must never be violated: Do not write on the face or the reverse side of a photograph with a ballpoint or felt-tip pen, since the pressure may damage the photograph and the ink may bleed through. A soft lead pencil may be used for writing on the back or the margin, but the impression should be wiped with a soft cloth so that excess graphite does not remain to make smudges.

In storing prints, keep in mind all the possible sources of damage. As Margery S. Long has observed, photographs "are made of potentially unstable materials that tarnish, fade, stain, discolor, grow fungus and are attacked by insects and gases. If they are in color, the dyes may fade, change color or bleed, destroying the color balance. The supporting material may become deteriorated and affect the images on them. Even the enclosures intended to protect them may contribute to their undoing." Thus, photos must be protected against light, moisture, contamination, pollutants in the atmosphere, insects, and human handling. Optimal conditions for a photo archive are therefore similar to those for archives of any type: darkness, humidity between 20 and 30 percent, and temperature kept below 70 degrees; in addition, folders and storage boxes should be free of acid-based material and of substances that give off harmful fumes, dusts, and gases.

Some very specific rules are too frequently violated by household archivists, at great cost to photographs they may cherish: Never bundle prints together with rubber bands; rubber bands dry out and stick to prints. Never fasten prints to anything with paper clips, since most paper clips rust, and even if they do not, they leave impressions in the photographs. Never allow prints to be touched for any purpose by cellophane tape; and never attempt to repair them with it, since cellophane tape breaks down and leaves a sticky residue. Never mount photographs with rubber cement, which contains sulfur and will eventually fade or stain a print. Firms that specialize in providing technical supplies for libraries and archives provide the best adhesive to use for mounting photographs as well as the acid-free paper on which they should be mounted.

Negatives should always be stored separately from the photographs. Although negatives of 35mm film fit nicely in commercially available plastic holders that will hold as many as thirty-six negatives from which proof sheets (contact prints) can readily be made, some of these holders can seriously damage them or reduce their life expectancy (despite the claims of their manufacturers). Acid-free envelopes or Mylar sleeves should be used instead. The proof sheets are useful in filing pictures in a way that makes them most accessible. To provide maximum protection against the total loss of a collection of pictures by fire or other catastrophe, it is a good idea to keep photographs and negatives in separate locations.

It is possible to minimize the fading of color photographs and the negatives from which they are printed by storing them in cool and dry places and away from bright light. If the color prints are displayed, tungsten lighting under fifty footcandles should be used. Fluorescent light is harmful because it contains more ultraviolet rays, and daylight, particularly direct sunlight, is even more harmful.

The preservation of new photographs begins with selection of film and the paper used for the prints. If color photographs are necessary or desired, it is advisable to shoot them as Kodachrome slides and then have Ilfochrome prints made from the slides; the stability of such prints is greater than those produced from color film. For black-and-white prints, only the traditional silver-grain film should be used, because the popular chromogenic black-and-white films (Ilford XP2 and Kodak T400CN) that can be processed in color chemistry by one-hour color minilabs degrade more rapidly. Black-and-white prints on resin-coated paper, introduced in the 1970s and popular ever since, especially for machine-made mass prints, are not nearly as archival as are those on conventional fiber-based paper. Well-treated and stored resin-coated prints may last for decades, but recent tests reveal that especially when framed behind glass, even archivally washed resin-coated black-and-white prints can start deteriorating in a matter of months if they are not toned or treated with an archival wash designed for that purpose (such as Agfa's Sistan). Keep in mind, though, that the likelihood of unimaginably superior digital copy and scanning options becoming available in the next decade or so will provide the most desirable method of preserving images.

COPYING PHOTOGRAPHS

Sometimes historians would like to use photographs that cannot be removed from their mountings without damage and for which no negative exists. Such photographs can be copied simply by taking pictures of them—simply, that is, if you have the right equipment and observe basic guidelines. Perhaps this is a good place to mention that the basic equipment of the nearby historian-photographer probably starts with a 35mm single-lens reflex camera. The normal lens, probably about 40–55mm, will not allow one close enough to a print to copy it, but a "macro" lens will; so will the use of extension rings that fit between the camera and the lens. If the camera lens cannot be removed, it can be adapted for close-up work by the addition of thin lenses that fit on the basic lens like filters. Using close-up fittings of this sort in various combinations enables one to place the camera at just the right distance from the photograph to make an acceptable copy of it.

The use of a copy stand, or possibly a tripod, to hold the camera perfectly still is essential. If one plans to do a great deal of copying, a stand with controlled artificial light should be used. Specifications for such stands and lighting are available in the books dealing with technical aspects of photography mentioned at the end of this chapter. Natural lighting may be used, but one must be careful to guard against glare and shadows. It may be necessary to place glass over the print to hold it flat, but this could interfere with the clarity of the copy. Anchoring the corners with small pieces of masking tape is preferable if the picture can be held flat by this means without damaging it.

The camera's shutter should be released by means of a short cable or the self-timer, if the camera has one, to prevent jiggling and thus blurring the picture. Sharper pictures are likely to result when a small lens aperture (for example, $f11$ rather than $f2.8$) is used. It is a good idea to take three shots of each picture, one at the f-stop that seems to be the best exposure and one each at the f-stops just above and below this one.

Once equipment is set up for copying, all kinds of possibilities appear. While it is a good idea to take at least one picture of the entire original, for the record and for study, the photographer may shoot parts of the original as well, reframing them, bringing out detail or eliminating extraneous material. Stains on prints and documents can be minimized or eliminated by using a filter of the same color as the stain.

Patience, care, and experimentation make possible the production of excellent copies of original photographs. In fact, the copies often turn out to be better photographs, from a technical point of view, than the originals.

COPYRIGHT ISSUES

Legal questions concerning the use of photographs (and all visual documents) are unavoidable and must be addressed carefully. The fact that a photograph is in the possession of an archive or museum, or even in a family album or community collection, does not necessarily mean that the holders are authorized to grant permission for its use. In each instance, users must ask whether they have the right to reproduce photographs that seem to satisfy their needs and purposes. If they do not enjoy such a right, it is necessary for them to know how to acquire it and to comply with legal restrictions in using it. This is true also of images conveyed electronically, that is, by television, film, the Internet, or CD-ROM.

Copyright laws governing visual documents are complicated, but their purpose is clear: to protect the rights of their creators or those to whom the creators have specifically assigned the rights through sale, loan, deposit, or donation. Copyrights protecting old photographs may have expired, which means that they are in the public domain, as are works produced and published by the United States government, but prospective users must verify the accuracy of their assumptions regarding the status of any photograph they wish to reproduce, exhibit, or publish. It is also prudent to be careful in making claims of "fair use," that is, the use of visual works in ways that have little effect on the value of the originals. As this book is being written copyright laws are being revised, with particular concern centered on the protection of ownership rights of texts and images transmitted electronically. Under the existing law, which took effect in 1978, copyright protection for all creative works is in effect for seventy years after the death of the author. This means that works produced on or after January 1 of that year are protected until at least 2048; in some circumstances the duration can be as long as ninety-five or 120 years.

Under the law in effect before 1978, the initial copyright endured for a term of twenty-eight years from the date it was secured and was eligible for renewal for another twenty-eight years. A revision of the law in 1978 extended the renewal term to forty-seven years, making a total of seventy-five years possible. In 1998 the renewal term of copyrights was extended to sixty-seven years and a total term of protection of ninety-five years. Because of the complexity and changing nature of copyright law, readers should consult the Register of Copyrights at the Library of Congress : <lcweb.loc.gov/copyright/>.

How do would-be users gain permission to use a copyrighted image? The first step is to identify and locate the holder of the copyright. The next is to get in touch with that person or institution to determine the terms and conditions under which use is permitted. If the intended use is publication in a book, the holder of the image may indicate that the cost will depend on such things as the size in which the image will be reproduced, the number of copies in the print run of the first edition, and whether permission is sought for North American or worldwide publication. The precise wording of the credit line accompanying the published image will also be prescribed. In some instances the owner provides an image that must be returned within a specified time period, in others the user may be given a new copy, for which there will be a copying charge. Although some institutions, such as the Library of Congress, which has a vast collection of images, do not charge for the use of material that is not copyrighted, users can expect to pay modest sums for the copies reproduced for their use. (John Schultz and Barbara Schultz provide comprehensive counsel on these matters in a forty-one-page chapter of *Picture Research: A Practical Guide.* However, because copyright laws change, readers should be sure to use the most up-to-date guidance possible when addressing permission and copyright issues.)

A final note: A photograph is a special kind of document, a special kind of artifact. Using photographs in historical research requires some knowledge of technical matters, many of which we have considered in this chapter. But the mystical element in photography is as important as the technical. Researchers and writers have not used photographs well if the mystifying merely becomes commonplace.

MOTION PICTURES

Our concern so far has been with still photography. Much of what we have said, apart from some of the technical considerations, applies also to the use of motion pictures. Historians of the nearby past should not overlook home movies as potential sources of information. Films produced by local businesses and industries, locally produced inserts for newsreels that once played in theaters, promotional shorts packaged by such groups as the local chamber of commerce, and footage shot by local television stations also merit historians' attention. Like photographs, motion pictures reveal changes in fashion, the landscape, family composition and relationships, community leadership, business practices, recreational styles, and opinions as to what is worth capturing on film.

There are important differences in usage, however, between photographs and motion pictures. The most obvious, of course, is that motion pictures are in motion. Consequently, they lend themselves to a different kind of analysis than that to which still photographs are susceptible, in part because it is difficult to locate and isolate the specific frames in a given reel that yield the greatest historical value. Treating the motion of the pictures as they move across the screen as an essential part of the message makes sense. In other words, the medium and the message are inseparable.

Running old movies is a favorite pastime, and the very causes of laughter they provoke are likely to be the main points of interest for historians. Showing such movies to members of the community can stimulate memories and produce more resources for those engaged in research. Showing them, however, requires equipment that is rapidly become obsolete, particularly the 8mm projectors on which many movies were filmed by amateurs. Indeed, one wonders how many reels of such film rest in historical society archives, as well as in attics and closets, never to be viewed again. A warning about movies is in order: old nitrate-based film may explode, especially if maintained in sealed storage. Immediate transfer to modern safety film, or possibly to videotape, is essential.

VIDEOTAPES

Film recorded by video cameras and camcorders helps to account for the obsolescence of 8mm and 16mm motion pictures. Videotapes have much in common with motion pictures as far as usefulness is concerned, but differences can also be noted. For one thing, the recording equipment is easy to use, as are the VCRs on which the film is played. Although obsolescence has not yet set in, the equipment is being steadily improved and "miniaturized," and the arrival of high-resolution television will complicate the consequences for users of camcorders and VCRs. For another, so commonplace have camcorders become, and so abundant are the videocassettes they have recorded and continue to record, that historians face what will soon be an embarrassment of riches. Or so it might seem. Using the riches is another matter. Attempting to locate useful material that was recorded for uncertain purposes is extremely time-consuming and often unproductive. Accordingly, historians of the nearby past may find that their main role with respect to video recordings will be to produce carefully designed and crafted tapes to be used by future generations.

NOTES AND FURTHER READING

Works mentioned or quoted in this chapter are: Andreas Feininger, *Photographic Seeing* (Englewood Cliffs, NJ: Prentice-Hall, 1973); Wright Morris, "Photographs, Images, and Words," *American Scholar* (summer 1979): 457–69; Margery S. Long, quoted in Robert A. Weinstein and Larry Booth, *The Collection, Use, and Care of Historical Photographs* (Nashville: American Association for State and Local History, 1977), p. 124; and Robert U. Akeret (Thomas Humber, ed.), *Photoanalysis: How to Interpret the Hidden Psychological Meaning of Personal and Public Photographs* (New York: Peter H. Wyden, 1973); Richard Chalfen's critical review of the Akeret essay in *Studies in the Anthropology of Visual Communication* 1, no. 1 (1974): 57–60, is perhaps more useful than the book itself.

For general works on visual literacy, see Donis Dondis, *A Primer of Visual Literacy* (Cambridge, MA: MIT Press, 1973); and Stewart Kranz and Robert Fisher, *Understanding Visual Forms: Fundamentals of Two- and Three-Dimensional Design* (New York: Van Nostrand Reinhold, 1976). Related books include Rudolph Arnheim, *Visual Thinking* (Berkeley: University of California Press, 1969); Estelle Jussim, *Visual Communication and the Graphic Arts: Photographic Technologies of the Nineteenth Century* (New York: Bowker, 1974)—particularly the first and last chapters; and William Ivins, *Prints and Visual Communications* (New York: DaCapo Press, 1953, reprinted 1969).

On reading photographs, in addition to Feininger's work cited above, see: Jonathan Bayer: *Reading Photographs: Understanding the Aesthetics of Photography* (New York: Pantheon, 1977); James T. Brooke, *A Viewer's Guide to Looking at Photographs* (Wilmette, IL: Aurelia, 1977); Graham Clarke, "How Do We Read a Photograph," in *The Photograph* (New York: Oxford University Press, 1997), 27–39; Thomas L. Davies, *Shoots: A Guide to Your Family's Photographic Heritage* (Danbury, NH: Addison House, 1977); David Finn, *How to Look at Photographs: Reflections on the Art of Seeing* (New York: Harry N. Abrams, Inc., 1994); Madelyn Moeller, "Photography and History: Using Photographs in Interpreting Our Cultural Past," *Journal of American Culture* 6, no. 1 (1983): 3–17; Karin Becker Ohrn, "Re-viewing Photographs: Unexplored Resources for Communication Research," *Journal of Communication Inquiry* 2 (winter 1977): 31–39; Marsh Peters and Bernard Mergen, "Doing the Rest: The Uses of Photographs in America Studies," *American Quarterly* 29, no. 3 (1977): 280–303; and John Szarkowski, *Looking at Photographs: 100 Pictures from the Collection of the Museum of Modern Art* (New York: Museum of Modern Art, 1973) and *The Photographer's Eye* (New York: Museum of Modern Art, 1966).

Practical applications of reading photographs are offered in Glen E. Holt, "Chicago through a Camera Lens: An Essay on Photography as History," *Chicago History* 1, no. 3 (1971): 158–69; and Harold M. Mayer and Richard C. Wade, *Chicago: Growth of a Metropolis* (Chicago: University of Chicago Press, 1969). Carefully assembled photographs on various themes that justify a second look include: William Crawford, *The Keepers of the Light* (Dobbs Ferry, NY: Morgan and Morgan, 1979); Chester Higgins, Jr., and Orde Coombs, *Some Time Ago: A Historical Portrait of Black Americans, 1860–1950* (Garden City, NY: Doubleday, 1980); Paul Kagan, *New World Utopia: A Photographic History of the Search for Community* (New York: Penguin, 1975); Julia Hirsch, *Family Photographs: Content, Meaning, and Effect* (New York: Oxford University Press, 1981); Peter Seixas, "Lewis Hine: From 'Social' to 'Interpretive' Photographer," *American Quarterly* 39, no. 3 (1987): 381–409; Jeffrey Simpson, *The American Family: A History in Photographs* (New

York: Viking, 1976); and George Talbot, *At Home: Domestic Life in the Post-Centennial Era, 1876–1920* (Madison: State Historical Society of Wisconsin, 1976).

For a comprehensive handbook on historians' uses of photography, see John Schultz and Barbara Schultz, *Picture Research: A Practical Guide* (New York: Van Nostrand Reinhold, 1991); the chapters on "Legal Issues" and "Electronic Picture Transmission and Research," as well as the Glossary and Bibliography, are particularly valuable, although it must be noted that technological advancements since the book was published are many and complex. Photography as a research tool is discussed in Howard Becker, "Photography and Sociology," *Studies in the Anthropology of Visual Communication* (fall 1974): 3–26; John Collier, *Visual Anthropology: Photography as a Research Method* (New York: Rinehart and Winston, 1967; revised and expanded edition, Albuquerque: University of New Mexico Press, 1986); J. Robert Davison, "Turning a Blind Eye: The Historian's Use of Photographs," *BC Studies* no. 52 (winter 1981–82): 16–38; Mary-Ellen Jones, *Photographing Tombstones,* Technical Leaflet no. 92 (Nashville: American Association for State and Local History, 1977); and Walter Rundell, Jr., "Photographs as Historical Evidence: Early Texas Oil," *American Archivist* 41, no. 4 (1978): 373–98; Christopher Taylor, "The Photograph as an Aid to Historical Research," *The Photographic Journal* 127 (February 1987): 54–56; and Jon Wagner, ed., *Images of Information: Still Photography in the Social Sciences* (Beverly Hills: Sage, 1979). Technical aspects of lens choices are laid out simply by Gary Gore in "Zooming in on History: Basic Camera Lenses," *History News* 35, no. 9 (September 1980): 9.

Among the most important works on the technical aspects of the collection, care, and use of historical photographs are Weinstein and Booth, cited above; Henry Wilhelm, with Carol Brower, *The Permanence and Care of Color Photographs: Traditional and Digital Color Prints, Color Negatives, Slides, and Motion Pictures* (Grinnell, IA: Preservation Publishing Company, 1993); George Eaton, *Conservation of Photographs* (Rochester, NY: Eastman Kodak Co., 1985); James M. Reilly, *Care and Identification of 19th-Century Photographic Prints* (Rochester, NY: Eastman Kodak Co., 1986) and *Storage Guide for Color Photographic Materials* (Albany: State University of New York, 1998). Also to be noted are Eddie Ephraums, "Not Fade Away," *The British Journal of Photography* (December 3, 1992): 11–12; Georgia Eubanks, "Building a Photo Archive," *Public Libraries* 18, no. 2 (summer 1979): 27–28; Peter Krause, "How to Care for Vintage Photos," *Historic Preservation* 39 (March/April 1987): 14–16; and Paul Vanderbilt, *Evaluating Historical Photographs: A Personal Perspective,* Technical Leaflet no. 120 (Nashville: American Association for State and Local History, 1979). Also useful is James H. Conrad, *Copying Historical Photographs: Equipment and Methods,* Technical Leaflet no. 139 (Nashville: American Association for State and Local History, 1981). The "Light Impressions" catalog is a source of information on supplies for all aspects of photography, useful even for those who prefer another supplier (P.O. Box 940, Rochester, NY 14603-0940; phone 1-800-828-6216; <www.lightimpressionsdirect.com>). See appendix C for a listing of suppliers of archival equipment of all kinds.

An interesting analysis of photography is offered by Otto Bettmann, *The Good Old Days: They Were Terrible* (New York: Random House, 1974); another, by Janet Malcolm, is *Diana and Nikon: Essays on the Aesthetic of Photography* (Boston: David R. Godine, 1980).

Works on the history of photography abound. Among the better ones are Ian Jeffrey, *Photography: A Concise History* (New York: Oxford University Press, 1981); Ben Maddow, *Faces: A Narrative History of the Portrait in Photography* (Boston: New York Graphic Society and Little, Brown, 1977); and three by Beaumont Newhall: *The Daguerreotype in America* (New York: Duell, Sloan, and Pierce, 1961), *The History of Photography* (New York: Museum of Modern Art, 1964), and *Photography: A Short Critical History* (New York: Museum of Modern Art, 1958); Naomi Rosenblum, *A World History of Photography* (New York: Abbeville Press, 1984); John Szarkowski, *Photography Until Now* (New York: Museum of Modern Art, 1989; distributed by Bulfinch Press, Boston). A very interesting essay on a slice of the history of photography is James C. Curtis and Sheila Grannon, "Let Us Now Appraise Famous Photographs: Walker Evans and Documentary Photography," *Wintherthur Portfolio* 15 (spring 1980): 1–23. See also Richard Conniff, "When 'Fiends' Pressed the Button, There Was Nowhere to Hide," *Smithsonian* (June 1988): 106–16; and Kathryn Humphreys, "Looking Backward: History, Nostalgia, and American Photography, *American Literary History* 5, no. 4 (1993): 686–99.

On movies as a resource, see Dorothy Weyer Creigh, *Old Movies: A Source of Local History Program,* Technical Leaflet no. 100 (Nashville: American Association for State and Local History, 1977); the author recounts the history of home movie-making and gives information on how to acquire films from the National Archives and Record Service. See also Richard Noble's *Archival Preservation of Motion Pictures: A Summary of Current Findings,* Technical Leaflet no. 126 (Nashville: American Association for State and Local History, 1980). The December 1988 *American Historical Review* (Vol. 93, no. 5) includes a forum on the problems and possibilities of portraying history on film: Robert A. Rosenstone, "History in Images/History in Words: Reflections on the Possibility of Really Putting History onto Film," 1173–1185; David Herlihy, "Am I a Camera?: Other Reflections on Film and History," 1186–1192; Hayden White, "Historiography and Historiophoty," 1193–1199; John E. O'Connor, "History in Images/Images in History: Reflections on the Importance of Film and Television Study for an Understanding of the Past," 1200–1209; and Robert Brent Toplin, "The Filmmaker as Historian," 1210–1227.

8

Artifacts

Traces of historical events are found in things as well as words and images. Taken together, things are known as "material culture" but they are in fact only the creations and products of culture. The inspiration for making them comes from the bundle of knowledge, beliefs, norms, and values that compose a culture, and they therefore represent events and ideas in the lives of people. Expressed another way, material culture is the part of the physical environment that has been transformed from the natural state by human action for human purposes. To understand human action and human purposes in a community, it makes sense to look carefully and in many different ways at things, called artifacts, from its past.

Studying the material culture of a community gives one the chance to learn from anonymous men and women who left no written record but played important parts in events. Because until our own era relatively little written history has been recorded by or about women, the study of material culture is particularly useful in learning about many aspects of women's history. Examining traces in the material culture helps historians halt the flow of history at a given point, to extract a thin slice of time, and to probe it carefully. Artifacts place the past in three-dimensional terms. Perhaps there is even a fourth dimension to the study of things, for seeing and touching things from the past gives one also a sense of what it was like to have lived in an earlier time.

Changing the subject of study from words and images to artifacts is to shift from the conceptual world to the perceptual world, a move begun in the previous chapter. Words and pictures are abstractions. In contrast, artifacts are concrete. They can be seen, heard, touched, smelled, and tasted. They are real things, subject to weighing, measuring, and counting. If artifacts are to be more than merely seen and appreciated, they must be understood in words, that is, handled conceptually.

Before turning to a model for the study of artifacts, a more specific definition is necessary. Work done initially by Robert G. Chenhall is helpful for that purpose. He developed "a logical system for naming things" to be used in museum

8.1   Scenes showing the interiors of homes, factories, and businesses with people going about their daily lives are, unfortunately, rare. What questions can such photographs suggest and answer about individuals or the community? (Photo courtesy of the National Archives and Records Administration.)

cataloging, that is, for identifying things with words. His categories showed the range of artifacts subject to study by historians and suggested starting points for individuals who wish to extend the range for their own purposes.

Chenhall's *Nomenclature for Museum Cataloging* was soon used by many museums and historical societies. Its users offered ideas for additional guidelines, and when it went out of print, Robert G. Blackaby and Patricia Greeno became editors of a revision. Building on Chenhall's work, they and their committee and advisors advanced a system built on these categories, with subcategories described in all instances:

1. Structures. "Artifacts originally created to define space for human activities or to be used as components of space defining artifacts."
2. Building furnishings. "Artifacts originally created to facilitate human activity and to provide for physical needs of people generally by offering comfort, convenience or protection," but not including clothing.
3. Personal artifacts. "Artifacts originally created to serve the personal needs of an individual [such] as clothing, adornment, body protection, or an aid for grooming."

4. Tools and equipment for materials. "Tools, equipment, and supplies originally created to manage, oversee, capture, harvest, or collect resources and to transform or modify particular materials, both raw and processed."
5. Tools and equipment for science and technology. "Tools, equipment, and supplies used for the observation of natural phenomena or to apply knowledge gained from such observation."
6. Tools and equipment for communication. "Tools, equipment, and supplies used to enable communication.," but not including "things produced as communication, such as works of art and documents."
7. Distribution and transportation artifacts. "Artifacts originally created to transport or distribute animate and inanimate things."
8. Communication artifacts. "Artifacts originally created as expressions of human thought," including such things as advertising media, art, ceremonial artifacts, documentary artifacts, media of exchange (such as coins and currency), and personal symbols.
9. Recreational artifacts. "Artifacts originally created to be used as toys or to carry on the activities of sports, games, gambling, or public entertainment."
10. Unclassifiable artifacts. "Artifacts originally created to serve a purpose that cannot be identified at the time the object is cataloged." The subcategories are "remnant," "function unknown," and "multiple use" artifacts.

ANALYZING ARTIFACTS

The categories listed above suggest that artifacts are the silent carriers of vast amounts of information about the past, which historians must find ways of extracting.

When we examine an artifact, a number of questions spring immediately to mind: Who made it? Of what is it made? For what was it used? How old is it? But rather than querying at random, it is preferable to approach artifacts with knowledgeable, systematically devised sets of questions.

A classic, comprehensive model for devising questions to ask of artifacts was developed years ago by E. McClung Fleming of the Winterthur Museum in Delaware. The general framework of that model is as useful for beginning students of nearby history as it is for the most advanced of scholars, and it provides the basis for the questions that we propose in coming to terms with artifacts. The Fleming model is built around an analysis of five basic properties, and it suggests four operations as essential to artifactual analysis.

The five basic properties provide a formula for including and interrelating all the significant facts about an artifact. The properties of an artifact are its history, material, construction, design, and function. *History* includes where and when it was made, by whom and for whom and why and successive changes in ownership condition, and function. *Material* involves what the object is made of—woods, fibers, ceramic

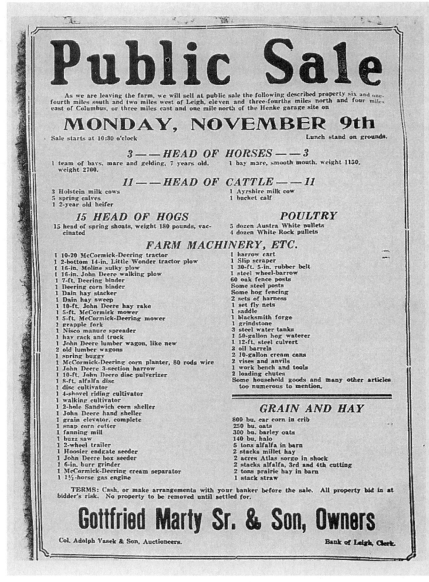

8.2 *This advertisement reveals something about the sellers' material possessions and the business practices connected with their sale. Why would one need to know the year of the sale (1942) to draw accurate inferences about their relative economic circumstances? (Photo courtesy of the Marty family collection and copyright © Myron Marty.)*

bodies, metals, glass, and so on. *Construction* has to do with the techniques of manufacture employed, workmanship, and the way parts are organized to bring about the object's function. *Design* includes the structure, form, style, ornament, and iconography of the object. *Function* embraces both the uses (intended functions) and the roles (unintended functions) of the object in its culture, including utility, delight, and communication.

Four operations performed on the five properties yield answers to most of the important questions we want to ask about an artifact. The operations are *identification* (including classification, authentication, and description), which results in a body of distinctive facts about the artifact; *evaluation*, which results in a set of judgments about the artifact, usually based on comparisons with other examples of its kind; *cultural analysis*, which examines the various interrelationships of an artifact and its contemporary culture; and *interpretation*, which suggests the meaning and significance of the artifact in relation to aspects of our own culture. The questions used to grasp the meaning and significance of artifacts may involve each of the five properties of the artifact, and each successive operation is dependent upon those preceding it. Identification is the foundation for everything that follows; interpretation is the crown. [Emphasis added]

Taking the first of the four operations as the starting point suggests the initial question to ask about an artifact: What is it? To answer that question and those that logically follow, one relies on information that the artifact itself yields upon direct examination (intrinsic data) and information brought to bear on it from outside sources (extrinsic data). The quest for intrinsic data can lead one to submit an artifact to laboratory analysis, perhaps to determine the kind of wood or metal or other material of which it is made. Searching for extrinsic data may send one to guidebooks or catalogs or may call for comparisons with artifacts already identified. In other words, answering the questions about an artifact may require considerable research.

To say what an artifact is, as Fleming suggests, requires first that it be classified, perhaps by function (for what it was used), by the material of which it is made, by construction, or by subject matter (the classification system developed by Chenhall, referred to above, is a subject-matter system, with the subject matter defined in part by the artifact's function). It also requires authentication (as to the genuineness of its materials, its construction, and other claims made for it), and description (exact specification of its dimensions, weight, color, shape, texture, and so on). To be systematic in the use of the model, one would ask "What is it?" about the artifact's history, material, construction, design, and function. This is not an effort one accomplishes with a glance at the object and a stroke of the pen.

Evaluation may be even more demanding. The first kind is rendered as a subjective judgment concerning the artifact's aesthetic quality and workmanship, the skill and taste of the craftsmanship that went into it, the effectiveness of its overall design, and the expressiveness of the form, style, and ornament it displays. In

8.3 Attics can be filled with artifactual treasures that give tangible evidence of earlier practices, tastes, and interests. Their value as traces of the past can be enhanced if those who put them into storage or recall them attach a written record of their memories and a precise identification of each object. (Photo courtesy of the National Archives and Records Administration.)

the other kind of evaluation, the artifact is compared in objective terms with similar artifacts as to size, cost, rarity, and date of origin. Again, both sorts are applied to all five properties of the artifact.

So, too, is the third operation, cultural analysis, which seeks to examine the relation of the artifact to aspects of the culture that created it. It is in the application of this operation that the historian clearly goes beyond the antique collector, to whom this matter is of incidental concern. The principal focus is on the function of the artifact, examination of which touches directly on questions of human action and human purpose referred to at the beginning of this chapter. Whether the function is utilitarian (as with a tool), social (as with an instrument of communication), or artistic (as with a decorative object), it provides the key to the knowledge, beliefs, ideas, norms, and values of the culture from which the artifact comes.

Obviously, great knowledge and skill are required in using this key in the most sophisticated way, but untrained persons can use it if they are mindful of their own limitations and sensitive to the rules regarding the use of historical traces spelled out in chapter 3. It is helpful, too, to keep in mind that the practices governing the use of artifacts are similar to those for the use of written documents (and remember, too, the origin of the term "document" in *docere,* "to teach"). Material documents "teach" in much the same way as written documents.

The fourth of the operations, interpretation, is concerned with the relationship between what is learned about the artifact and some key feature of contemporary life. This relationship, Fleming says, must be sufficiently intense or rich to have self-evident meaning, significance, or relevance. It may have to do with a person or event important to the audience to whom the interpretation is directed, to some distinctive feature of the artifact that might be especially appreciated in a given context, to a special accomplishment—perhaps a first or a biggest or a fastest—in which it played a part, or to some notable characteristic of the times.

Cracking the subtle code of the artifact, to use the apt expression of one writer, is a task that is fraught with temptations, five of which are sufficiently common and serious to merit mention here. The first is the temptation to examine an artifact in isolation, as a thing separate from the culture of which it is a part and thus to draw erroneous conclusions about it. The second is almost the opposite: the tendency to see the artifact as representing a larger piece of a culture than it does. A single object should not be asked to explain too much about those who made and used it. Third, people often view an artifact only in terms of the present; that is, they identify, evaluate, analyze, and interpret it too exclusively in terms of the culture and the time period of the person studying it. Fourth, concern for the function of artifacts sometimes prompts disregard for their aesthetic value. Finally, there is the temptation, to which Americans are particularly vulnerable, to see all artifacts on a progress continuum, with each one accounting for a step in the long march from the primitive to the modern. This continuum requires each artifact to be genealogically relevant, and many are not.

WHY USE ARTIFACTS?

The study of an artifact, it is easy to see, is a rigorous exercise. What benefits does it hold for historians of the nearby? It helps them understand how earlier generations solved daily problems; it reveals the interplay between the aesthetic and the practical, the decorative and the functional; it gives us a feel for the quality of life in another time and place; and it provides insights into tastes, customs, manners, and styles of living. In sum, it helps historians to know and understand an earlier culture and the events that went into the making of it.

LOCATING ARTIFACTS

A natural question arises at this point: Who finds the artifacts worthy of study, and where do they find them? In the most fundamental sense, artifacts are the principal concern of archaeologists, but archaeologists do more than discover material for study. They verify it, provide for its preservation, measure and describe it, photograph it—especially if relocation to another site is impossible or infeasible—classify and arrange it in logical order, and prepare it for analysis by others. Their purpose is to prepare artifacts for historical study, but that is not to say that archaeologists must abandon them to historians. Nor is it to be inferred that the archaeological processes enumerated here are off limits to historians. The fields of archaeology and history may be distinct, but those who operate in them cannot avoid crossing field lines.

Archaeologists dig. When the digging requires unearthing, literally, historians are well advised to know their limits. Locating lost sites, identifying known sites, determining their nature and extent, locating known features within them, securing data for restoration or reconstruction, actual excavation of a site, salvaging threatened sites—these are all tasks best left to trained archaeologists.

But when archaeology is defined as a "technique for discovering and conserving evidence of all times and places, both above and below ground," the limits for historians are expanded, and most particularly so for historians of the nearby past. The cardinal rule in doing above-ground archaeology is: Do not damage, disturb, or destroy any material that is potentially the subject of archaeological and historical study. Furthermore, archaeological material should be removed from its location only if it cannot be studied there or if removal is essential to its protection. For advice and assistance on archaeological questions, historians should turn to the state historic preservation officer (who is required by law to employ professional archaeologists) or to the National Park Service, the Corps of Engineers, state geological and archaeological agencies, or to archaeologists in academic institutions.

A relatively new area of study within the broader field of archaeology is filled with challenges for the local historian. It is called "industrial archaeology," defined by Kenneth Hudson, one of its preeminent practitioners, as "the discovery, recording, and study of the physical remains of yesterday's industries and communications." The technique of his specialty, Hudson says, is to examine such matters as the conditions of work in a particular period and the attitude of employers, workers, and the general public to those conditions; what the different parties—workers, owners, managers, financiers, investors—derived from the process, plant, or method of working in the way of income, satisfaction, accidents, ill health, and standards of living; the techniques and equipment used in getting the job done; the scale of an industrial operation; and the condition of the physical environment in which workers and their families lived. This is a broad undertaking; in fact, it is a virtual invitation to historians to help, for the artifacts of industry cannot reveal all these things by themselves. The insights and knowledge of historians must be brought to bear on them.

If industrial archaeology holds a natural appeal for historians of the nearby past, and it should, especially if industries have played a part in the history of the

8.4 Advertising devices are one variety of artifact. During the early years of the automobile era, businesses trying to attract the attention of passing motorists erected buildings representing their product or service (an oil derrick or a coffee pot, for instance) or put on other unusual structures to catch the eye (Dutch windmills were quite popular). The artifacts suggest a different approach to advertising as well as a different type of business organization from the standardized emblems of modern day road signs. The cowboy hat and boots structures of this distinctive gas station lasted longer than many structures of this type. (Photo courtesy of and copyright © Roger Grant.)

locale, another area of study probably holds greater appeal. The only reason for calling the study of artifacts found around the house "household archaeology" is to point out that the methods of identification, evaluation, analysis, and interpretation are applicable to them in the same way that they are to things found underground or at industrial sites.

That such household artifacts as old furniture, tools, dishes, pottery, clothing, and decorative art are called antiques should pose no problem for historians. They can and should be studied in the same way as other cultural artifacts, and the information they yield is similar. In some respects the precise effort and intense care that antique collectors and dealers put into identifying and authenticating antiques set an example for historians. The difference is that antique collectors stop short; cultural analysis and interpretation are not their principal concerns, as they are for historians. Another difference is that for historians an artifact does not have to be old to be of interest or value; for antique collectors and dealers it is often age that confers value, and it is value expressed in monetary terms that inspires interest.

Purists would exclude persons interested in antiques from the fraternity of historians. Instead, historians say: broaden your interests and join us; meanwhile we will learn what we can from you.

MUSEUMS

Of what use are museums to students of material culture? That depends, of course, on the museum. In their broadest purpose, museums are conservatories of material culture. The good ones are also interpreters of it. They subject their holdings, one by one, to the scrutiny called for in the model used in this chapter, and they arrange their exhibits so that the artifacts in them tell the story of another time and place in terms that make sense today.

But museum directors are caught in an array of dilemmas. To name a few:

- Tax and private voluntary support are unpredictable, and funds for such basic activities as research and collections preservation are often severely limited.
- To satisfy the priorities of governments and private foundations, museums are increasingly asked to justify their contributions to local economic development and demonstrate their social cultural impact.
- Without charging admission, many museums cannot survive, but if fees are too high, public use declines.
- Museums are teaching institutions, but many of their users regard them as places to spend leisure time as they look for entertaining diversions. They compete with shopping malls, sporting events, casinos, and with pervasive Disney influences in American life. In their competition for visitors, they can hardly avoid packaging some of what they do in Disneyesque forms.
- To teach well museums must offer carefully planned exhibits, but preparation of exhibits is often too costly for museum budgets.
- Museums collect and attempt to preserve objects of material culture that were made to be used and discarded. Even under the best of conditions, preservation sometimes proves to be impossible.
- When exhibitions are underwritten by corporate or other sponsors, the stories presented face criticism for being slanted.
- Some donations come to museums with strings attached that curators cannot in good conscience honor.
- Deaccessioning, the act of formally removing nonrelevant objects from the collection for transfer to another museum or to sell at auction, has created controversy for some history museums. While deaccessioning is a logical way to strengthen and improve collections, it is sometimes viewed by the public, donors, and sometimes trustees as a breach of trust.
- Controversial exhibitions, no matter how honest the messages they convey, are susceptible to attack by interest groups and, in turn, by politicians.

• Perhaps the greatest dilemma for museums is that while they are called upon to preserve with the greatest of care the objects in their collections, especially since many of the objects are appropriately called "one of a kind," they also want to see those objects studied and used, which means exposing them to the wear and tear that come with handling.

That points to a problem for users of museums, including historians: Too often the use that is allowed is merely passive. The object, locked under glass or secured behind ropes and railings, may merely be looked at. Another problem associated with the use of museum-held artifacts in historical research derives from the fact that the artifacts are not only lifted out of contexts that give them meaning but are placed, quite often at least, next to completely incongruous artifacts, thus detracting from meaning all around. This problem occurs on the most grandiose scale at Henry Ford's Greenfield Village at Dearborn, Michigan, as noted in chapter 1.

Furthermore, museum curators and users sometimes lean toward a "good old days" approach, tending to simplify and glorify the past. At one museum they call this the "goodness and granola" approach: "Life was simpler and better then, and if America would only return to the old values, the old ways of doing things. . . ." In this approach it is natural to emphasize white, male, middle- and upper-class success stories. Knowing the history of a museum helps one understand the biases appearing there: Henry Ford's at Greenfield Village, for example, and the Rockefellers' at Colonial Williamsburg. To their credit, in recent years these museums have made significant efforts to make the stories they tell more complete and better balanced. Indeed, in recent decades good museums have generally become better sources for learning about the lives of blacks and women, and they have addressed such matters as labor conflict, populist discontent, and feminist or minority protest.

Government-sponsored museums, such as the Smithsonian Institution, tend to be more multifaceted in their ways of doing things because of their sources of support and the constituencies they serve, but they too face constraints and are vulnerable to political attacks. The Smithsonian's attempt to look at the use of atomic bombs on Japan in 1945 from Japanese as well as American perspectives, for example, raised such a storm of criticism, including in the Congress, that the head of the Institution canceled the exhibition. The whole episode threatened the ability of the Smithsonian to deal candidly with controversial issues, and museums across the nation felt shock waves from it. It became clear that museums do not enjoy the academic freedom that is essential to overcome myth and reconstruct stories from the past based upon the widest range of evidence and best available perspectives.

Still another problem museums face is that the artifacts they hold are select samples; the museum user must trust that the curator's choices are representative of a given time, place, and culture; that they are genuinely credible evidence of an event; and that the uniqueness of each item justifies its inclusion in a museum collection. Furthermore, a museum's artifacts are not always cataloged and indexed in the same way that written documents are recorded in archives, although properly operated museums know where their artifacts are. In any case, finding the precise object one is looking for often requires considerable effort. It is no wonder, then, that museums are better at evoking wonder and excitement and stimulating interest in the past than they are at focusing on specific problems.

Museologists and curators are aware of these problems, and many are striving to overcome them. Some museums are working diligently to catalog and index their holdings. Some are distinguishing between serious students and casual visitors and are making objects available under controlled conditions for scholarly study. Some are abandoning the practice of taking contributions of objects, willy-nilly, from the good citizens of the community in return for promises of prominent display, which means that the eclectic jumbles that have characterized many exhibits can be discontinued. Conscious efforts are being made to create exhibits that tell a story with learning rather than entertainment in mind. The story is told through imaginative arrangement of the exhibits rather than by placing long explanations next to each object.

Some museums teach by creating living, functioning museums. Conner Prairie Pioneer Settlement, north of Indianapolis, for example, is a frontier village fixed in 1836. Instead of listening to the prepared speeches by interpreters, visitors chat with the storekeeper, attend school, watch the blacksmith and the potter at work, smell the bread being baked in the fireplaces (and perspire with the cook if they visit in summer months), stroll through the barns, and generally make themselves at home. The interpreters, speaking in the first person, present tense, engage in conversations with visitors. (Visitor: "Was this house an underground railroad stop?" Interpreter, with a suspicious look: "You with the law?" Who else would ask about the underground railroad in 1836?) This is entertainment, of course, but it is also education.

Through artifacts, demonstrations, and the use of professional and volunteer interpreters, Living History Farms, near Des Moines, Iowa, tells the story of changes in agricultural and rural life. Staff members in period clothing interpret the everyday activities of rural Iowa covering a span of 300 years. Because the emphasis is on changes in methods of farming and the daily functions of a frontier town, the interpreters provide information on developments, both past and expected in the future, that place artifacts and methods in their appropriate contexts. Very little first-person role playing occurs, but visitors can see the work of farm families, blacksmiths, lawyers, doctors, veterinarians, potters, and undertakers as it is performed by the interpreters.

Museums of this kind, spread across the countryside, have a particular problem in addressing a situation that challenges all museums; that is, making their facilities accessible to persons with disabilities in compliance with the 1990 Americans with Disabilities Act. Historic properties are covered by the ADA, and adjustments are re-

Like Conner Prairie, Living History Farms offers interactive programs for students, who have opportunities to spend a day working as "hired hands" on either a turn-of-the-century farm, complete with draft horses, or an 1850 farm with oxen and a log cabin. Or, among other things, they may visit the 1875 frontier town, learning the activities of skilled trades people or attending class in the one-room school-house. Here are excerpts from letters by student participants:

We got to see many interesting things. I think it was neat to see the potter spin a bowl right in front of us. I also liked the colorful hats in the Millinery. At the drug store [we saw] how they used to make pills back in 1875. . . . I also liked the house that the [1700 Ioway] Indians lived in. They were made of sticks, bark, twigs, and leaves. I learned that they were very resourceful and used plants for many reasons. We also went to the doctor's office, and the lady showed us the tools they used to amputate. I thought the animals were one of the best parts. (8th grade)

Thank you for showing me around the farm. My favorite thing was to throw hay down to the horses. The hay stack was fun to stand on. I learned that you had a lot of chores in 1900 [and] that you have to have a lot or responsibility to do it all. (4th grade)

Adult visitors also write letters:

My folks, farmers for all their lives, were in their early 80s at the time they visited Living History Farms. My father-in-law was starting to lose some of his sharpness and it hurt to watch. But the day we took them there we watched the years roll away. It was August, hot and muggy with a storm threatening, the corn was getting it['s] final cultivation. Dinnertime came, the horses were taken to the barn, and the men washed up at the pump in the rear. We followed them into the house, where the cookstove was pumping out the heat and all the good smells of noontime dinner. My mother-in-law stood there with tears glistening in her eyes, my father-in-law was choked up. Even our children, who were 8 and 10, remember this as the day we took Grandpa and Grandma back in time to their childhood. It was the best gift we ever gave them. . . . one we will never forget. (Visitor from Santa Maria, California.)

quired even if no rehabilitation or restoration work on the property is anticipated. The law is specific in spelling out how its requirements must be met, but it does make special provisions for historic properties that cannot be made accessible without destroying their historical significance. All institutions would do well to seek guidance of the kind provided in a leaflet authored by Thomas C. Jester and published by the National Park Service, "Preserving the Past and Making It Accessible for People with Disabilities" (1992, revised in August 1996).

Ideally, historians should come to see themselves as partners with museums in their communities. In so doing, they can become part of a movement to open up museums and make them more responsive to community interests. They can assist in acquiring museum-worthy objects; perhaps they can help in researching and caring for them. Certainly, by observation and personal study, historians can learn something from museums about the conservation of artifacts in their own possession.

This chapter began by asserting that traces of historical events are found in things as well as words. Not only will persons who work with artifacts in ways recommended here come to see the past differently, but their sensitivity to the importance of things as carriers of meaning will help them see their own environment as a living museum.

NOTES AND FURTHER READING

This chapter has referred to and quoted from James R. Blackaby, Patricia Greeno, and the Nomenclature Committee, eds., *The Revised Nomenclature for Museum Cataloging: A Revised and Expanded Version of Robert G. Chenhall's System for Classifying Man-Made Objects* (Walnut Creek, CA: AltaMira Press, 1988); E. McClung Fleming, "Artifact Study: A Proposed Model," *Winterthur Portfolio* 9 (1974): 153–73; and Kenneth Hudson, *World Industrial Archaeology* (Cambridge: Cambridge University Press, 1979), pp. 2, 13–14.

Thomas J. Schlereth is widely recognized as the leading scholar in American material culture studies. His *Artifacts and the American Past* (Nashville: American Association for State and Local History, 1980) contains nine essays, some of them previously published (and cited below in their original place of publication). Also by Schlereth are *Cultural History and Material Culture: Everyday Life, Landscapes, Museums* (Ann Arbor, MI: UMI Research Press, 1990); *Material Culture: A Research Guide* (Lawrence: University Press of Kansas, 1984); and *Reading the Road: U.S. 40 and the American Landscape* (Knoxville: University of Tennessee Press, 1997). Schlereth is also the editor of an anthology, *Material Culture Studies* (Nashville, TN: American Association for State and Local History, 1982; republished, AltaMira Press, 1996). Since 1989 Schlereth has served as the contributing editor for the "Exhibition Reviews" that appear in the June and December issues of the *Journal of American History.*

Another comprehensive collection of essays on topics treated in this chapter is Ian M. Quimby, ed., *Material Culture and the Study of American Life* (New York: Norton, 1978); two essays that merit special mention are "How Much Is a Piece of the True Cross Worth?" by Brooke Hindle and "Doing History with Material Culture" by Cary Carson.

Other works on artifacts and their use include: Kenneth Ames, "Material Culture as Non-Verbal Communication: A Historical Case Study," *Journal of American Culture* 3 (1980): 619–41; Simon J. Bronner, *Grasping Things: Folk Material Culture and Mass Society in America* (Lexington, KY: University Press of Kentucky, 1986); Simon J. Bronner, ed., *American Material Culture and Folklife: A Prologue and Dialogue* (Logan, UT: Utah State University Press, 1992); John Chavis, "The Artifact and the Study of History," *Curator* 7, no. 2 (1964): 156–62; Craig Gilborn, "Pop Pedagogy," *Museum News* 47, no. 4 (December 1968): 12–18; John A. Kouwenhoven, "American Studies: Words or Things?" in *American Studies in Transition,* edited by Marshall Fishwick (Philadelphia: University of Pennsylvania Press, 1964), 1–16; Kurt E. Leichtle, "Bits and Pieces: Interpreting Culture," *Journal of American Culture* 12 (summer 1989): 49–54; Steven Lubar and W. David Kingery, *History from Things: Essays on Material Culture* (Washington, DC: Smithsonian Institution Press, 1993); Edith Mayo, ed., *American Material Culture: The Shape of Things Around Us* (Bowling Green, OH: Bowling Green University Popular Press, 1984); Harold Skramstad, "American Things: A Neglected Material Culture," *American Studies: An In-*

ternational Newsletter 10, no. 3 (spring 1972): 11–22; John T. Schlebecker, "The Use of Objects in Historical Research," *Agricultural History* 51 (1977): 200–208; Alexander Wall, "The Voice of the Artifact," *History News* 27, no. 10 (October 1972): 3–8; and Wilcomb E. Washburn, "Manuscripts and Manufacts," *American Archivist* 27 (1964): 245–50. *Pioneer America: The Journal of Historic American Material Culture* was published by the Pioneer America Society at Louisiana State University. Another journal, begun in 1964, added a subtitle in 1979: *Winterthur Portfolio: A Journal of American Material Culture* (Chicago: University of Chicago Press). An occasional article in *Technology and Culture,* such as Ruth Schwartz Cowan's "The Industrial Revolution in the Home: Household Technology and Social Change in the Twentieth Century" 17, no. 1 (1976): 1–23, may be helpful to students of artifacts.

These works emphasize theoretical aspects of material culture: Ray B. Browne and Pat Browne, eds., *Digging into Popular Culture: Theories and Methodologies in Archaeology, Anthropology, and Other Fields* (Bowling Green, OH: Bowling Green State University Popular Press, 1991); R. R. Dipert, "Some Issues in the Theory of Artifacts: Defining 'Artifact' and Related Notions," *The Monist* 78, no. 2 (1995): 119–35; Margaret J. M. Ezell and Katherine O'Brien O'Keeffe, eds., *Cultural Artifacts and the Production of Meaning: The Page, the Image, and the Body* (Ann Arbor: University of Michigan Press, 1994); James G. Gibb and Karen Lee Davis, "History Exhibits and Theories of Material Culture," *Journal of American Culture* 12 (summer 1989): 27–33; W. David Kingery, *Learning from Things: Method and Theory of Material Culture Studies* (Washington, DC: Smithsonian Institution Press, 1996); Jules David Prown, "Mind in Matter: An Introduction to Material Culture Theory and Method," *Winterthur Portfolio* 17 (1982): 1–19; and Sari Thomas, "Artifactual Study in the Analysis of Culture: A Defense of Content Analysis in a Postmodern Age," *Communication Research* 21, no. 6 (December 1994): 683–97.

Franklin Folsom and Mary Elting Folsom, *America's Ancient Treasures: A Guide to Archeological Sites and Museums in the United States and Canada* (Albuquerque: University of New Mexico Press, 4th ed., 1993) is an excellent guide to artifacts of Native American peoples found in forty-nine states, ten Canadian provinces, and the Northwest and Yukon Territories. Works on material culture in early American life include: James Deetz, *In Small Things Forgotten: The Archaeology of Early American Life* (New York: Doubleday, 1977); E. McClung Fleming, "Early American Decorative Arts as Social Documents," *Mississippi Valley Historical Review* 45, no. 2 (September 1958): 276–84; Brooke Hindle, *Technology in Early America: Needs and Opportunities for Study* (Chapel Hill: University of North Carolina Press, 1966); Ivor Noel Hume, *All the Best Rubbish: Being an Antiquary's Account for the Pleasures and Perils of Studying and Collecting Everyday Objects from the Past* (New York: Harper and Row, 1974) and *A Guide to Artifacts of Colonial America* (New York: Knopf, 1970); and Robert Blair St. George, ed., *Material Life in America, 1600–1860* (Boston: Northeastern University Press, 1987).

Books that deal with artifacts in the contexts in which they are found include: John A. Kouwenhoven, *Made in America: The Arts in Modern Civilization* (New York: Doubleday, 1948); Russell Lynes, *The Domesticated Americans* (New York: Harper and Row, 1957), an exploration of the interplay between material culture and manners; and Richard E. Meyer, ed., *Cemeteries and Grave Markers: Voices of American Culture* (Logan, UT: Utah State University Press, 1992).

Works on specific kinds of artifacts are virtually limitless in number. Examples include: Robert Abels, *Early American Firearms* (New York: World Publishing, 1950);

Michael and Ariane Batterberry, *Mirror, Mirror: A Social History of Fashion* (New York: Holt, Rinehart and Winston, 1977); Patricia A. Cunningham and Susan Voso Lab, eds., *Dress in American Culture* (Bowling Green, OH: Bowling Green State University Popular Press, 1993); Roger A. Fischer, *Tippecanoe and Trinkets Too: The Material Culture of American Presidential Campaigns, 1828–1984* (Urbana: University of Illinois Press, 1988); Claudia B. Kidwell and Margaret C. Christman, *Suiting Everyone: The Democratization of Clothing in America* (Washington, DC: Smithsonian Institution Press, 1974); John Michael Vlach, *The Afro-American Tradition in Decorative Arts* (Cleveland: Cleveland Museum Art, 1978); and Philip D. Zimmerman, "A Methodological Study in the Identification of Some Important Philadelphia Chippendale Furniture," *Winterthur Portfolio* 13 (1979): 192–208.

For books on specific kinds of antiques—such as books, bottles, china, clothing, coins, dolls, and more—as well as for annual guides and price lists, the best advice is to visit local libraries and bookstores. Some of the better more general books are: Paul Atterbury and Lars Tharp, eds., *The Bulfinch Encyclopedia of Antiques* (Boston: Little, Brown, 1994); Louise A. Boger and H. Batterson Boger, comps. and eds., *The Dictionary of Antiques and the Decorative Arts: A Book of Reference for Glass, Furniture, Ceramics, Silver, Periods, Styles, Technical Terms, Etc.* (New York: Scribner's, 1957); Joseph T. Butler, *Field Guide to American Antique Furniture* (New York: Henry Holt, 1987); Mary Durant, *The American Heritage Guide to Antiques* (New York: American Heritage Press, 1970); F. Lewis Hinckley, *A Directory Antique Furniture: The Authentic Classification of European and American Designs for Professionals and Connoisseurs* (New York: Crown, 1953); Eric Knowles, *Discovering Antiques: A Guide to the World of Antiques and Collectibles* (London: De Agostini, Ltd., 1996); Judith Miller and Martin Miller, eds., *Miller's Understanding Antiques* (London: Reed International, Ltd., 1987; rev. ed., 1997); Judith Miller, *Care and Repair of Everyday Treasures: A Step-by-Step Guide to Cleaning and Restoring Your Antiques and Collectibles* (Pleasantville, NY: Reader's Digest, 1997); and "Antique Farm Equipment: Researching and Identifying," *History News*, Technical Leaflet no. 101 (Nashville: American Association for State and Local History, 1977).

On industrial archaeology, see: R. A. S. Hennessey, "Industrial Archaeology in Education," *History Teacher* 9, no. 1 (1975): 29–41; Kenneth Hudson, *Industrial Archaeology: An Introduction* (London: John Baker, 1963); J. B. Lane, "Oral History and Industrial Heritage Museums," *Journal of American History* 80, no. 2 (September 1993): 607–18. Theodore Anton Sande, *Industrial Archeology: A New Look at the American Heritage* (Brattleboro, VT: Stephen Greene Press, 1976); and David Weitzman, *Traces of the Past: A Field Guide to Industrial Archaeology* (New York: Scribner's, 1980).

A volume designed to "bridge the gap between memory and history, between popular and professional approaches to making history" is Gaynor Kavanagh, ed., *Making Histories in Museums* (New York: Leicester University Press, 1996). General works on museums are: Edward P. Alexander, *Museums in Motion: An Introduction to the History and Functions of Museums* (Nashville: American Association for State and Local History, 1979); Tim Ambrose, *Museum Basics* (London: ICOM in conjunction with Routledge, 1993); G. Ellis Burcaw, *Introduction to Museum Work* (Nashville: American Association for State and Local History, 1975); Gary Edson and David Dean, *The Handbook for Museums* (London: Routledge, 1994); Kenneth Hudson, *Museums of Influence* (Cambridge: Cambridge University Press, 1987); Warren Leon and Roy Rosenzweig, eds., *History Museums in the United States: A Critical Assessment* (Urbana: University of Illinois Press,

1989); Ralph H. Lewis, *A Manual for Museums* (Washington, DC: National Park Service, 1976); Stephen E. Weil, *Rethinking the Museum and Other Meditations* (Washington, DC: Smithsonian Institution Press, 1990); and Alma S. Wittlin, *Museums: In Search of a Usable Future* (Cambridge, MA: MIT Press, 1970).

More specialized works are: Richard Chase, "Museums as Learning Environments," *Museum News* 54 (September/October 1975): 37–43; Victor J. Danilov, *Museum Careers and Training: A Professional Guide* (Westport, CT: Greenwood Press, 1994); Graeme Gardiner, "The Conservation Survey: Identifying Preservation Problems," *Museum International* 48, no. 2 (1996): 55–58; Jane R. Glaser and Artemis A. Zenetou, eds., *Gender Perspectives: Essays on Women in Museums* (Washington, DC: Smithsonian Institution Press, 1994); Per E. Guldbeck, *The Care of Historical Collections* (Nashville: American Association for State and Local History, 1972); Amy Henderson and Adrienne L. Kaeppler, eds., *Exhibiting Dilemmas: Issues of Representation at the Smithsonian* (Washington, DC: Smithsonian Institution Press, 1996); Ivan Karp and Steven Lavine, eds. *Exhibiting Cultures: The Poetics and Politics of Museum Display* (Washington, DC: Smithsonian Institution Press, 1992); Arminta Neal, *Exhibits for Small Museum: A Handbook* (Nashville: American Association for State and Local History, 1976); Daniel Porter, *Developing a Collections Management Manual* (Nashville: American Association for State and Local History, 1986); Frederick L. Rath, Jr., *Care and Conservation of Collections: A Bibliography on Historical Organization Practices* (Nashville: American Association for State and Local History, 1977); Fred Schroeder, "Designing Your Exhibits: Seven Ways to Look at an Artifact," Technical Leaflet no. 91 (Nashville: American Association for State and Local History, 1977); Michael Steven Shapiro, ed., *The Museum: A Reference Guide* (Westport, CT: Greenwood Press, 1990); Mike Wallace, *Mickey Mouse History and Other Essays on American Memory* (Philadelphia: Temple University Press, 1996); National Park Service, *Tools of the Trade: A Listing of Materials and Equipment for Managing Museum Collections* (Washington, DC: Curatorial Division, National Park Service, 1994); Thomas J. Schlereth "Historic Houses as Learning Laboratories: Seven Teaching Strategies," Technical Leaflet no. 105 (Nashville: American Association for State and Local History, 1978) and "The Historic Museum Village as a Learning Environment," *Museologist* (June 1977): 10–18.

An interesting controversy regarding the purpose and future of museums took shape in a pair of articles in *Museum News:* Wilcomb Washburn, "Are Museums Necessary?," 47, no. 2 (October 1968): 9–10 and Ian Quimby, "Reply to Washburn," 47, no. 4 (December 1968): 10–11. A pair of articles in the winter 1996 *History News*, pp. 22–25, dealt with the question, "Is There Enough History to Go Around?" Jerome Thompson's is titled "Overgrazing the Commons," and Tom McKay's "Standing in the Local Societies' Shoes." Other provocative articles relating to museums include: Loris Russell, "Problems and Potentialities of the History Museum," *Curator* 6, no. 4 (1963): 341–49; and Robert B. Ronsheim, "Is the Past Dead?" *Museum News* 53 no. 3 (November 1974): 16–18, 62.

For discussions of the controversy surrounding the *Enola Gay* exhibition at the Smithsonian Institution in 1994–95, see Martin Harwit, *An Exhibit Denied: Lobbying the History of Enola Gay* (New York: Copernicus/Springer-Verlag, 1996); Edward T. Linenthal and Tom Engelhardt, *History Wars: The* Enola Gay *and Other Battles for the American Past* (New York: Henry Holt, 1996); Philip Nobile, ed., *Judgment at the Smithsonian* (New York: Marlowe and Co., 1995); and "History and the Public: What Can We Handle? A Roundtable About History after the *Enola Gay* Controversy," *Journal of American History*

82, no. 3 (December 1995): 1029–144. Mike Wallace, in *Mickey Mouse History,* cited above, also devotes several chapters to the controversy.

Many museums now provide information about their holdings, and some invite "virtual visits" through their Web sites. The Association of Living History, Farm and Agricultural Museums <www.alhfam.org> provides links to sixty-three museums in the United States, fifteen in Europe, and two in New Zealand. Among them are: Hancock Shaker Village <www.hancockshakervillage.org>; Colonial Williamsburg <www.history.org>; Conner Prairie <www.connerprairie.org>; the Henry Ford Museum and Greenfield Village <www.hfmgv.org>; Historic Cold Spring Village <www.hcsv.org>; Living History Farms <www.lhf.org>; Old Sturbridge Village <www.osv.org>; and the Smithsonian Institution <www.si.edu>. See also the sites of other museums, such as the Chicago Historical Society <www.chicagohs.org> and the United States Historical Holocaust Museum <www.ushmm.org>.

For information about software for use in museum management, see "PastPerfect Museum Software," <www.museumsoftware.com> published by AltaMira Press.

9

Landscapes and Buildings

Culture, defined simply, is what one needs to know to be one of the folk. Material culture is what the folk have made with what they know.

Where can you go to see a natural landscape that has not been affected by the intrusions of material culture? Roads, bridges, and automobiles are everywhere. Lining the roads are billboards, power lines and towers, silos, motels, restaurants, convenience stores, and gas stations. On the horizon you see the urban skyline, with its office buildings, factories, warehouses, and churches; airplanes circle overhead. The natural surroundings have been so thoroughly altered by the doings of people that they are intertwined with, even lost in, the cultural landscape. And yet, most people take the cultural landscape as something that is just there; they seldom stop to think about what surrounds them.

SURVEYING THE CULTURAL LANDSCAPE

A survey of the cultural landscape shows the nature and extent of change over time. In urban areas, particularly, there is a commonly appearing cycle of: (1) construction, (2) abandonment, (3) conversion, (4) abandonment, (5) demolition, and (6) new construction. Sometimes the cycle skips a phase, but its essential motion persists. In rural areas the full cycle is less frequent and slower, and for this reason and others rural areas often hold greater appeal for local historians and preservationists than urban areas, but the cycle occurs there, too. The process ends with abandonment.

Studying change over time in the cultural landscape invites consideration of migration patterns, the opening and closing of transportation routes, evolving architectural fashions and changing tastes in living space, and the displacement of older commercial districts by new shopping centers. In every instance, of course, the historical evidence found in the landscape must be supplemented by information derived from written documents.

The cultural landscape also offers evidence of neighborhood or regional differences. In a city, the differences might be apparent in the width of streets or size of lots; regionally, in house styles and in materials used in construction. At the same time, the cultural landscape shows the growing similarities of cities and towns in one part of the country with those in others. Put another way, our surroundings reveal the wide diffusion of the more common ingredients of material culture.

Shopping centers provide an object lesson for study. A century ago, the general stores, dispensers of goods that were largely homegrown, homemade, and home packaged, began to give way to mass production and distribution of standardized products. Mail-order houses, chain store outlets, large department and discount stores, and specialty shops that handled these products displaced general stores, gradually at first, then swiftly.

Today downtown shopping areas and their smaller counterparts in scattered parts of cities, and even the town squares in smaller communities, have been supplanted by look-alike shopping centers and strip malls. Visitors to Disneyland or Walt Disney World must surely be struck by the similarities between these plastic, self-conscious entertainment centers and the bright, shiny, world within-a-world shopping centers, such as the Mall of America in Bloomington, Minnesota.

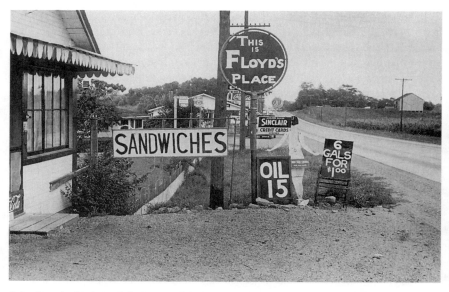

9.1   Popularization of the automobile had remarkable consequences for the landscape, not only for the streets, roads, bridges, and parking spaces cars required, but also for the facilities built to service them and devices employed to attract their drivers' attention. The transformation of the landscape by the automobile is everywhere—apparent in cities, in towns, at the edge of town (as shown here), and in the country. (Photo courtesy of the Library of Congress.)

The chain stores that occupy them, the brand-name merchandise they offer, and the national advertising they display, all in compliance with the uniform restrictions imposed by the center's management, make them astonishingly predictable. As we contemplate the place of shopping centers in American life, we might ask what became of the central commercial districts and town squares left behind. What happened to the men and women who once shopped there, and where do those who live near the abandoned areas now shop?

Also giving the cultural landscape the appearance of a growing sameness are the ubiquitous fast-food restaurants. They offer everyone something to study: Sociologists can consider relationships between their increasing popularity and changes in family size, greater numbers of mothers who are employed, and the increase in single-parent homes. Economists can examine the effect on American life of these restaurants' dependence on a labor force of young people paid at minimum wage, as well as the ties between efficiency and waste in fast-food marketing techniques. Anthropologists can study the symbolism of the rituals of fast-food restaurants. And nutritionists can concern themselves with the long-term effects of a steady fare of burgers and french fries on the health of those who eat them regularly.

Historians are interested in all of these matters, of course, but perhaps most interesting are the ways in which fast-food restaurants are indicators of change over time. What do such places, these virtual extensions of the automobile, say about mobility in American life? How have they helped to encourage ideas of equality? If equality is taken to mean "indistinction" (and there is significance to the assumption that it can be so taken), indistinction is apparent in the customary self-service, the attire of the patrons, the time of the day the restaurants may be patronized, the absence of tipping, and the age of their patrons. Historians might want to know how erasing distinctions has become important through the years.

People who investigate the past of the local cultural landscape will also have more specific interests: How have fast-food restaurants resulted from changed traffic patterns? Or, in turn, how have they changed such patterns? What structures, if any, were demolished to make room for them? Were they the first commercial structures on a given strip? In a given locality, how many are in the abandoned or converted stage while new ones are being built? What has been their effect on the neighborhoods in which they are located?

UNDERSTANDING THE CULTURAL LANDSCAPE

To see the cultural landscape more intelligently and to give order to questions about it, models for analysis and interpretation are helpful. As a general principle, the starting point is to see the whole and to see its parts. Seeing the landscape whole means looking for relationships between buildings and open spaces, between building and building, between the cultural and the natural landscapes, between commercial and residential areas, between old and new. It means looking for *form* (the principle of coherence), *balance* (one element offsets another), *harmony* (good visual sounds), and *unity* (things fit together to give the impression of oneness) in its constituent parts. And it means also looking for shapelessness, imbalance, incongruity, and disorder.

Seeing the cultural landscape whole also involves identifying time points on the cycle of construction, abandonment, conversion, and demolition. It may entail observing the effects of distinctive features of the natural and cultural landscapes on the geographic space. How did natural features, a river, for example, shape a city? How did a railroad reshape it? And how did an interstate highway or an airport reshape it again?

Changes in the built landscape of the community are clues to movement in the location of various activities, alteration of economic patterns, and quite possibly other developments. Perhaps nothing has signified the rearrangement of twentieth-century communities as much as the rise of shopping centers. Exploring the consequences of their evolution is a worthy and sizable task, as historian Neil Harris hints in this capsule description of their development.

Early shopping centers, like so many modern innovations, developed in California during the 1920s and '30s. Living in the first set of urban communities built entirely around the automobile, Californians quickly discovered the advantages of placing groups of stores around or within parking areas. Similar arrangements soon appeared in other parts of the country. Richard Neutra designed a small shopping center for Lexington, Kentucky; New Jersey had the Big Bear Shopping Centers, built around giant groceries, with parking space for up to 1,000 cars.

In the '30s also, chain and department stores, both vital to the future centers, began to adapt their businesses to the increasingly affluent suburbs and the ever mobile automobile. Until then, retail location in large American cities had been generally a function of existing transportation lines. But as automobile usage spread, downtown location became more problematic. "The automobile emancipated the consumer but not the merchant," the *Architectural Forum* noted in 1949, and well before the firms like Macy's and Sears Roebuck had begun building in the suburbs or on the peripheries of metropolitan centers.

It was the union of department stores with the older ideal of grouping easily accessible smaller stores that produced the first regional centers. This was supplemented, of course, by the explosion of highway construction during the Eisenhower era. The years from the early '50s to the late '60s were the golden era of shopping center construction. By the end of the '60s more than 10,000 shopping centers of every size and shape had been built. The huge shift of wealth and population to the suburbs guaranteed their profits. Large department stores—like Hudson's in Detroit and Dayton's in Minneapolis—were eager to get a piece of this action. Instead of simply opening up more branches, department stores began to organize their own centers, hire architects and developers, and get mortgages from life insurance companies, whose huge supply of capital enabled them to influence the suburban landscape as powerfully as their huge downtown skyscrapers shaped the center cities.

Source: Neil Harris, "Spaced-Out at the Shopping Center," New Republic, December 13, 1975, p. 23.

Seeing the parts means focusing on traffic patterns, perhaps on changes in the character of neighborhoods caused by highways or railroad tracks. It means considering pronounced changes in the nature of communities at night and by day, and examining places where things are produced, where deals are made, and where the action is. Seeing the parts means seeing dumps, green spaces, woods, cemeteries, and pavement.

Grouping the parts of the landscape by categories prepares you to use them in historical research. Variations in streetlights, for example, prompt one to ask why one style stops and another begins in a given community in which the houses show little age difference. Sidewalks and curbs lead the observer to wonder why some parts of a community have them and others do not. Counting churches and church-related agencies in one area invites one to consider why those of one denomination predominate. What effect did the country clubs and cemeteries surrounding a residential subdivision have on its development? How did the developers exploit these features in their plans and promotions? What explains the survival of one old, incongruous business establishment, such as a feed store and grain elevator, on the edge of a ghetto? In rural areas, why does a town at one bend in the road prosper while another becomes a ghost town? Why do farms in some areas seem so similar, in others so different?

9.2   Horse-drawn vehicles still dominated city streets when this photograph was taken, but the rails embedded in the thoroughfare serve the observant historian as a trace of the technological changes occurring in the late-nineteenth-century urban landscape. (Photo courtesy of and copyright © Summit County Historical Society.)

> *Apparently minor changes in technology or practice can have large consequences for community life. The introduction of parking meters on the streets of a central business district produced conflict and change in a Minnesota town.*
>
> In Old Benson, one could stop one's car in the middle of the street while one exchanged civilities with a neighbor. The street operated like a general all-purpose meeting place where the ladies stopped to chat, where children shouted greetings to one another, where boys gathered with their bicycles to plan a raid on one of the nearby apple orchards, and where young men and women made a date. The street symbolized the sociability and sharing of a self-oriented community.
>
> In New Benson, the street is being converted into an efficient thoroughfare and municipal parking area calculated to speed individuals on their business or to return a small fine for overparking into the public treasury. To the new-style Bensonite the stalling, traffic-blocking proclivities of the old-timers are "dog-patchy" examples of rural nostalgia. They wish to give their town the look of streamlined efficiency of the metropolis.
>
> *Farmers, who regarded their patronage as vital to Benson's prosperity, saw the meters as an indication that they were no longer as welcome as before. In other communities, downtown parking meters have been credited with encouraging patronage of suburban shopping centers with free parking and thus have stimulated a fundamental shift in community commercial patterns, tax revenues, and crime rates. Small and indirect influences should not be overlooked in seeking explanations for complicated changes, such as the decline of a central business district.*
>
> Source: *Don Martindale and R. Galen Hanson,* Small Town and the Nation: The Conflict of Local and Translocal Forces *(Westport, CT: Greenwood, 1969), p. 173.*

Focusing narrowly on one specific type of artifact invites the use of the Fleming model outlined in the previous chapter. A study of manhole covers (as reported, for example, in *The Manhole Covers of Los Angeles,* by Robert and Mimi Melnick) or fire hydrants in a locality calls for comparative identification and descriptions, evaluations, cultural analyses, and interpretations. Their history, materials, construction, design, and function all invite attention. Indeed, the model is applicable to artifacts of all sizes and varieties, from decorative doorknobs to street signs to grave markers to statues and monuments and even to buildings.

Buildings deserve special attention here because they are not only the most prominent artifacts on the cultural landscape but the centers of human activity as well. People walk around them, go into them, move up and down and about in them; look at them from the outside and out of them from the inside; work, play, eat, sleep, relax, entertain, make love, worry, and squabble in them. Buildings interact with the economic, social, aesthetic, and physical lives of those who use them. People and buildings exist in an organic relationship.

As the centers of human activity, buildings can correctly be called functional entities on the cultural landscape. They are also structural entities, made of concrete materials and ordered according to certain forms and design principles. And

9.3. *Aerial views of a neighborhood may help historians trace and question its development. At the center of this view is the little frame church shown in photos 3.1–3.4. A look at that church in these surroundings prompts one to ask: How did proximity to a streetcar line affect the church's growth and outlook? What were the reasons for locating the church one block off the main thoroughfare? What were the consequences of this decision? How did the absence of a street to connect this subdivision with the more modest one adjacent to it affect the character of the congregation? What effect did the apparently blatant violation of zoning ordinances—placing a modest frame structure in a community of substantial brick homes—have on relations with the community? (Photo courtesy of and copyright © Unity Lutheran Church, Bel-Nor, Missouri.)*

9.4 *Buildings and streets take on a different character at night. (Photo courtesy of and copyright © Summit County Historical Society.)*

they are symbolic, representing at least the necessities of one or more persons at a given time and place. They may also carry messages about the hopes, circumstances, and traditions of those who built them.

To understand buildings, then, historians must pay attention to their function, structure, and symbolism. Sensitivity to the relationship between these three elements is of critical importance in studying buildings, but it is often useful to examine them separately. Although providing an architectural primer is beyond the scope of this chapter, some suggestions for looking at buildings may prepare one for more detailed study of styles and types.

In considering a building's *function,* one should try to determine what the architect and the builders conceived to be its main purposes, the organizational idea they used to accomplish these purposes, the relationship between spatial arrangements and purposes, the provisions made for movement within the spaces, allowances for adaptation in the event that the building's purposes changed, and the sensitivity of the architect to the personal and performance needs of the people for whose use the building was intended.

Regarding the *structure* itself, one should look for signs of originality and imagination in its design, creative use of materials, appropriateness to the site and surroundings, evidence of concern for proportion (the relations of the parts to each other and to the whole), scale (the proportions as they relate to people), balance (symmetrical or asymmetrical), rhythm (repeated elements giving order), unity (indications that the building is a whole), and character (the distinctive blend of features).

Sometimes one finds buildings that exhibit few or none of the design qualities traditionally regarded as particularly desirable, such as those listed. More often than not this lack results from the architect's or builder's ineptitude, but be aware that some contemporary architects have consciously sought to reject the traditional and to display instead permissiveness, chaos, ambiguity, wit, and whimsy. For them, the character of a building can be defined as well by these qualities as by the traditional ones.

Finding *symbolism* in a building is trickier than identifying either its functions or its structural design features. It is tempting to see symbolism where none exists, and it is probably incorrect more often than not to assert that a given piece of architecture represents "the spirit of the age." More accurately, it represents the spirit of the architect, who may or may not have been in touch with the spirit of the age, assuming that one existed. For example, postmodern architecture of the late 1960s and 1970s, the kind referred to in the previous paragraph, may reflect the frenzy, restlessness, and disillusionment with reason that is thought to have characterized these years. But maybe architects sensed this mood more keenly than others, and therefore their work is not really representative or symbolic. The same could be said of the work of great architects like Louis Sullivan and Frank Lloyd Wright; perhaps their creations are notable because they were out of step with their age, not because they reflected the values and spirit of the times.

9.5   As this industrial scene in Ensley, Alabama, shows, rural remnants survived for a time in the shadow of sprouting smokestacks. What multiple effects did the advent of industry bring farmers? (Photo courtesy of the Library of Congress.)

In what sense, then, is there symbolism in buildings? Buildings express things unintentionally, and such expressions are worth observing. For example, until around 1970 architects could assume the continuing availability of cheap energy. The energy required to run a skyscraper, with its seasonal climate controls, elevators, and other services, and to bring people to there could be discounted as a cost consideration. The buildings of the cheap energy era symbolize an attitude; those of the new era are likely to reflect new necessities. It is not the spirit of the age, then, but its realities that initiate changes in style. Changes dictated by necessity are worth looking for.

We can look at the Gothic cathedral, a great architectural invention, for another example. It is tempting to regard the Gothic cathedral as symbolic of the spirit of an age, as evidence of the grandeur of devotion and single-minded godliness. The structure was in fact a solution to a very practical problem. The kings and bishops found that if they could ally themselves with the rich burghers by erecting new buildings, they could break the power of the monastic orders and feudal lords. The spirit of later ages that built Gothic cathedrals was probably the spirit of imitation.

The best thing to do, then, is to look for the economic and social realities that are reflected in architecture and to be cautious about drawing inferences about things to be seen symbolically, about something as amorphous as the spirit of the times.

Once one becomes sensitive to the interplay between function, structure, and symbolism, it is natural to turn one's attention to architectural styles and to learn to identify them. Persons who wish to gain some real competence in identification should carry with them one of the guides listed at the end of this chapter. But the use of appropriate terminology is only the first step in preparing the history of a building. Consider the case of a house. It will contain much more than a visual account of its style. The whole facade—foundation, exterior covering material, roof, chimney, windows, doorways—needs to be described; so, too, do attachments, outbuildings, nearby grounds, and walkways. Comparisons with nearby houses are helpful. The descriptions should be accompanied by measurements. If the plans for the structure are available, they should be verified, for actual construction often fails to follow plans. One will want to discover the date of construction, which should appear in the property abstract, ordinarily in the possession of the owner or the mortgage holder. This document should also include details regarding legal transactions involving the house, particularly its ownership. The original plat, possibly available at the city hall or county courthouse, gives dates for the development of an area; shows street, driveway, sewer, and other utility locations; gives a sense of the larger scene in which the house is located; and often contains the building code of the community and the restrictions imposed by the developer. If insurance documents can be traced, they are likely sources of information, and city directories, some that go back many years, provide at least the names (and possibly the occupations) of people who lived in the house at given times. The names enable the researcher to go to federal census reports, now available to 1920, for additional details. Photographs show the house as it appeared before and after adaptations as well as how it was used. Scrapbooks, diaries, and letters, if they can be located, offer clues to the dynamic relationship between the house and those who lived in it.

Pieces of furniture once used in the house may suggest how the house was lived in. Impressions stamped in the underside of porcelain fixtures in bathrooms and kitchens, particularly in older houses, may provide useful dates, but inferences must be drawn from such traces with great care. The dates may apply to remodeling rather than to original construction. Sleuthing in the house might reveal sliding or pocket doors that have been hidden, walls that have been removed, and doors that have been relocated. Careful removal of paint and wallpaper lets one discover layers of interior decorations of the past.

Another way of finding out how the people lived in an old house is to become a backyard archaeologist. The trash pit, long since covered over, may lead to the recovery of traces from another day. Since bottles are the hardiest survivors, medicinal practices and tastes in liquor might be discerned. Flatware is a favorite find because it is so datable. Almost everything found in a trash pit is an ordinary object not likely to have been preserved otherwise.

All of this activity may be very interesting for the historian of a single house, but does it have any usefulness in a universal sense? Potentially, yes, if one studies a number of houses. "For most people in most cultures," cultural geographer Peirce F. Lewis writes, "a house is the single most important and expensive thing they will ever build or buy. Most people avoid building eccentric houses for the same reason they avoid eccentricity in haircuts, clothing, styles, speech patterns, and religion— each is such a basic expression of unspoken cultural values that deviations from accepted standards are taken as evidence of an unstable and untrustworthy personality and invite unfavorable comment from one's neighbors. In short, one's house is more than mere shelter; it is a personal and social testament. Axiomatically, no major changes in domestic house-types will occur in most cultures without basic shifts in the culture itself." For this reason, he argues, studying houses is an excellent way to gain insights into a culture, into diversity between regions of a larger culture, and into the nature of slow but steady change over time.

Inventions can alter the way people live and interact with one another within a community. Memories of the arrival of indoor plumbing, electricity, automobiles, or television are often vivid and revealing. They are well worth seeking out. This reminiscence of one small town's early experience with another vital innovation, the telephone, suggests more than one effect.

Father went down [to] the school house to a meeting, and the next morning he was telling us that they were organizing a telephone company to build a line and put in phones for the farmers. Mother said, "We don't need any!" Father thought we better join as it would cost more if we waited and had to build our own line from the school house up to our place. Now when they were building the line they would build it up to our gate, and we would only have to pay for the line up our long lane. We lived about a quarter of a mile back in the field.

When they started to build our line, they called it the 400 line. I think it was the first farmer-owned built out of town. Our number was 406, and our ring was one short and two longs. The 500 line was built about the same time, and it went out to the folks that lived in and around Section Six. The 600 line went south out of town and ended up in Gilbert. The Gilbert Co-op Grain Company's number was 617.

I can remember when the men started to build the line. All of the neighbors worked. Some of them dug holes and put in the poles. Others rolled out the wire. Mr. Springman fixed a hook on the end of a long slim rod to lift the wire up from the ground to the bracket on the telephone pole. Then the men could pull the wire tight. I thought that was something when he came along lifting up the wire.

A lot of things went on over a country phone. Sometimes there was plenty of "rubbernecks." One winter evening I got bored and asked Mother if I could call Uncle Julius and have him play a few Edison phonograph records so I could hear them over the telephone. I called up and thought I talked to Uncle Julius. He said to hang up and he would ring me back. It would take a little time to set the phonograph up so it would play right into the phone. He got it fixed and played me three or four records. I thanked him and thought I had a lot of fun. A day or so later Mother was telling Uncle Martin what a kick I got when Uncle Julius played the records for me over the phone. Then Uncle Martin laughed and said, "That was me that played the records." Uncle Martin and Mother thought they had a good joke on me. To make matters worse I learned some time later that four or five other folks heard me make the call and listened in on music too.

Source: Guy Johnson, "The Boy on Kiegley's Creek," unpublished manuscript in the possession of the authors.

Pursuing this idea, historians of the environs nearby will discover that the amount and use of space within houses can tell us about the activities carried out there, the degree of individual privacy, the relative standing of children and adults or of males and females, and the concern for amenities of the people who lived in them. Here are clues to the place and roles of women in earlier times.

This chapter has attempted to show that the cultural landscape is filled with material evidence from the past. The task for the historian is to see it and then use it to understand and reconstruct events and ideas of earlier times. The suggestions given here are starting points.

NOTES AND FURTHER READING

Works quoted or cited in this chapter are: Peirce F. Lewis, "The Geography of Old Houses," *Earth and Mineral Sciences* 39 (1970): 33–37; Robert and Mimi Melnick, *Manhole Covers of Los Angeles* (Los Angeles: Dawson's Book Shop, 1974).

John J. G. Blumenson, *Identifying American Architecture: A Pictorial Guide to Styles and Terms, 1600–1945* (Nashville: American Association for State and Local History, 2nd ed., rev., 1981) is particularly helpful to persons who deal specifically with individual buildings or groups of buildings in their research, for it contains a pictorial glossary of terms they will want to use in building descriptions. Another useful book is Carole Rifkind's *A Field Guide to American Architecture* (New York: New American Library, 1980). A third is John Poppeliers, S. Allen Chambers, and Nancy B. Schwartz, *What Style Is It?* (Washington, DC: Preservation Press, 1983; reprint ed., New York: J. Wiley, 1995).

General and interpretive works on the cultural landscape, many of which are well illustrated, include: Peter Blake, *God's Own Junkyard: The Planned Deterioration of America's Landscape* (New York: Holt, Rinehart and Winston, 1964) written, the author says, not in anger but in fury; Grady Clay, *Close-Up: How to Read the American City* (New York: Praeger, 1973) and *Real Places: An Unconventional Guide to America's Generic Landscape* (Chicago: University of Chicago Press, 1994); Gerald Danzer, *Public Places: Exploring Their History* (Nashville: American Association for State and Local History, 1987; reprint ed., AltaMira Press, 1997); Mira Engler, "Drive-Thru History: Theme Towns in Iowa," *Landscape* 32, no. 1 (1993): 8–18; Fran P. Hosken, *The Language of Cities* (New York: Macmillan, 1968); Lawrence Halprin, *Cities* (Cambridge, MA: MIT Press, rev. ed., 1972); John Brinckerhoff Jackson, *American Space* (New York: Norton, 1972); Peirce F. Lewis, "Axioms of the Landscape: Some Guides to the American Scene," *Journal of Architectural Education* 30 (September 1976): 6–9; Penelope Lively, *The Presence of the Past: An Introduction to Landscape History* (London: William Collins, 1976); Kevin Lynch, *What Time Is This Place?* (Cambridge, MA: MIT Press, 1972); John Stilgoe, *Borderland: Origins of the American Suburb, 1820–1939* (New Haven: Yale University Press, 1988); Christopher Tunnard and Boris Pushkarev, *Man-Made America: Chaos or Control* (New Haven: Yale University Press, 1963); Mary T. Watts, *Reading the Landscape of America* (New York: Macmillan, rev. ed., 1975); Richard Saul Wurman, *Making the City Observable* (Cambridge, MA: MIT Press, 1971); Ervin H. Zube, ed., *Landscapes: Selected Writings of J. B. Jackson* (Amherst: University of Massachusetts Press, 1970); Paul Zucker, *Town and Square from the Agora to the Village Green* (Cambridge, MA: MIT Press, 1970). Journals include *Landscape,* published three times a year, and *Landscape Architecture,* a bi-monthly publication of the American Society of Landscape Architects.

On shopping centers and malls, see Neil Harris, "American Space: Spaced-Out at the Shopping Center," *New Republic,* December 13, 1975, pp. 23–26; William Severini Kowinski, "The Malling of America," *New Times,* May 1, 1978, pp. 30–55; Louis G. Redstone, *New Dimensions in Shopping Centers and Stores* (New York: McGraw-Hill, 1973), a comprehensive work intended for architects, designers, and developers; and Francesca Turchiano, "The [Un]malling of America" *American Demographics* 12 (April 1990): 36–39. Cultural implications of fast-food restaurants are treated in Marshall Fishwick, ed., *Ronald Revisited: The World of Ronald McDonald* (Bowling Green, OH: Bowling Green University Popular Press, 1983); and Max Boas and Steve Chain touch on landscape considerations in *Big Mac: The Unauthorized Story of McDonald's* (New York: Mentor, 1977); also see Paul Hirshorn and Steven Izenour, *White Towers* (Cambridge, MA: MIT Press, 1979).

Streets and their adornments are the subject of Robert I. Alotta, *Street Names of Philadelphia* (Philadelphia: Temple University Press, 1975); Frederick Fried and Edmund Gillon, *New York Civic Sculpture* (New York: Dover, 1976); James Goode, *The Outdoor Sculpture of Washington, D.C.* (Washington, DC: Smithsonian Institution Press, 1974); Robert Grist and Glenn Herbert, "Measuring Billboard Blight," *Landscape Architecture* 77 (May/June 1987): 100–102; Carole Rifkind, *Main Street: The Face of Urban America* (New York: Harper and Row, 1977); and Bernard Rudofsky, *Streets for People: A Primer for Americans* (Garden City, NY: Doubleday, 1969).

Specific features of the cultural landscape are considered in: T. Allen Comp, *Bridge Truss Types: A Guide to Dating and Identifying,* Technical Leaflet no. 95 (Nashville: American Association for State and Local History, 1977); Ronald E. Butchart, *Local Schools: Exploring Their History* (Nashville: American Association for State and Local History, 1986); Wayne Craven, *Sculpture in America* (New York: Crowell, 1968); H. Roger Grant and Charles W. Bohi, *The Country Railroad Station in America* (Boulder, CO: Pruett, 1978), and "The Country Railroad Station as Corporate Logo," *Pioneer America* 11 (August 1979): 117–29; Sara Pressey Noreen, *Public Street Illumination in Washington, D.C.: An Illustrated History* (Washington, DC: George Washington University, 1975); Rene Smeets, *Signs, Symbols and Ornaments* (New York: Van Nostrand Reinhold, 1975), Susan and Michael Southworth, *Ornamental Iron-work: An Illustrated Guide to Its Design, History and Use in American Architecture* (Boston: David R. Godine, 1978); Robert Sommer, *The Mind's Eye: Imagery in Everyday Life* (New York: Delacorte, 1978) offers useful ideas for improving one's sensitivity to the material environment; James P. Wind, *Places of Worship: Exploring Their History* (Nashville: American Association for State and Local History, 1990; reprint ed., AltaMira Press, 1997); Wilbur Zelinsky, "Where Every Town Is Above Average: Welcoming Signs along America's Highways," *Landscape* 30, no. 1 (1988): 1–10, and "On the Superabundance of Signs in Our Landscape: Selections from a Slide Lecture," *Landscape* 31, no. 3 (1992): 30–38.

On grave markers, see: Roberta Halporn, *Lessons from the Dead: The Graveyard as a Classroom for the Study of the Life Cycle* (Brooklyn: Highly Specialized Promotions, 1979); Leonard Huber, *New Orleans Architecture: The Cemeteries* (Gretna, LA: Pelican, 1974), contains a useful bibliography; Mary-Ellen Jones, *Photographing Tombstones: Equipment Techniques,* Technical Leaflet no. 92 (Nashville: American Association for

State and Local History, 1977); John J. Newman, *Cemetery Transcribing: Preparations and Procedures,* Technical Leaflet no. 9 (Nashville: American Association for State and Local History, 1971); Jack G. Voller, "The Textuality of Death: Notes on the Reading of Cemeteries," *Journal of American Culture* 14 (winter 1991); David Weitzman, "Resting Places," the best chapter in *Underfoot: An Everyday Guide to Exploring the American Past* (New York: Scribner's, 1976).

Books and articles intended to foster understanding of architecture include: R. W. Brunskill, *Illustrated Handbook of Vernacular Architecture* (New York: Universe, 1971); William Caudill, William M. Pena, and Paul Kennon, *Architecture and You: How to Experience and Enjoy Buildings* (New York: Watson-Guptill, 1978); Carl W. Condit, "Technology and Symbol in Architecture," *Humanities in Society* 1, no. 3 (1978): 203–19; Gerald A. Danzer, "Buildings as Sources: Architecture and the Social Studies," *High School Journal* 57, no. 5 (1974): 204–13; Andrea Oppenheimer Dean, "The Architect and Society," *Architecture* 78 (July 1989): 50–53; David R. Goldfield, "Living History: The Physical City as Artifact and Teaching Tool," *History Teacher* 8, no. 4 (1975): 535–56; and Robert T. Packard and Balthazar Korab, *Encyclopedia of American Architecture* (New York: McGraw-Hill, 1995); Beverly Russell, *Architecture and Design, 1970–1990: New Ideas in America* (New York: Henry N. Abrams, Inc., 1989).

On architectural styles, see the volumes by John J. G. Blumenson, Carol Rifkind, and John Poppeliers et al. cited above. Also Dell Upton and John Michael Vlatch, eds., *Common Places: Readings in American Vernacular Architecture* (Athens: University of Georgia Press, 1986); and Marcus Whitten, *American Architecture since 1780: A Guide to Styles* (Cambridge, MA: MIT Press, 1969).

The better commentaries on American architecture include: Wayne Andrews, *Architecture, Ambition and Americans* (New York: Harper, 1947) and *Architecture in America: A Photographic History from the Colonial Period to the Present* (New York: Atheneum, 1980); Carl W. Condit, *American Building: Materials and Techniques from First Colonial Settlements to the Present* (Chicago: University of Chicago Press, 1969) and *American Building Art: The Nineteenth Century* (New York: Oxford University Press, 1960); James Marston Fitch, *American Building:* vol. 1, *The Historical Forces That Shaped It* (Boston: Houghton Mifflin, 2nd ed., 1966), and *American Building:* vol. 2, *The Environmental Forces That Shaped It* (Boston: Houghton Mifflin, 2nd ed., 1976); Siegfried Giedion, *Space, Time and Architecture: The Growth of a New Tradition* (Cambridge, MA: Harvard University Press, 3rd ed., 1954); Alan Gowans, *Images of American Living: Four Centuries of Architecture and Furniture as Cultural Expression* (Philadelphia: Lippincott, 1964); and *Styles and Types of North American Architecture: Social Function and Cultural Expression* (New York: Icon Editions, 1992); Henry Russell Hitchcock, *Architecture: Nineteenth and Twentieth Centuries* (New York: Penguin, 1977); Vincent Scully, *American Architecture and Urbanism* (New York: Praeger, 1969); and G. E. Kidder Smith, *The Architecture of the United States: An Illustrated Guide to Notable Buildings,* 3 vols. (Garden City, NY: Doubleday, 1981): vol. 1, *New England and the Mid-Atlantic States;* vol. 2, *The South and the Midwest;* vol. 3, *The Plains States and the Far West.*

On modern architecture, see John Peter, *An Oral History of Modern Architecture: Interviews with the Greatest Architects of the Twentieth Century* (New York: Henry N. Abrams, Inc., 1994). On postmodern architecture: Christopher Mead, ed., *The Architecture of Robert Venturi* (Albuquerque: University of New Mexico Press, 1989); C. Ray Smith, *Supermannerism: New Attitudes in Post-Modern Architecture* (New York: Dutton, 1977);

and Robert Venturi, *Complexity and Contradiction in Architecture* (New York: Museum of Modern Art, 1977) and *Learning from Las Vegas* (Cambridge, MA: MIT Press, 1977). Psychological aspects of architecture are treated in Robert Sommer, *Tight Spaces: Hard Architecture and How to Humanize It* (Englewood Cliffs, NJ: Prentice-Hall, 1974).

Analytical works on house forms are: Lucius F. and Linda V. Ellsworth, "House Reading: How to Study Historic Houses as Symbols of Society," *History News* 35, no. 5 (May 1980): 9–13; Henry Glassie, *Folk Housing in Middle Virginia* (Knoxville: University of Tennessee Press, 1975), and "Eighteenth-Century Cultural Process in Delaware Valley Folk Building," *Winterthur Portfolio* 7 (1972): 29–57; John Fraser Hart, *The Look of the Land* (Englewood Cliffs, NJ: Prentice-Hall, 1975) examines houses in rural environments; D. Geoffrey Hayward, "Home as an Environmental and Psychological Concept," *Landscape* 20 (October 1975): 2–9, offers a five-step method for analyzing American homes; Fred Kniffen, "Folk Housing: Key to Diffusion," *Annals of the Association of American Geographers* 55 (1965): 549–77; Amos Rapoport, *House Form and Culture* (Englewood Cliffs, NJ: Prentice-Hall, 1969); John E. Rickert, "House Facades of the Northeastern United States: A Tool of Geographic Analysis," *Annals, Association of American Geographers* 57 (1967): 211–38.

Barbara J. Howe, Dolores A. Fleming, Emory L. Kemp, and Ruth Ann Overbeck, *Houses and Homes* (Nashville: American Association for State and Local History, 1987; reprint ed., AltaMira Press, 1997) offers a good starting point for doing the history of a house. Also on houses are: Linda Ellsworth, *The History of a House and How to Trace It,* Technical Leaflet no. 89 (Nashville: American Association for State and Local History, 1976); Ettore Camesasca ed., *History of the House* (New York: Putnam's, 1971), a large and attractive book; Jan Cohn, *The Palace or the Poorhouse: The American House as a Cultural Symbol* (East Lansing: Michigan State University Press, 1979); David P. Handlin, *The American Home: Architecture and Society, 1815–1915* (Boston: Little, Brown, 1979); Stephen Gardiner, *The Evolution of the House* (New York: Macmillan, 1974). On house interiors: William Seale, *The Tasteful Interlude: American Interiors through the Camera's Eye* (Nashville: American Association for State and Local History, 2nd. ed., rev., 1981) and *Recreating the Historic House Interior* (Nashville: American Association for State and Local History, 1979); and Gwendolyn Wright, *Building the Dream: A Social History of Housing in America* (New York: Pantheon, 1981).

Three works on the urban landscape that suggest new directions for historical research are: Devereaux Bowly, Jr., *The Poorhouse: Subsidized Housing in Chicago, 1895–1976* (Carbondale: Southern Illinois University Press, 1978); Louis Cain, *Sanitation Strategy for a Lakefront Metropolis* (DeKalb: Northern Illinois University Press, 1978); and Ann Durkin Keating, *Invisible Networks: Exploring the History of Local Utilities and Public Works* (Malabar, FL: Krieger Publishing Company, 1994).

Four works with interpretation as their theme are: William T. Alderson and Shirley Payne Low, *Interpretation of Historic Sites* (Nashville: American Association for State an Local History, 1976); Paul L. Benedict, *Historic Site Interpretation: The Student Field Trip,* Technical Leaflet no. 19 (Nashville: American Association for State and Local History, 1971); Shirley Payne Low, *Historic Site Interpretation: The Human Approach,* Technical Leaflet no. 32 (Nashville: American Association for State and Local History, 1965); and Freeman J. Tilden, *Interpreting Our Heritage* (Chapel Hill: University of North Carolina Press, 1967), reflects a National Park Service point of view.

On archaeology and its variations: John L. Cotter, "Above-Ground Archaeology," *American Quarterly* 27, no. 3 (August 1974): 266–80; James Deetz, *Invitation to Archaeology*

(Garden City, NY: Natural History Press, 1967); Jean C. Harrington, *Archaeology and the Historical Society* (Nashville: American Association for State and Local History, 1965); Ivor Noel Hume, *Historic Archaeology: A Comprehensive Guide for Both Amateurs and Professionals to the Techniques and Methods of Excavating Historical Sites* (New York: Knopf, 1969); and "Archaeology: Handmaiden to History," *North Carolina Historical Review* 41 (1964): 215–25; and Thomas J. Schlereth, "Above-Ground Archaeology: Discovering a Community's History through Local Artifacts," in *Local History Today,* edited by Thomas Krasean (Indianapolis: Indiana Historical Society, 1979), 53–83; this excellent essay appears in revised form as chapter 9 in Schlereth's *Artifacts and the American Past* (Nashville: American Association for State and Local History, 1980), pp. 184–203.

10

Preserving Material Traces

"All at once heritage is everywhere," writes historian David Lowenthal. "It is the chief focus of patriotism and a prime lure of tourism. One can barely move without bumping into a heritage site. . . . [T]he whole world is lauding—or lamenting—some past, be it fact or fiction."

What accounts for this "rash of backward-looking concern?" Why is heritage such a "growth industry"? Because, according to Lowenthal, much that we inherit is indeed a "goodly heritage," for it "links us with ancestors and offspring, bonds neighbors and patriots, certifies identity, roots us in time-honored ways." But "heritage is also oppressive, defeatist, decadent. . . . Debasing the 'true' past for greedy or chauvinist ends, heritage is accused of undermining historical truth with twisted myth."

Observations like these indicate the need for wisdom and care in preserving the material traces that help sustain the "goodly heritage" of a locale, a region, a state, and the nation. Moreover, they suggest that historians of the nearby past have a role to play in cultivating the wisdom and care necessary in the cause known as historic preservation. Their involvement is important even if they serve mainly in consultative or supporting roles, working with preservation experts whose daily tasks connect them with an impressive network of persons and organizations that provide guidance, examples, ideas, and assistance.

Historic preservation has experienced many changes in the past several decades—changes in definition, mission, scope, and practice. Organizations and institutions have evolved, laws have been amended and new ones enacted, and publications on preservation have poured forth. Reflected in all these changes has been the development of impressive grassroots preservation efforts. Volunteers across the nation, working with local government officials and state and federal agencies, can claim significant accomplishments in small communities and large.

The intent of this chapter is to consider the purposes and benefits of historic preservation, review the background to contemporary preservation movements, survey challenges preservationists face, and identify sources of further information for practitioners in preservation causes. Historians of the nearby past who work with specialists in historic preservation and wish to stay current with changes in the field are its primary audience, along with students interested in preservation. Although its emphasis is on the preservation of structures and districts regarded as having historic value, implicit throughout is the understanding that principles and problems applicable there apply also to the preservation of landmarks, battlefields, rivers, and archaeological and other sites historic in character. (Preservation of oral and visual documents, artifacts, and the landscape has been treated in previous chapters.)

PURPOSES AND BENEFITS

Historic preservation, as defined in the Secretary of the Interior's Standards for the Treatment of Historic Properties (1995), "is the act or process of applying measures necessary to sustain the existing form, integrity, and materials of an historic property." A definition provided by the National Park Service's Cultural Resources Programs places preservation in a larger context, calling it "a process of steps designed to protect significant cultural resources for the benefit of future generations." Its purpose is "to make sure people can see, visit, work, or live in a real historic place"—in other words, to give people a sense of "what it was like to have been there." Seeing, touching, and moving about in the remains of the past permit us to feel their scale, their texture, their uses of space and distance, and their attitude toward time and place. Meeting the past in a material way sometimes stirs feelings of pride, patriotism, or admiration. Sometimes it gives insights into such things as work, hardship, illness, eating habits, and forms of education, recreation, and entertainment in other times and places.

But are there practical arguments for preservation, tangible benefits to be gained from it? There are indeed. First, preservation makes good economic sense, especially when it is less costly than building anew. Site clearance and excavation are unnecessary, and construction time and expense and cost of materials may be reduced. Streets and utility lines are already in place, and landscaping costs are likely to be lower than they would be for new structures. Preservation enhances property values and helps restrain urban sprawl, thus serving the interests of whole communities. Not least, preservation can contribute substantially to tourism, bringing in outside dollars.

Indeed, tourism based on preservation is the lifeblood of many communities. Almost every state is dotted with sites celebrating heritage in one way or another. In Iowa, for example, where tourism is the state's third leading industry (after agriculture and manufacturing), Mira Engler has identified ten ethnic heritage villages, twenty-three historical villages or museums, seven country or antique centers, and two towns with artifacts collections. These tourist attractions, she says, represent the four faces of the past Iowans have in common: Old World, Frontier America, Old Town, and Agrarian America. Not included in Engler's count are the many county museums and the museum and the historic sites maintained by the State Historical Society and the Department of Natural Resources, all of them also designed to attract tourists.

A second benefit of preservation is aesthetic. Stylish old buildings, or even unstylish ones with distinctive character, are marks of beauty, stability, and continuity on the cultural landscape, especially as they stand in contrast to the structures likely to replace them after demolition. They diversify the environment. Third, preserved buildings offer specific educational benefits: The structures themselves and their contents are usually worthy subjects for study, and it is natural to use them as centers for historical exhibits and for the broader study of history, architecture, and material culture. Fourth, preservation contributes to community spirit and pride when people work together to restore a single building as a centerpiece in their community or, better, when individuals and families restore an entire neighborhood. Fifth, preservation can also be used to approach social problems in intelligent ways. The high social and economic cost of low-rent, high-rise public housing has increased the attractiveness of preserving, restoring, and putting to use existing structures for subsidized housing. In some cities, converting warehouses that have outlasted their purposes into apartments and condominiums has attracted residents back to downtown

10.1 One Midwestern community tried to "save" its downtown by making it look like a suburban shopping center, but the arcade wrecked the facades of some grand old buildings. (Photo courtesy of the Marty family collection and copyright © Myron Marty.)

areas. Given all these benefits, historic preservation offers many opportunities for learning experiences for both children and adults.

If the cultural values of historic preservation are so obvious and significant, how is it possible to explain the demolition of so many of the buildings that have been listed on the National Register of Historic Places and more that might have been so listed? That landmarks have regularly been turned into rubble and hauled away? Has "progress at any price" been the prevailing American outlook? Are the arguments for preservation so weak, the benefits so trifling, that they fail to persuade? Or are the people who must be convinced simply dense, indifferent, and insensitive? Fortunately, through education and hard work, preservationists have achieved notable success in building sentiment for preservation and stirring to action citizens in communities across the nation.

HISTORICAL BACKGROUND OF PRESERVATION LAWS

The history of the most significant laws affecting the preservation of historic places shows an evolving commitment to making preservation possible and successful. The first act of Congress having to do with historic preservation, the Antiquities Act of 1906, gave the president power to designate nationally significant historic resources and authorized cabinet members to grant permits for archaeological work; the actions of the president and cabinet members could apply only to lands belonging to the United States. Ten years later, the National Park Service Act created the Park Service and gave it authority to administer historic sites as well as scenic parks.

In 1935, with the enactment of the Historic Sites Act, a national policy was established for preserving sites, buildings, and objects of national significance, regardless of ownership. The law authorized the secretary of the interior to identify historic buildings and sites by conducting surveys, to acquire some of them, and to administer the ones acquired while aiding in the preservation of others through cooperative agreements. The act also created the National Historic Landmarks Program.

In 1966, a Conference of Mayors report, *With Heritage So Rich,* indicated a growing interest in preservation and pointed to the need for a more comprehensive, coordinated national preservation program focusing on the cultural environment as a whole rather than on its outstanding parts. Four new laws broadened and strengthened the federal role in historic preservation. The Department of Transportation Act and the Federal Highway Act declared it a national policy of making special efforts to preserve the natural beauty of the countryside. The Demonstration Cities and Metropolitan Development Act relaxed restrictions that had previously prevented the use of urban renewal funds for historic preservation, and it authorized new historic preservation programs in urban areas.

The most important of the four 1966 laws was the National Historic Preservation Act. This act considerably strengthened the 1935 legislation by calling for the creation of the National Register of Historic Places to foster preservation of districts, sites, buildings, structures, and objects significant in American history, and it afforded limited protection for properties listed in the Register by requiring that federal agencies take them into consideration in the evaluation of federally funded, licensed, or permitted projects. It also inaugurated a matching grants-in-aid program to states and the National Trust for Historic Preservation (a federally chartered private organization) and established an Advisory Council on Historic Preservation to review federal actions related to preservation and to advise the president and Congress on these matters. The National Environmental Policy Act of 1969 enlarged the interpretation of impact to include the man-made environment. Under this act, federal agencies are required to evaluate and explain publicly the impact of their projects on both natural and cultural resources and to make every effort to eliminate or mitigate damaging effects.

Executive Order No. 11593 ("Protection and Enhancement of the Cultural Environment") issued by the president on May 13, 1971, and codified by Congress in 1980, explicitly requires every federal agency to make an inventory of historic properties in their custody, to nominate them to the National Register of Historic Places, and to adopt measures to ensure their preservation. Because some federal agencies have been slow to comply, citizens should be alert for violations.

For many years, all preservation activities were centered in the National Park Service in the Department of the Interior. To cope with the demands on the Park Service brought by the growing size and scope of preservation efforts, the Advisory Council on Historic Preservation was recently made an independent agency of the executive branch, and in 1978 the National Register of Historic Places and three other agencies sharing responsibility for preservation were pulled together in the Heritage Conservation and Recreation Service (HCRS), still in the Department of the Interior. In 1981 the HCRS was abolished, and its programs were returned to the National Park Service, where several units are now responsible for a wide variety of preservation activities and services.

CHALLENGES

Mechanisms for historic preservation, we can see, are in place, so it is fair to ask why preservationists sometimes falter in their efforts—why, so to speak, they run into brick walls. Sometimes the many challenges encountered in saving and restoring old structures are too formidable. It cannot be done without a lot of hard work and long hours. Further, if their goal is to place the structures on the National Register of Historic Places, they may find the nomination processes daunting in their complexity.

Another challenge involves attempts to balance cultural benefits with economic costs. Although in many instances both the economic and cultural benefits make a strong case for preservation, what happens when cost-benefit analyses show that demolishing a structure, even a treasured one, is less costly than replacing it with a new one? If taxpayer dollars are involved, as they sometimes are, even in preserving privately owned structures, how are the expenditures justified?

On the other hand, what are the consequences when the economic benefits of preserving a historic district or building prove to be too great? Can the character of a structure be maintained when it attracts so many tourists that normal operations become difficult? In most communities and with most structures this is not a problem, but in others it clearly is. Frank Lloyd Wright's Taliesin in Spring Green, Wisconsin, and Taliesin West in Scottsdale, Arizona, provide examples. These sites attract hundreds of thousands of visitors annually, and preserving them depends in large part on the fees paid by the visitors. At both sites, however, working professionals and apprentices in the resident architectural firm and school of architecture must cope with the distractions caused by the visitors. Many tourists attracted to the Frank Lloyd Wright Home and Studio in Oak Park, Illinois, want also to see the many privately owned prairie-style homes that Wright designed in that Chicago suburb. During parts of each year the owners of these homes and their neighbors encounter automobile and pedestrian traffic that many of them consider a nuisance, and sometimes their private property is invaded.

The preservation of neighborhoods, particularly in urban areas, is also problematical at times. When blocks of row houses become the target of middle-class preservers—sometimes styled "urban frontiersmen" engaged in "gentrification"—property values rise so much and so rapidly that the resident population is displaced. By the time this happens the early residents of the area are typically long gone, their places having been taken successively by poorer and poorer residents. What is to become of such persons when a neighborhood undergoes renewal? How can the charge of elitism be addressed in situations that displace people?

Then, too, how are decisions made regarding what should be preserved? Structures that were at one time ordinary quickly become extraordinary when they are preserved. Their value rises, they attract attention, and imitators appear. When the extraordinary, the distinctive structure in a community, is preserved it does not take long for it to be idealized, to become regarded as typical and representational when in fact it is not. The Campbell House and Eugene Field House in St. Louis are examples. Still, choices must be made. Just as we cannot remember everything we have ever learned, so a society cannot retain everything it has ever built or made. The whole landscape cannot be locked in time.

Also problematical is the realization that much so-called historic preservation is merely preservation. Individuals who are romantic, sentimental, or nostalgic pay little heed to the historic—that is, to the significant—when they preserve buildings. If heritage continues to be a growth industry, some nonhistoric creations of the preservation movement are likely to be its most important products. Preserving old structures may almost always be desirable, but *historic* preservation should be what the designation implies.

ALLIES AND RESOURCES

Preservation movements quite naturally attract men and women with strong commitments to the idea and promise of preservation. Perhaps they see the recycling of buildings as environmentally sound. Perhaps they regard preservation as a way of resisting urban sprawl. Perhaps they appreciate such things as the wood and masonry found in old structures. Whatever the inspiration for their commitments, they almost always discover that preservation requires some measure of compromise. But they also discover that the resources for addressing the issues they face and the network of alliances at their disposal bring success within their reach. This is true not only for those engaged in the museum/tourism end of preservation, but also of efforts to preserve historic, privately owned properties. In the paragraphs that follow, we provide mailing and Web site addresses for sources of information.

For beginners and veterans alike, considerable assistance in doing preservation is available. Much of it is provided through the Certified Local Government (CLG) Program created by amendments in 1982 to the National Historic Preservation Act. This program, initiated and coordinated by the National Park Service, is designed to stimulate and support preservation at the local level. Each state structures the program to conform with state-enabling legislation and most State Historic Preservation Offices provide CLG assistance. Typically, designated persons work directly with preservationists at the local level, providing essential technical and other assistance. The starting point in most cases should therefore be the State Historic Preservation Office, although one can go directly to the national office for information: Certified Local Government Program, Heritage Preservation Services, National Park Service, 1849 C Street, N.W., NC330, Washington, DC 20240; <www2.cr.nps.gov/clg>. From this agency or from the State Historic Preservation Offices one can receive "Local Preservation Briefs."

In addition, information on a wide variety of preservation concerns is available through *Cultural Resources Management,* "a professional magazine published by the National Park Service to promote and maintain high standards for preserving and managing cultural resources." Now in its twenty-third year, *CRM* is accessible on-line at <www.cr.nps.gov/crm>; back issues and a searchable database are included at this site.

An indispensable source of information for preservationists is *Preservation: The Magazine of the National Trust for Historic Preservation.* Published bimonthly, it contains news, features, editorials on preservation issues, advertisements for supplies and historic properties, and more. The current volume is the fifty-second (although the name has changed on occasion), making it a good resource for understanding changes in preservation through the years. Information is available from the National Trust for Historic Preservation, 1785 Massachusetts Avenue, N.W. Washington, DC 20306; <www.nthp.org>. Other publications

Research in the National Archives helped Michael Musick find a historical house to buy. "I always wanted to live in an old home," he explained, "particularly one associated with the Civil War." He visited Bolivar, West Virginia, a small community adjacent to Harpers Ferry, which had served as the background for an 1862 Mathew Brady Civil War photograph he had found in the archives. The buildings shown in the picture that were still standing included the circled house. Neighbors gave him the name of the owner.

Armed with this evidence, Musick returned to the archives to consult maps and Civil War claim files. He found that the house's original owner had petitioned for government compensation, attaching a receipt from a colonel acknowledging that Union soldiers had occupied the house during the war and used the picket fence around the house for firewood. Census records for 1850 through 1900 provided further information about owners and tenants of the house. After he had verified his discovery and learned more, Musick was able to buy and restore the house of which he had dreamed.

10.2   The Twenty-second New York State Militia, Bolivar, West Virginia, 1862, by Mathew Brady. (Photo courtesy of the National Archives and Records Administration.)

10.3 The historic house that Michael Musick bought for restoration in Bolivar, West Virginia, after tracing it through National Archives records and a Mathew Brady Civil War photograph. (Photo courtesy of and copyright © Michael Musick.)

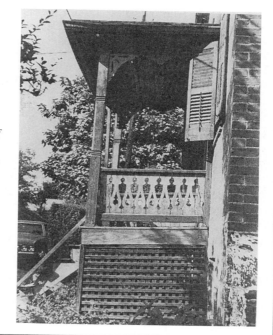

10.4 A prerestoration detail of the well-preserved decorative woodwork on the Musick house. (Photo courtesy of the National Archives and Records Administration.)

of the National Trust are listed in the "Notes and Further Reading" section of this chapter. Some states, incidentally, have counterpart organizations that are affiliated in varying degrees with the National Trust.

See also *The Alliance Review,* the newsletter of the National Alliance of Preservation Commissions, University of Georgia, School of Environmental Design, 609 Caldwell Hall, Athens, GA 30602. Again, some states have counterpart alliances.

Here are some specific issues preservationists encounter, along with sources of information for addressing them (and bear in mind that most sources provide information applicable to many issues, not only those under which their addresses appear):

What to Do with a Building that Calls for Preservation

It is obvious that "preserving" a historic property is not a simple matter. The Secretary of the Interior's Standards for the Treatment of Historic Properties (1995) identifies four distinct but interrelated approaches for treatment of such properties:

> *Preservation* focuses on the maintenance and repair of existing historic materials and retention of a property's form as it has evolved over time (Protection and Stabilization have now been consolidated under this treatment.) *Rehabilitation* acknowledges the need to alter or add to a historic property to meet continuing or changing uses while retaining the property's historic character. *Restoration* depicts a property at a particular period of time in its history, while removing evidence of other periods. *Reconstruction* recreates vanished or non-surviving portions of a property for interpretive purposes.

The statement by the Secretary also provides guidance for choosing an appropriate treatment, outlines standards for each of the treatments, and explains when the standards are mandatory.

Within each of the approaches there are questions. For example: To which point in its history should the property be restored, if restoration is the approach taken? Is restoration worthwhile if only the facade can be returned to its original appearance? If it is restored, who will be responsible for maintaining the property? What if it is necessary to relocate the property? Can the property be adapted for new uses? Answers to these questions and many more can be found through the Heritage Preservation Services, a unit in the National Park Service's National Center for Cultural Resource Stewardship and Partnership Programs, 1849 C Street, N.W., Washington, DC 20240; <www.cr.nps.gov/whatwedo.htm#HPS>.

Buildings and Neighborhoods

Preservationism was once conceived almost entirely as the saving of isolated, representative, or unique structures. House museums in urban areas show consequences that are in many instances unavoidable. Yet, does it not make sense to avoid such consequences where possible by saving entire districts rather than isolated buildings? An important source of information, in addition to those cited above, is the National Trust for Historic Preservation's "Main Street Program," which focuses on the revitalization of historic or traditional commercial areas in towns with populations under 50,000 by building on their inherent assets, including their architecture. (It must be noted that Main Street has recently begun programs in larger cities.) The program shows preservationists how to learn from the experiences of others to whom they might turn for advice, how they can acquire the skills and expertise necessary to revitalize their communities, and where they can find accurate, up-to-date information relevant to their downtowns. Contact the National Main Street Center of the National Trust for Historic Preservation, 1785 Massachusetts Avenue, N.W., Washington, DC 20036; <www.mainst.org>.

Technical Demands

Preservation is an exciting but demanding business. Some historic buildings have been maintained very well through the years, and continuing their preservation may be relatively easy. However, anyone who has worked with old buildings that have not been maintained knows how difficult it is to cope with deterioration of inside and outside walls, foundations, floors, ceilings, and roofs; to know how to combat crumbling masonry, peeling paint, falling plaster, and broken windows; to find ways of conserving energy or of remedying plumbing and electrical deficiencies—to say nothing of solving landscaping and parking problems.

Technical guidance is provided by the National Register of Historic Places through such publications as the "National Register Bulletins" (more than twenty-five in number, most of them on-line at <www.cr.nps.gov/nr/nrpubs.html>). For additional practical assistance the place to turn is the Heritage Preservation Services of the National Park Service's National Center for Cultural Resource Stewardship and Partnership Programs, 1849 C Street, N.W., Washington, DC 20240; <www.cr.nps.gov/whatwedo.htm#HPS>. Particularly valuable are the "Preservation Briefs" (forty-two presently), available on-line at <www2.cr.nps.gov/tps_1.htm#briefs>.

Money

Acquisition of properties to be preserved can be expensive for both individuals and communities. Repairing or restoring them and then maintaining them is also costly. If private investors provide the money, how are the public interests protected? If nonprofit organizations are involved, how can they raise enough money through donations to be effective? What government funds are available, how can they be obtained, and how should they be used? How can various tax incentives be used? With guidance provided by publications of the National Trust for Historic Preservation and other organizations, individuals and communities are often able to demonstrate convincingly the economic benefits of preservation, but doing so requires careful documentation.

Federal laws as well as laws in states and many communities provide incentives for preservation. For example, following the Tax Reform Act of 1976, tax laws at the federal level became more favorable to preservation than they had been previously. Although they have been revised several times since then, they continue to be designed to foster private-sector rehabilitation of historic buildings and promote economic revitalization.

The Federal Historic Preservation Tax Incentives program is administered through a partnership among the National Park Service, the Internal Revenue Service, and State Historic Preservation officers. The incentives are available for buildings that are National Historic Landmarks, that are listed in the National Register, and that contribute to National Register Historic Districts and certain local historic districts. The properties must be income producing and must be rehabilitated according to standards set by the Secretary of the Interior.

The entire tax incentive picture is complicated, and local preservationists should be equipped with the latest information about it. To obtain such information, contact Federal Historic Preservation Tax Incentives, Heritage Preservation Services (2255), National Park Service, 1849 C Street, N.W., Washington, DC 20240; <www2.cr.nps.gov/tps/tax/tax_p.htm>. A good summary is "Preservation Tax Incentives for Historic Buildings" (1996), prepared by Michael J. Auer for the Historic Preservation Services.

State and local governments also provide tax incentives of various kinds, and preservationists are advised to take advantage of them, too. These might include such things as grants and loans, tax abatement, exemptions from parking requirements, and exemptions from building codes or zoning requirements. In some instances, tax incentives include deductions for charitable contributions of partial interests in historic property, principally easements.

In seeking tax incentives, the obvious question is, How can they be used most effectively? But one must also ask other questions, such as whether tax abatement might lower a community's tax base and lead to reduction in government services and whether tax incentives benefit the upper class's interests at the expense of the welfare of the lower classes.

Building Codes and Zoning Laws

Suppose a property is acquired. Will zoning laws permit its use in ways that may be at odds with the character or design of the community in which it is located? If not, will exemptions be granted? Can it be brought into conformity with building codes without destroying its own character? If not, again, will exemptions be granted? Can it retain its integrity when it is also made safe and user-friendly by the installation of a sprinkler system and air conditioning? How do the changes required to bring a structure into compliance with the Americans with

Disabilities Act affect the integrity of a building? If such changes cannot be made, under what circumstances are exemptions granted? On the latter two of these questions, see Thomas C. Jester's brochure, "Preserving the Past and Making It Accessible for People with Disabilities" (1996), published by the National Park Service's Heritage Preservation Services.

Property Rights

What is to keep property owners from doing as they please with their property—including tearing it down or altering it beyond recognition? Who has the right to impose the "public good" on owners of private property? This issue, of course, involves zoning, understood as the tool by which people collectively establish standards to preserve the beauty and integrity of their communities. In the 1980s a "property rights movement" gained influence, and by the 1990s it was scoring successes in the courts. Its advocates oppose zoning and other ordinances, and they object to such things as federal land ownership, federal regulation of wetlands and other resources, designations to the National Wild and Scenic River System, and even the National Register of Historic Places. They contend that land use ordinances, regulations, and designations amount to a "taking" of the value of private property, and they insist that, according to the Fifth Amendment to the Constitution, "taking" requires "just compensation." By the mid-1990s, "takings" legislation had been introduced in almost all states and passed in some form in many of them, and support for it existed in the Congress of the United States.

Progress

Perhaps it is true that, until very recently at least, America's past has always seemed to lie somewhere out in the future. Plans for tomorrow were always more important than remembrances of yesterday. The future called for bigger, faster, and more—more in quantity, more comfortable, more convenient. Such plans were not necessarily inspired by builders and designers and wreckers of the landscape. These persons simply planned the instruments to satisfy the desires of people and businesses, to give them what they thought they had a right to have. Destruction of the landscape can rightly be regarded as reflecting the collective will of the people, or at least the indifference of those who might have helped preserve it. How, the preservationist must ask, can the will or indifference be changed to produce different understandings of progress?

Urban Renewal and Government Programs

Despite commitments to preservation going back at least to 1906, government programs have sometimes been destructive forces in urban areas. What do you suppose occupied the land where government-financed urban-renewal projects now stand or where motorists now speed along? When you drive on an interstate highway through the heart of a city, notice the rows of once-stately buildings to one side or the other. Then ask what once stood where the highway came through.

The National Historic Preservation Act of 1966, Section 106, states that "Federal agency officials must consider the impact of their programs and projects on places of historic value. They incorporate ways to protect and enhance historic resources through their land-use planning, funding, and licensing actions. . . . The Section 106 review process guarantees that State and local governments, Indian tribes, private citizens, and organizations will have meaningful involvement in Federal project planning when proposed actions affect historic resources they care about." Recently issued guidelines give this statement more force than it enjoyed in the past. More information is available from the Advisory Council on Historic Preservation, 1100 Pennsylvania Avenue N.W., Suite 809, Washington, DC 20004; <www.achp.gov/aboutcouncil.html>.

Education

Historic preservation offers many educational opportunities, both for practitioners and young people. For information on seminars conducted by the National Preservation Institute, P.O. Box 1702, Alexandria, VA 22313; <www.npi.org>. For materials for children, see "Teaching with Historic Places, NRHP, National Park Service, P.O. Box 37127, Suite 250, Washington, DC 20013; <www.cr.nps.gov/nr/twhp/home.html>. State and local agencies also provide many educational opportunities, which have the effect of building community support for preservation.

THE NATIONAL REGISTER OF HISTORIC PLACES

Historic preservation efforts are frequently aimed at placing structures or districts on the National Register of Historic Places. Comprehensive information about the National Register can be obtained by writing to it at the National Park Service, U.S. Department of the Interior, P.O. Box 37127, Washington, DC 20013-7127 and through this Web site: <www.cr.nps.gov/nr>. Besides general introductions to the Register and its operations and The Secretary of the Interior's Standards for the Treatment of Historic Properties (cited earlier), the Register provides such documents as "How to Apply the National Register Criteria for Evaluation" and "How to Complete the National Register Registration Form," as well as a complete list of National Register Publications, including forms.

It is useful here, however, to provide a brief introduction to the National Register, since it is the key element in the preservation laws. Listing on the Register provides some protection against destruction and may make it possible to secure funding for restoration. Protection was weakened in 1980 with the enactment of a provision allowing the owner's objection to block the placement of a property on the Register.

In the event of such objection, the property may still be listed as eligible, so that it is at least protected from the negative effects of federal projects.

Persons seeking to preserve historic places in their communities must know how to register them. Each state designates an agency headed by a state historic preservation officer to work with the Register, most commonly the state historical society, department of natural resources, department of conservation, or department of cultural affairs. The criteria for evaluation of places nominated are uniform nationally. They read as follows:

The quality of significance in American history, architecture, archaeology, and culture is present in districts, sites, buildings, structures, and objects that possess integrity of location, design, setting, materials, workmanship, feeling, and association, and:

a. that are associated with events that have made a significant contribution to the broad patterns of our history; or

b. that are associated with the lives of persons significant in our past; or

c. that embody the distinctive characteristics of a type, period, or method of construction, or that represent a significant and distinguishable entity whose components may lack individual distinction; or

d. that have yielded, or may be likely to yield, information important in prehistory or history.

Criteria considerations: Ordinarily cemeteries, birthplaces, or graves of historical figures, properties owned by religious institutions or used for religious purposes, structures that have been moved from their original locations, reconstructed historic buildings, properties primarily commemorative in nature, and properties that have achieved significance within the past 50 years shall not be considered eligible for the National Register. However, such properties will qualify if they are integral parts of districts that do meet the criteria or if they fall within the following categories:

a. a religious property deriving primary significance from architectural or artistic distinction or historical importance; or

b. a building or structure removed from its original location but which is significant primarily for architectural value, or which is the surviving structure most importantly associated with a historic person or event; or

c. a birthplace or grave of a historical figure of outstanding importance if there is no other appropriate site or building directly associated with his productive life; or

d. a cemetery that derives its primary significance from graves of persons of transcendent importance, from age, from distinctive design features, or from association with historic events; or

e. a reconstructed building when accurately executed in a suitable environment and presented in a dignified manner as part of a restoration master plan, and when no other building or structure with the same association has survived; or

f. a property primarily commemorative in intent if design, age, tradition, or symbolic value has invested it with its own historical significance; or

g. a property achieving significance within the past 50 years if it is of exceptional importance.

Working with the designated State Historic Preservation officer is essential in the registration process. This officer provides the nomination forms that are required if the property is to be considered by a state review board, and approval of this board is a necessary step in the quest for a place on the National Register.

The essential part of the nomination to the National Register is an inventory or survey of the property in question. Forms for this purpose are available from the National Park Service, but this general guidance provided in a Register publication provides a starting point for those wishing to know what is involved:

> A person wishing to prepare a nomination needs a thorough knowledge of the property. By physically inspecting the property and conducting historical research, applicants can gather facts such as the physical characteristics of the property, date of construction, changes to the property over time, historic functions and activities, association with events and persons, and the role of the property in the history of the community, State, or the nation.
>
> When gathering information, keep in mind how it will fit into the final form. The form, first of all, is a record of the property at the time of listing: giving its location, defining its boundaries, identifying its historic characteristics, and describing its current condition. Second, it is a statement of how the property qualifies for National Register listing. Claims for historical significance and integrity are supported in the form by facts about the property. These facts link the property to one or more of the four National Register criteria, on the one hand, and to the history of its community, State, or the nation, on the other.

Once this is done, persons should turn entirely to the forms and guidance of the National Register.

A survey along these lines gives the information needed for nomination forms, but local historians interested in preserving the building will want to analyze the information and draw further conclusions about the architectural, historical, and archaeological significance of the building as they consider possible uses for it should preservation seem feasible. Various questions will need to be considered, such as: How extensive and how costly would the required repairs be? Can it be rehabilitated or restored? To be useful, would it have to be reconstructed or possibly even relocated?

While placement on the National Register carries prestige and is very important if federal grants are to be used for acquisition or restoration of a property, local inventories and landmark legislation can be equally important. Preservationists should therefore work closely with local officials and, as indicated below, with the State Historic Preservation officer.

CONCLUSION

Historic preservation is not an endeavor to be undertaken lightly or alone. Assistance should be utilized at every stage of the process. Preservationists should be prepared to maintain ties not only with the appropriate local and state agencies, but also with local landmark commissions and historic properties advisory councils. They too should be prepared to call on persons specially trained and well experienced in historic preservation. Of what does special training consist? A recent survey of degree programs in colleges and universities shows a variety of emphases, including urban planning, architecture, art history, architectural history, urban affairs, landscape architecture, geography, law, management, history, American studies, and, of course, historic preservation.

If the processes of preservation are so complicated and the work so hard, some people might wonder whether the effort is worthwhile. Those who believe in the importance of historic preservation, however, will make it possible for more and more people to find links with the past, to develop a sense of what it was like to have been there.

How does one start? By starting. As someone who has been active in state historic preservation remarked, it may be best for people simply to take a foolhardy plunge into preservation projects, since reliance on absolute logic is not always helpful in such work; a touch of insanity helps, and "if most folks knew the frustrations they were in for, probably nothing would ever be taken on." Perhaps such people consider the frustrations a small price for great rewards.

NOTES AND FURTHER READING

References in this chapter for which mailing and Web site addresses were not given were to Mira Engler, "Drive-Thru History: Theme Towns in Iowa," *Landscape* 32, no. 1 (1993): 8–18; and David Lowenthal, *Possessed by the Past: The Heritage Crusade and the Spoils of History* (New York: Free Press, 1996).

Interesting speculation about the future of historic preservation appears in "Millions for the Millennium? How Federal Largesse Could Best Benefit the Nation," *Preservation* 50, no. 3 (May/June 1998): 16–17. Among the many publications of the National Trust's Preservation Press, several merit mention here: Richard C. Collins, *America's Downtowns: Growth, Politics, and Preservation* (1991); Carol Highsmith, *America Restored* (1994); Diane Maddex, ed., *The Brown Book: A Directory of Preservation Information* (1983); Carl L. Nelson, *Protecting the Past from Natural Disaster* (1991); *All About Old Buildings: The Whole Preservation Catalog* (1985); *American Landmarks: Historic Properties of the National Trust for Historic Preservation* (1980); *Landmark Yellow Pages: Where to Find All the Names, Addresses, Facts and Figures You Need* (1993).

Federal involvement in preservation efforts has a long history. An interesting introduction is found in F. Ross Holland, Jr., "The Park Service as Curator," *National Parks and Conservation Magazine* (August 1979): 10–15. How extensive the involvement has been is evident in the listing of more than 68,000 structures and sites in the National Register of Historic Places. The cumulative listing through 1994 is available in *The National Register of Historic Places* (New York: John Wiley and Sons, 1995). The National Register's Web site includes a searchable database that includes the up-to-date list. Some NPS publications are much less voluminous, such as the brochure, "My Property Is Important to America's Heritage: What Does That Mean? Answers to Questions for Owners of Historic Properties" (1997). See also "Federal Preservation Laws" published by the Cultural Resources Program of the National Park Service (1993) and *A Handbook on Historic Preservation Law* (Washington, DC: Conservation Foundation, National Center for Preservation Law, 1983). A complete set of preservation laws is accessible at <www.cr.nps.gov/linklaws.htm#LAW>.

Information about federal funding for preservation is found in Lesley Slavitt (edited by Susan Escherich), *Preserving and Revitalizing Older Communities: Sources of Federal Assistance* (Washington, DC: Preservation Assistance Division, National Park Service, 1993).

Of related interest is Harley J. McKee, *Recording Historic Buildings: The Historic American Buildings Survey* (Washington, DC: National Park Service, 1970). The roots of this publication lie in the Historic American Buildings Survey begun as a New Deal program in 1933 and published with additional material bringing it up to date from time to time since then.

A brochure published by the National Endowment for the Humanities, "Preserving America's Heritage" (Washington, DC, 1997), shows that books, photographs, and films must also be included in preservation causes; contact <www.neh.fed.us>.

Historic preservation has been the subject of much controversy, involving political, social, economic, aesthetic, legal, and other questions. For years, it seems, historic preservation has been in crisis. Betty Doak Elder, "Crossroads: Congress to Decide Preservations Future," *History News* 35, no. 4 (April 1980): 7–13, describes alternatives as they looked at the beginning of a new decade. See also Pamela Thurber, ed., *Controversies in Historic Preservation: Understanding the Preservation Movement Today* (Washington, DC: National Trust for Historic Preservation, 1985).

Other works touching on controversial or problematical aspects of preservation include Walter L. Bailey, "Historic Districts: A Neglected Resource," *North Dakota History* 43 (1976): 22–24; David A. Clary, "Historic Preservation and Environmental Protection: The Role of the Historian," *Public Historian* 1 (fall 1978): 61–75; Grady Clay, "Townscape and Landscape: The Coming Battleground," *Historic Preservation* 24 (1972): 34–43; E. Blaine Cliver, "Reconstruction: Valid or Invalid?" *Historic Preservation* 24 (1972): 22–24; Larry Tice, "Let's Put History Back into Historic Preservation," *Preservation News* (October 1979): 5; Larry Ford, "Historic Preservation and the Stream of Time," *Historical Geography Newsletter* 5 (winter 1975): 1–15; Kevin Lynch, *What Time Is This Place?* (Cambridge, MA: MIT Press, 1972); and Robert M. Utley, "Historic Preservation and the Environment," *Colorado Magazine* 51 (winter 1974): 1–12.

A good introduction to the roots of the legislation that has been a part of the historic preservation movement is found in *With Heritage So Rich* (New York: Random House, 1966), a report of the United States Conference of Mayors. A good case for preservation is made in Randolph Langenbach, *A Future from the Past: The Case for Conservation and Reuse of Old Buildings in Industrial Communities* (Washington, DC: Department of Housing and Urban Development, 1977).

Charles B. Hosmer, Jr., lays out the history of historic preservation in *Presence of the Past: A History of the Preservation Movement in the United States before Williamsburg* (New York: Putnam's, 1965) and *Preservation Comes of Age: From Williamsburg to the National Trust* (Charlottesville: University Press of Virginia, 1981). See also William J. Murtagh, *Keeping Time: The History and Theory of Preservation in America* (New York: John Wiley and Sons, rev. ed., 1997); Deborah Slaton and Rebecca A. Shiffer, *Preserving the Recent Past* (Washington, DC: Historic Preservation Education Foundation, 1995).

Among the many surveys of developments in the preservation movement are: Alice Cromie, *Restored Towns and Historic Districts of America: A Tour Guide* (New York: Dutton, 1979); Elizabeth Kendall Thompson, ed., *Recycling Buildings: Renovations, Remod-*

elings, Restorations, and Reuses (New York: McGraw-Hill, 1977); Louis Redstone, *The New Downtowns: Rebuilding Business Districts* (New York: McGraw-Hill, 1976); Nathan Weinberg, *Preservation in American Cities and Towns* (Boulder, CO: Westview Press, 1979); and Tony P. Wrenn and Elizabeth D. Mulloy, *America's Forgotten Architecture* (New York: Pantheon, 1976).

That preservation efforts are often too little, too late is apparent in James M. Goode, *Capital Losses: A Cultural History of Washington's Destroyed Buildings* (Washington, DC: Smithsonian Institution Press, 1979). Also in Mary Cable, *Lost New Orleans* (Boston: Houghton Mifflin, 1980); Jane H. Kay, *Lost Boston* (Boston: Houghton Mifflin, 1980); David Lowe, *Lost Chicago* (Boston: Houghton Mifflin, 1975); Nathan Silver, *Lost New York* (New York: Schocken, 1971); and Carla Lind, *Lost Wright: Frank Lloyd Wright's Vanished Masterpieces* (New York: Simon & Schuster, 1996).

Among the better guides for doing preservation or for coping with preservation problems are: James Marston Fitch, *Historic Preservation: Curatorial Management of the Built World* (Charlottesville: University Press of Virginia, 1990); Marsha Glenn, *Historic Preservation: A Handbook for Architectural Students* (Washington, DC: American Institute of Architects, 1974); Harrison Goodall and Renee Friedman, *Log Structures: Preservation and Problem-Solving* (Nashville: American Association for State and Local History, 1980); Marya Morris, *Innovative Tools for Historic Preservation* (Chicago: American Planning Association, 1992); Morgan W. Phillips, *The Eight Most Common Mistakes in Restoring Houses,* Technical Leaflet no. 118 (Nashville: American Association for State and Local History, 1979); Richard Ernie Reed, *Return to the City: How to Restore Old Buildings and Ourselves in America's Historic Urban Neighborhoods* (Garden City, NY: Doubleday, 1979); Kenneth Smith, et al., eds., *Revitalizing Downtown* (Washington, DC: National Main Street Center, 1996); Elinor R. Snow, *Historic Preservation Resources* (Beltsville, MD: National Agricultural Library, 1994); Samuel N. Stokes, A. Elizabeth Watson, and Shelley S. Mastran, *Saving America's Countryside: A Guide to Rural Conservation* (Baltimore: Johns Hopkins University Press, 2nd ed., 1997); Bradford J. White, *Preparing a Historic Preservation Plan* (Chicago: American Planning Association, 1994); Arthur P. Ziegler, Jr., *Historic Preservation in Inner City Areas: A Manual of Practice* (Pittsburgh: Ober Park Associates, rev. ed., 1974); Robert E. Stipe, ed., *New Directions in Rural Preservation* (Washington, DC: U.S. Department of the Interior, 1980); Arthur P. Ziegler, Jr., and Walter C. Kidney, *Historic Preservation in Small Towns: A Manual of Practice* (Nashville: American Association for State and Local History, 1979); and Thomas J. Martin, et al., *Adaptive Use: Development Economics, Process, and Profiles* (Washington, DC: Urban Land Institute, 1978). Historic preservation frequently entails legal questions. Although such questions require the special knowledge and skills of lawyers, a helpful reference book for lay persons is Nicholas Robinson, *Historic Preservation Law* (New York: Practicing Law Institute, 1979). For help in local situations, see Stephen N. Dennis, *Recommended Model Provisions for a Preservation Ordinance, with Annotations* (Washington, DC: National Trust for Historic Preservation, 1980).

The most comprehensive bibliography of materials on historic preservation is Frederick L. Rath, Jr., and Merrilyn O'Connell, *Historic Preservation: A Bibliography on Historical Organization Practices,* vol. 1 (Nashville: American Association for State and Local History, 1975). John A. Jakle, *Past Landscapes* (Monticello, IL: Council of Planning Librarians, 1973), is a bibliography of work done by cultural geographers in historic preservation. *The Old House Journal,* 199 Berkeley Pl., Brooklyn, NY 11217; and Lawrence Grow, comp., *The Old House Catalogue* (New York: Main Street Press, 1976) merit attention.

11

Research, Writing, and Leaving a Record

The preceding chapters have discussed a wide variety of research methods, some of them quite specialized. Those chapters have emphasized discovering historical traces—written, oral, visual, material, and immaterial—and interpreting them. Using them purposefully to communicate information about the nearby past, however, requires moving beyond the excitement of discovery and insight to bring the evidence under control. It is therefore important to record the discoveries of the moment. If they are registered in a sloppy or indifferent manner, even the best research is wasted. But careful, organized recording with a view toward future use is an aspect of historical research that pays off in understanding, time saved, quality, and satisfaction. Observing just a few sound principles of research, writing, and record keeping will help you avoid common mistakes, make your work more effective, and enable you to accomplish more in the time available.

TAKING NOTES

Few people can remember great quantities of detailed information for long. Taking notes becomes essential for an accurate record. While it is possible to scribble notes on any scrap of paper that is handy at the moment, such jottings often prove awkward to use later. It is far better in the long run to work out a method of note taking at the outset of a project and to follow it consistently thereafter.

The format in which you choose to record information is a matter of personal preference, of course, and that choice should be dictated by the way in which you plan to present your findings. Some researchers find notebooks most satisfactory, while others prefer loose sheets or cards that can later be sorted and rearranged. Laptop or desktop computers offer convenience, but at a price as well as at a somewhat higher risk of loss of material accumulated. Choose a note-keeping format that suits your research and writing styles and stick with it. (One of the authors prefers five-by-eight-inch index cards, which he color codes according to topic by drawing narrow lines with felt-tip markers across the tops. This method facilitates sorting and assimilating when the time to write arrives. The other author dislikes the bulk of cards and uses five-by-eight-inch slips of paper instead; he also forgoes the color coding. Both like the security of hard copy. While both have experimented successfully with computer data files for some projects, they frequently back up those files and sometimes print them out as well.) Changing format increases storage problems and the likelihood that items will be overlooked.

The cardinal rule of note taking is to identify on every item the source of the information you are recording. This practice allows you to go back and check if necessary. It is also a good idea to leave some space on each note for adding information later or for coding as you prepare for writing. If you choose to use a notebook from which pages can only be removed by tearing them out, be sure to devise some system of cross-referencing and organizing so that the sources of your notes is not lost to you. Do likewise with computer files so that cutting and pasting does not separate information from an identified source.

There is no substitute for neatness and accuracy in recording information, whatever the format. Scribbling in haste, taking down too little information, or using abbreviations that later become unintelligible may mean effort wasted. An unclear note may require going back to the source at a later time to verify information that might have been carefully recorded the first time. Using a pen rather than a pencil (except where the rules of the archival research room prohibit it) reduces the likelihood of smudging. Writing on only one side of a card prevents you from overlooking notes later and makes card flipping unnecessary. Consistency in spelling of names and terms will allow you to retrieve every reference in a text if you use a computer.

As you proceed to gather information, ideas for organizing and analyzing may come to you. Jot down these thoughts also, or keep them in a separate computer file. If you do not write them down until later, they may disappear altogether. Be alert, too, for illustrative material that could make your story more vivid. Here is where a photocopying machine may be used most effectively. Make a copy of the visual document you consider to be potentially useful, write on it where you found it, and file it with others that you are accumulating so that you have a set to choose from when you prepare your presentation.

Photocopiers come in handy for other purposes as well, but they must be used judiciously. Some researchers make extra work for themselves by photocopying indiscriminately everything they find. Selections must be made sooner or later; by making them sooner you are likely to save yourself time and money without damaging your finished product.

WRITING

Eventually the time will come for you to write. Even if you choose to present your findings in an audiovisual form, such presentations require a script, and the better the writing, the better the final product. Writing on a computer using a word processing program with cut and paste capacities, spelling and grammar checkers, a thesaurus, and outlining and footnoting features can ease the labor of writing and lead more quickly to a polished piece of work, but basic techniques remain the same. Effective writing, after all, is nothing other than a process of putting ideas and credible supporting evidence in a logical order and comprehensible language so that a reader or listener can understand them. If writers present a worthwhile topic in this way, they stand a good chance of interesting and persuading the audience.

The nature and extent of preparation for writing depends on the envisioned finished product. The range of options for historians of people and things nearby is broad, both in medium and in scope. End results might be presented in an audiovisual medium. A sound recording might be made to accompany a set of printed pictures or merely for use by itself. A slide-tape show can effectively convey a wide variety of information. Videotape is becoming a more accessible and economical format. Computer-generated presentations that can combine material of your own creation with audio or video material downloaded from the Internet or CD-ROM databases and then be used interactively, sent over the Internet, or projected onto a large screen are within the capacity of most Macintosh or Windows users. More elaborate film presentations are possible, though they can be expensive and technologically complex and can demand professional involvement. Some groups have had great success communicating their research in dramatic form, either as stage presentations or through role playing in historical surroundings. Written pieces can range from short essays on single topics to full-length books. Possibilities between these extremes include scrapbooks, photo-essays, collections of vignettes, and extended articles. Sometimes short pieces can be used to present findings at early stages and as parts of longer works later. Whatever form your finished product takes, it will be more effective if you prepare it with its intended audience in mind.

Starting to write is often very difficult, even painful. The first step involves thinking through the topic and deciding what to say about it. If you are like many people, you will be tempted, when the time for writing arrives, to find an excuse to do something else. You will think of another source to check, another book to read, another library or archives to visit, another person to interview. But at some point you will have to stop gathering information and put words together in coherent form to meet a deadline, to seek funds for a preservation project, or simply to assess for yourself the work you have done.

Some people, ourselves included, find it helpful to begin their writing with an outline they work out and rearrange as suits them on paper or a computer screen. Some are committed to very formal and detailed outlines, while others are satisfied with a general idea as to how they hope to develop their story. An outline, formal or informal, grows from a conceptual scheme. Typically there is an interplay between a rudimentary notion of the purpose you have in mind and the material with which you are working. The lack of any idea, at least as a starting point, is likely to be a handicap, since that means that you are working aimlessly, without a goal.

Some writers find that catastrophes offer a good focus for stories. They are dramatic, they unfold in a natural sequence, and they can cause important changes. The response of individuals and institutions to a crisis can provide clues to their character and role within the community. Of course, the importance of one event in the overall history of a family or community ought not to be exaggerated. This description of a northern Indiana disaster, written by a student, provides an example of how both narrative and analysis can be incorporated into an interesting account.

The worst explosion and fire in the Calumet Region's history were caused by the world's largest hydroformer on Saturday, August 27, 1955. The hydroformer made high octane fuel which was blended with other gasoline stocks to create fuel for high compression auto engines. The explosion occurred because an experiment backfired. When the hydroformer blew up at the Standard Oil Refinery, some of Whiting's residents did not know what to think; some thought an atomic bomb had hit their town. The first explosion and fire occurred at 6:15 A.M. and burned uncontrollably throughout the day. As the flames spread, a 60 million barrel storage tank blew up as late as 4:00 P.M.

The series of explosions that rocked the Standard Oil Refinery on that day blew out most of the windows in a three mile radius, including most of Whiting and parts of East Chicago and Indiana Harbor. The Stiglitz Park District of Whiting was the worst hit. The initial blast hurled hunks of two-inch steel up to 30 feet long out of the refinery. One chunk nearly 50 feet long flew two city blocks, smashed through a food store and flattened an automobile. At least 50 homes close to the explosion were demolished.

Firemen from ten cities responded to the explosion and fire, including firemen from Gary, Hammond, East Chicago, Whiting, Oak Forest, Midlothian, Oak Park, Blue Island, and Dolton.

A grocery store at 1829 129th Street in Whiting was demolished by the steel roof of the huge hydromate unit. When Douglas Stepullin, the owner of the grocery store, arrived on the scene, all that remained of his store was a huge scar on the earth. Some of the store's merchandise was thrown across the street.

The Plewniak household at 2638 Schrage Avenue in Whiting was slumbering at 6:14 A.M. on August 27,1955. Frank Plewniak and his wife, Joan, were sleeping in a front bedroom, while their two small sons were asleep in another bed in the rear of the house. Suddenly!—an ear-splitting explosion rocked the house. Seconds later, a 10-foot steel pipe torpedoed through the roof of the house. A child's scream pierced the air. The terrified parents rushed into the children's bedroom. Upon arrival in the room, they found Ronald Plewniak, 8, crying in his bed. His right leg had been severed by the 10-foot pipe. Ronald's three year old brother, Richard, was unconscious in his crib. He was pinned beneath the pipe. Richard Plewniak died one half hour later at Saint Catherine Hospital in East Chicago, Indiana.

Ronald Plewniak is now thirty years old. After his graduation from college, he was given a life-time job with the Standard Oil Company.

Twenty-five other people were injured. There was one death which was indirectly related to the explosion. Walter Rhea, 61, a foreman at the refinery, died of a heart attack as he arrived on the disaster scene.

Standard Oil bought up most of the residential property in the area worst hit by the explosion and fire. The area was bounded on the east by Indianapolis Boulevard, on the south by 129th Street and on the west by Louisa Avenue. Neither the newspapers nor the people that I interviewed mentioned where the owners of this property moved. . . .

Standard Oil's loss was estimated at 19 million dollars. They received 18 million dollars in insurance payments, but I could not find any records where the insurance company paid individuals for their damaged property. Due to the huge amount by the insurance company, Standard Oil was able to replace most of the equipment burned by the fire with new an improved facilities. By 1956, they were back to normal operating procedures.

This explosion has been described as the worst fire in the Calumet Region's history. However, most of the people who were interviewed cannot remember what happened on Saturday, August 27,1955. I believe that this is the case because the newspaper played the explosion down. They reported as little as possible. The release by Standard Oil was only a rehash of what was said in the newspapers. While researching this paper, Standard Oil refused to discuss the matter and offered no information technical or otherwise.

Source: Ruthie Williams, "The Explosion of Standard Oil, August 27, 1955," in Steel Shavings, *edited by Ronald D. Cohen (Gary: Indiana University Northwest, 1978), pp. 25–27.*

Conceptual schemes need not to be elaborate. Consider the possibilities, for instance, of the following simple elements for the history of a family, an organization, or a community:

Origins
Dynamics
Milestones
Character

It is natural to focus on origins, as many of the questions posed in chapter 2 imply. Origins lead you to the people who knew about them, to the time and place, and to much more. In examining dynamics, you will look at what moved people, how power was held and used, and how decisions were made. Again, people will be at the center of your examination. Contemplating milestones means considering times of marked change, great occasions, measuring points on the continuum of routine, and turning points. In discerning character you seek to identify distinctive features that set your subject apart from others of the same general type. You are seeking to answer the simple question: "Who were these people—really?" These elements must be woven into the story being told. They give substance and meaning to the story's plot.

Outlines, whether formal and detailed or loose and general, are most helpful when the parts in them are expressed as questions to be answered. Mere listing of topics to be treated gives little coherence or direction to the finished product, and these are two essential ingredients of good writing. Also important are simplicity and clarity. These four qualities: coherence, direction, simplicity, and clarity—are perhaps best defined in terms of their opposites. Thus prose manifesting them will not be rambling and disjointed, aimless, tangled and confused, or vague and murky.

Keep in mind that someone fifty or a hundred years from now may be interested in the same nearby past that has absorbed your attention. Your possibility of communicating with that person improves if you avoid slang or jargon that is popular at the moment but may be incomprehensible within a few years as "in" phrases change. Cryptic comments, sarcasm, and attempts at humor also run a high risk of being misinterpreted. If you write in simple, direct English with well-defined terminology, uncomplicated, straightforward sentences, and paragraphs that follow logically, you stand the best chance of being understood in the future as well as now.

Two further thoughts on writing. First, the best way to overcome the initial obstacle, how to start, is simply to write something relating to the beginning of your account. Never mind if the result later seems quite unusable. You can always revise or rewrite entirely. In fact, rewriting to put ideas and evidence in better order, clarify connections and transitions, avoid repetition, select more precise and effective language, and eliminate spelling, grammatical, and typographical errors is an essential aspect of good writing. Computer spelling and grammar checkers are useful tools, but they cannot help with properly spelled but misused words, awkward phrasing, faulty logic, or ineffective explanations. Only careful, critical, and sensitive review by the author—aided, in the best of circumstances by other readers—followed by thorough polishing of the prose offers a dependable path to the highest quality finished work.

Second, at some point in your writing you are likely to throw up your hands and say, "Everybody already knows what I am writing! Why should I write it down? It all seems so useless!" This is a common reaction. The fact is, though, that you *think* everybody knows only because you are so immersed in your material that it has become commonplace to you. How to solve the problem? Just keep writing.

Finally, writers and sponsors of publications or other creative presentations should be aware of copyright regulations, which protect for a time exclusive rights to print, record, translate, perform, or sell one's work. For information regarding copyright regulations, see under "Copyright Issues" in chapter 7.

PRESERVING A RECORD

You can leave a record of your work, of course, regardless of whether you write, tape, or film anything. The currently popular practice of establishing a computer Web site so that your material can be located on the World Wide Web is a possibility, but one that carries high risks if it becomes the sole preservation effort. It is far too early to know if the Web, much less individual Web sites, will long endure, especially in its present form. A better way to make your efforts available and useful to others for the long run is to contribute material prepared or collected to an archives, library, or museum or, if none exists with a particular interest in the history of your area, to establish one. The preservation of documents, oral in-

Writing about a person's personality or the nature of family and community life is seldom easy. Detailed descriptions usually provide greater accuracy and generate more interest than general labels. For example, Oliver Cook's grandfather might have been called stern, honest, quick tempered, and forgiving, but a reader has a much better sense of him from these brief stories.

Oliver Cook was born on March 6, 1897, in Green County, Bolligee, Alabama, the fourth of Mack and Fannie Cook's seven children. His mother died when he was very young, and his father, who worked for the Alabama-Georgia Railroad, was killed by a train. The children were then reared by their maternal grandparents. Having to go to work on the farm at nine years of age, they had little time for schooling. Oliver attended school for three sessions. When the children returned from school, they had to change clothes and go to the fields. There was always something to do.

Oliver's grandfather was an earlier riser than the other family members. He would drink his morning coffee. When he finished, he would tap his walking stick on the floor about three times. You had better get out of bed or you would feel the stick. To this day, Oliver enjoys sleeping late into the morning.

When Oliver was nine years old his grandfather sent him to the store with 45¢. The store owner had Oliver do some work such as bringing in wood and lard barrels for kindling. The storekeeper paid him 45¢ also. When he got home, he showed his grandmother the money, and she told his grandfather. The next morning, his grandfather hooked up the team and drove to the store to ask the storekeeper about the money.

Oliver remembered his encounter with a white man named Horton when he was seven or eight years old. He was walking down the road when they met and he said, "What you say, Horton?" The man got mad and went to tell Oliver's grandfather because no black addressed a white man that way.

His grandfather said he would take care of the situation. He was getting ready to punish Oliver when one of his uncles asked what was going on. His grandfather said, "He called Mr. Horton 'Horton.'"

His uncle said, "You aren't going to whip him for calling him 'Horton?' That's his name, Horton!" His grandmother added that Oliver was too young to know what he was saying. After that Horton wouldn't even look his way; if he saw him coming, he'd turn his horse around and go the other way.

Source: Family History Collection, American History Research Center, University of Akron, Akron, Ohio.

terview tapes or transcripts, and material objects that have enduring value and are not duplicated elsewhere ensures that other nearby historians later on will be able to achieve their own understanding of the past. Some future historian may have questions or ideas different from yours and may not be satisfied with your version of the past alone, any more than you would be content with only one source of information. If you ensure that worthwhile historical traces available to you are preserved along with the accounts you produce, then people who become interested in the same family, building, neighborhood, church, business, community, or whatever will be able to understand the basis for your view and will have as good or better an opportunity to draw their own conclusions. Such an endeavor can make a great contribution to nearby history.

11.1   Photographs of the nearby world are as important to preserve as any other historical document. Sometimes a photograph taken for a particular purpose can provide information on other matters as well. This picture of a city sewer project, for instance, records the appearance of a neighborhood's buildings, streets, and other public utilities. Proper identification, storage, and care of photographs will extend their life and usefulness. (Photo courtesy of and copyright © Summit County Historical Society.)

In the course of your own investigation of the nearby past, you may well have encountered one or more repositories with holdings relating to your locality or topic and with an interest in acquiring additional material, most likely part of a public or university library in the area, a local historical society or museum, or a similar institution. If no such facility exists, the creation of one in a local library, high school or college, church, community center, or other appropriate institution can be a worthwhile undertaking. Whether you place materials with an existing archives or museum or create a new repository, certain matters need to be considered in order to ensure that the materials will be well preserved and used.

The first standard for judging any repository must be the strength of its commitment to preserving and making accessible its holdings. If resources or interest in historical collections run low after a few years, materials may be lost to succeeding generations. Those institutions that already have a long history of caring for historical materials are most likely to survive and retain their interests in years to come. A library, which has the narrow purpose of acquiring and preserving documents and enjoys reasonably steady financial support, may be a better choice for a repository than a community center with a wide range of programs, changing leadership with varied interests, and uncertain funding. Of course, the library may be the victim of a taxpayers' revolt, while the community center may remain a stable and vital institution for generations, so there are no absolute guarantees. But whether you contribute to an existing repository or create a new one, it is wise to consider its possible circumstances fifty or a hundred years in the future. At the very least, it is worth knowing that should the institution at some time not wish or not be able to maintain historical collections, it will act responsibly to transfer them to other appropriate and capable hands rather than abandoning them.

A second important consideration is location with respect to your topic. In doing your own research, you have no doubt realized the value of having all related materials in a single place. Not only does such an arrangement save a researcher's time and expense, but it contributes to a better understanding by archivists, librarians, and curators of the range of sources available on a subject. It is therefore generally better, if possible, to add to an existing collection rather than to divide materials concerning an individual, family, organization, or community. While having a separate repository for your particular materials may seem attractive, in the long run they may as a result be overlooked. Of course, if no institution exists with an interest in or an ability to handle your material, or if the appropriate one is at too great a distance to allow reasonable access to those most interested, the establishment of a new repository may be the only solution.

Beyond having a firm commitment to maintaining materials, a repository needs to be prepared to provide adequate care and protection, publicity, and reasonable access for purposes of research. While the techniques of preserving historical documents and artifacts are logical and are not excessively complicated, they are rather specialized. In order to ensure that an existing institution or a newly created one can properly handle the materials entrusted to it, its personnel ought to have knowledge and training in appropriate archival or curatorial methods. The staff also need sensitivity to the past and concern for its preservation. A number of universities conduct courses in archival administration, museum curatorship, or historical preservation, while the Society of American Archivists (527 South Wells Street, Chicago, IL 60607 or <www.archivists.org>) and the American Association for State and Local History (530 Church St., Suite 600, Nashville, TN 37204 or <www.aaslh.org>) offer a wide variety of publications and programs to inform individuals and institutions about proper procedures and methods. This is not the place for an extended discussion of archival-curatorial theory and technique, but few comments on basic policies may be useful in assessing the capabilities of existing institutions to handle historical materials successfully and the standards that newly created repositories should be expected to meet.

Repositories must be able to make intelligent judgments regarding the value of material offered to them. Not everything from the past is equally worth keeping, especially when resources of time, money, and space are limited, as they always seem to be. Documents and objects must be appraised and their

A local history society that was encouraging the preservation of historically valuable records distributed this checklist so that the churches would have a clear idea of what to save or collect.

I. Church records to be preserved in perpetuity:
   A. *Constitutions and articles of incorporation,* at least one copy of each edition, including also auxiliaries, affiliated agencies, or subsidiaries;
   B. *Calls* issued and accepted by pastors and others who serve the parish; *assignments* of church workers by hierarchical officials;
   C. *Deeds,* leases, titles, policies, surveys. and descriptions of church properties;
   D. *Contracts,* blueprints, plans, specifications, and related documents;
   E. *Mortgages* (even if retired—don't burn them);
   F. *Membership lists,* possibly in serial, with designation of charter members;
   G. *Minutes* of voting bodies, boards, councils; related documents which have produced resolutions or actions;
   H. *Sunday bulletins,* newsletters, announcements to the members of the congregation, news releases;
   I. *Ledgers* of official acts: baptism, confirmation, marriage, and burial records;
   J. *Official correspondence* relating to membership status, pastors, and others employed by the congregation; relating to denominational or organizational affiliations;
   K. *Treasurers' reports* and financial files required by law;
   L. *Histories* of the congregation: narrative, statistical, and chronological;
   M. *Records of educational agencies* regarding such things as enrollments, teachers, policies, terms, materials, and tuition;
   N. *Reports* of all official committees and commissions;
   O. *Reports* filed with judicatories;
   P. *Membership changes,* transfers, disciplinary cases, excommunications, expulsions, etc.;
   Q. *Officers,* lists of the congregation and all boards, committees, commissions, auxiliary agencies and organizations, etc.;
   R. *Biographical* and vital data of members to the extent that it can be recorded.

II. Church records that we recommend be kept only temporarily:
   A. General correspondence (2 years);
   B. Copies of calls and contracts offered but not accepted (2 years);
   C. Communications with members that do not have legal or historical value (2 years);
   D. Programs and other printed materials not covered in any of the above categories: keep two copies in permanent files for programs of special occasions, one copy of others; discard duplicates periodically, perhaps annually;
   E. Communion announcement cards and related types (1 year);
   F. Financial records: remittance envelopes, deposit slips, canceled checks, weekly financial reports (5 years);
   G. Miscellaneous: when in doubt retain.

III. Materials to be actively sought for inclusion in church archives:
   A. Photographs related to the life of the church: formal ones may include confirmation pictures, for which a complete file (with identifications) is desirable; weddings, church staff, church officers; informal ones of picnics, socials, and gatherings; exterior and interior shots of buildings and properties; aerial views of church and community;

B. Community documents that relate to the place of the church in the community; examples of cooperation or conflict between church and community;

C. Written records and recollections of members willing to provide them;

D. Tapes of interviews with selected members; transcriptions of the tapes;

E. Tape recordings (audio or video) of sermons—randomly selected ones as well as those made on special occasions;

F. Tape recordings of choirs and renditions by organists;

G. Artifacts of the church "keepsake" variety.

Source: Normandy (Missouri) Area Historical Association. Parts I and II are adapted from bulletins of the Concordia Historical Institute, 801 DeMun Avenue, St. Louis, MO 63105.

historical importance assessed, so that valuable traces are preserved but not buried under a mountain of trivial or duplicate material. Appraisals are some of the most difficult judgments that archivists and curators must make. Items preserved must be those that seem likely to shed light on matters that either now or at some future time will be regarded as historically significant or interesting. Is the information contained in a document or an artifact unique, or can it be found elsewhere? Does its preservation present problems that outweigh its value? Is the material likely to be used? The more the archivist or curator knows about the past, other historical resources, and the process of research, the wiser the decisions he or she can make as to what to save. No wonder that the growing career fields of archives, museums, and historical preservation require individuals with training and interest in history.

Once a repository accepts material, it assumes an obligation to care for it and to make it accessible. Thus, an archivist or curator might conclude that something is worth preserving and might still feel that his or her particular institution should not accept it because it lacks relevance to that institution's other holdings or because there are no resources to care for it. Such a decision does not indicate indifference or hostility. No archives or museum can collect everything, and a different or new repository may be needed to provide an adequate home for worthwhile material.

A repository must be able to arrange newly acquired materials in good order, to provide safe, secure storage so that material will not be damaged or lost, and to take steps to preserve fragile, aged items. The staff must also keep track of each acquisition, record its provenance or history, and prepare catalogs, inventories, and other finding aids, so that potential users will be able to determine the contents of the repository and to locate those items they wish to examine. Furthermore, the institution must publicize its own existence and holdings through the *National Union Catalog of Manuscript Collections,* scholarly and popular publications, the Online Computer Library Catalog (OCLC) or the Research Libraries Information Network (RLIN), and other means so that interested parties will become aware of its resources. Protecting, arranging, describing, and publicizing materials in their care are important responsibilities for archivists and curators.

Aiding people who wish to use materials is an obvious duty but one that must be balanced with a responsibility to protect donors and guard the items for future use. Individuals and heirs, businesses, and institutions have rights and interests that deserve respect. Archives, manuscripts, audiovisual documents, and material objects are placed in repositories in the belief that they ought to be preserved but not necessarily that they should be made public immediately. Furthermore, many individuals identified in family, business, or government documents have not participated in the decision to deposit the information in an archives and may not wish to have their privacy invaded. Donors should consider such matters and discuss possible areas of concern with archivists or curators.

Any responsible institution will recognize and defend legitimate rights of privacy and will do its best to ensure that researchers do likewise. It is reasonable and appropriate for use of some types of sensitive material to be restricted for a period of time. In addition, donors may properly ask, and institutions may insist, that researchers not publish or otherwise publicly repeat names of living persons or other designated confidential information without permission of the repository, donor, and possibly other persons involved. Archivists and curators should explain the conditions under which materials may be used, and researchers should pay careful heed. If donor, protector, and user cooperate, traces of the past can be physically preserved and made available without damage.

If you decide to place material you own or for which you bear responsibility in a library, archives, or museum, you should reach an understanding with the institution about the nature of donation and the rights and obligations of the recipient. A written agreement to this effect is a normal and very important procedure by which both donor and repository acknowledge their acceptance of the specified terms. Satisfactory forms for gifts of family histories, documents, oral histories, and objects may be found in appendix B.

Depositing historical materials in an archives or museum is an act of generosity and concern for future generations, but nevertheless it requires thoughtful consideration to ensure proper care for the items. Creating a new repository is an even more weighty matter, for it involves assuming responsibility to see that traces of the past continue to be preserved, protected, and made available. Fortunately, in either case there are trained specialists, educational institutions, and professional organizations willing and able to provide advice and assistance. The creation and support of archives, libraries, museums, and similar institutions is a fine means of leaving a record. But whether you write about your own research, produce a tape, film, exhibit, or drama, or contribute to an historical repository, you are furthering in a valuable way the understanding of nearby history.

NOTES AND FURTHER READING

Other works on this subject, different in emphasis or less comprehensive, include: John Cummings, *A Guide for Writing Local History* (Lansing: Michigan Bicentennial Commission, 1974)—a very elementary book; Thomas E. Felt, *Researching, Writing, and Publishing Local History* (Nashville: American Association for State and Local History, 1976); W. G. Hoskins, *Fieldwork in Local History* (London: Faber and Faber, 1976) and *Local History in England* (London: Longman, 1972 [1959]); David Weitzman, *Underfoot: An Everyday Guide to Exploring the American Past* (New York: Scribner's, 1976); and Carol Kammen, *On Doing Local History: Reflections on What Local Historians Do, Why, and What It Means* (Walnut Creek, CA: AltaMira, 1986).

An excellent guide for high school students doing nearby history is Gerald A, Danzer and Lawrence W. McBride, *People, Space, and Time: An Introduction to Community History for Schools* (Washington, DC: University Press of America, 1985). A book that shows how to examine town newspapers, firehouses, post offices; how to make maps; how to create family museums and archives; and other things is James Robertson, ed., *Old Glory: A Pictorial Report on the Grass Roots History Movement and the First Hometown History Primer* (New York: Warner Paperback, 1973). A volume that seeks to place nearby history in a larger context and suggests different forms for future family and community histories is David Russo, *Families and Communities: A New View of American History* (Nashville: American Association for State and Local History, 1974).

The best handbook for researchers and writers of history, amateur as well as professional, is Jacques Barzun and Henry F. Graff, *The Modern Researcher* (New York: Harcourt Brace Jovanovich, 5th ed., 1992), although its information on the use of the Internet is badly out of date. Richard Marius, *A Short Guide to Writing about History,* 3rd ed. (New York: Longman, 1999) provides excellent advice. Mary Lynn Rampolla, *A Pocket Guide to Writing in History* (Boston: Bedford/St. Martin's, 2nd ed., 1998) is a useful brief guide to general issues, and its companion volume, Diana Hacker, *A Pocket Style Manual* (Boston: Bedford/St. Martin's, 3rd ed., 1999), is helpful as well. The Hacker volume is accessible through the World Wide Web at <www.bedfordbooks.com>.

On writing, of the many books available, see particularly Jacques Barzun, *Simple and Direct: A Rhetoric for Writers* (New York: Harper and Row, 1976); William Zinsser, *On Writing Well: An Informal Guide to Writing Nonfiction* (New York: Harper, 6th ed., 1998); and William Strunk and E. B. White, *The Elements of Style* (New York: Allyn & Bacon, 4th ed., 1999). An effective grammatical guide because of its humorous way of making its point is Patricia T. O'Conner, *Woe Is I: The Grammarphobe's Guide to Better English in Plain English* (New York: G. P. Putnam, 1996).

To find local institutions concerned with preserving, collecting, investigating, or celebrating the past, consult the latest edition of the *Directory of Historical Societies and Agencies in the United States and Canada* (Nashville: American Association for State and Local History).

Those establishing their own nearby history archives or attempting to assess the quality of an existing repository may wish to consult Theodore R. Schellenberg, *Modern Archives: Principles and Techniques* (Chicago: University of Chicago Press, 1956) and *The Management of Archives* (New York: Columbia University Press, 1965); Ruth B. Borden and Robert M. Warner, *The Modern Manuscripts Library* (New York: Scarecrow, 1966); Lucille M. Kane, *A Guide to the Care and Administration of Manuscripts,* 2nd ed. (Nashville: American Association for State and Local History, 1966); O. Lawrence Burnette, Jr., *Beneath the Footnote: A Guide to the Use and Preservation of American Historical Sources* (Madison: State Historical Society of Wisconsin, 1969); Kenneth W. Duckett, *Modern Manuscripts: A Practical Guide for Their Management, Care, and Use* (Nashville: American Association for State and Local History, 1975); and H. G. Jones, *Local Government Records: An Introduction to Their Management, Preservation, and Use* (Nashville: America Association for State and Local History, 1980). A very good brief overview is David H. Hoober, *Manuscript Collections: Initial Procedures and Policies,* Technical Leaflet no. 131 (Nashville: American Association for State and Local History, 1980).

The Society of American Archivists (527 South Wells Street, Chicago, IL 60607) regularly updates a series of basic how-to-do-it archives manuals. The latest versions are publicized at <www.archivists.org> and in the quarterly *American Archivist,* which also contains articles, book reviews, technical reports, and other information of value to those managing and doing historical research at local archives. A source of information on local museums and historical societies as well as archives is the American Association for State and Local History (530 Church St., Suite 600, Nashville, TN 37204 or <www.aaslh.org>). Special types of material are dealt with in Robert A. Einstein and Larry Booth, *The Collection, Use and Care of Historical Photographs* (Nashville: American Association for State and Local History, 1976); and James Bracelet and Douglas Marshall, *Maps in the Small Historical Society: Care and Cataloging,* Technical Leaflet no. 111 (Nashville: American Association for State and Local History, 1979).

12

Linking the Particular and the Universal

Each community, local institution, structure, and family is unique, and at the same time each shares characteristics with others of its kind. Every one occupies a different location in time, space, and circumstance that gives it an individual identity. Yet similarities in origin, design, motivation, or behavior join them with others in important respects. Uniqueness ensures that any exploration of nearby history will present its own challenges and revelations. The existence of shared characteristics, on the other hand, means that any historian of the nearby world can benefit from an awareness of what other students of the past have done, particularly those who have examined similar phenomena elsewhere.

The historian who wishes to understand a topic never regards it as existing in a vacuum. A much better appreciation of any particular subject can be attained by considering related matters, both the history of comparable phenomena and simultaneous developments in other areas that may affect the object of interest. The behavior of similar individuals or institutions and the nature of contemporary developments can often shed light on the subject of concern. If, as British historian H. P. R. Finberg suggests, family, community, national, and international history form a series of concentric circles, one must always be considered in relation to the others. Furthermore, all families in a community or communities in a society are circumscribed by the same conditions and thus have much in common. Therefore, any historian of the nearby past is wise to consider the questions, methods, and insights of other historians concerned with related times or topics. As a result, some of the links between the personal and the commonplace, the particular and the universal, may become evident.

There is also something to be gained from observing how others have examined the past. Whether or not their questions, methods, assumptions, and conclusions correspond to one's own, the process of comparing one's approach to others', past and present, can help clarify what one is doing and why. Historians approach their work differently from sociologists, economists, political scientists, and others who concentrate on a particular dimension of the human experience. Historians regard a broad variety of past conditions and phenomena—social, economic, political, cultural, and intellectual—as interrelated, and they have used many different techniques and analytic schemes to study the complex process of change over time. Furthermore, views on appropriate methods of exploring and interpreting the past evolve over time, generally in the direction of greater complexity, subtlety, and sophistication. Not every historian accepts the same approach to understanding the past, of course, and debates over various methods have long been and will undoubtedly continue to be a vital part of the study of history. Discussions of questions and techniques help all historians clarify their own assumptions, priorities, and beliefs.

During the last third of the twentieth century a growing number of academic historians became interested in family and community history, joining the many independent historians and genealogists already concerned about the past of a particular family or place. The academics brought new questions and research methods to the field, both broadening and altering the direction of study. At the same time, perceptive academics found they could often gain insight from the work of nonprofessional local historians. It is useful to consider the causes and effects of the rise of a "new social history" and thereafter a "new cultural history" as well as the gulf that previously separated academics from other historians. Doing so helps make apparent the relationship between the two and suggests the potential benefits to be gained from their intersection and collaboration. Such a consideration also makes clear that history, properly done, does not encompass the uncovering of a single absolute truth, but rather it involves a description of the past, using the best methods and evidence currently available, in terms of the ideas, issues, and perspective of the moment. History, whether nearby or international, should not be considered a fixed and limited reality but an interaction with the past that can provide fresh insight as needs and questions change.

THE EVOLUTION OF AMERICAN LOCAL HISTORY

American historical writing began as the consideration of the nearby past. William Bradford's *Of Plymouth Plantation,* accounts of early Massachusetts Bay by John Winthrop and Cotton Mather, and numerous similar works on New England villages reflected the initial Puritan concern with showing a corrupt world how their religiously committed community could, with God's favor, overcome hardship and establish a more moral society. The secular historiography of the seventeenth, eighteenth, and early nineteenth centuries focused as well on the settlement and development of individual colonies or towns, usually with an upper-class perspective and a large measure of local pride and self-promotion. Well after the Revolution came to an end that tumult was still being described colony by colony as Americans continued to identify themselves in state and local rather than national

12.1–12.2   *The growth of towns and cities produced arrangements for residents' well-being and acquisition of life's necessities that differed from rural arrangements and would themselves change over time. Careful examination of photographs such as these can reveal details of community life. What does the police patrol wagon suggest about policing concerns and practices at the start of the twentieth century? What does the small town general store delivery truck reveal about consumer credit and the local telephone network?*

(Photo courtesy of and copyright © Summit County Historical Society.)

(Photo courtesy of and copyright © Summit County Historical Society.)

terms. In the new nation, state and local historical societies began to gather records and present accounts of the past that were understandably self-centered. The Massachusetts Historical Society was founded in 1794, and similar institutions followed, in New York in 1804, thereafter in other Atlantic Coast states and, seemingly almost as soon as they were settled, in western states as well.

Only as the people of the young nation began to think of themselves as united with one another did they start reconstructing experiences once thought individual and distinctive as parts of a coordinated whole; their new present, in other words, revised their interpretation of their past and subsequent means of dealing with it. Not until George Bancroft's ten-volume *History of the United States America from the Discovery of the Continent* began to appear in 1834 (the last volume would not be published until forty years later) was a successful effort made to describe the American past from a national rather than a state or local perspective. Not for another fifty years would a national historical association be created, and an additional half century would pass before a national archives came into being. Preoccupation with local affairs and conditions, tinged perhaps with sectional self-justification, kept historical attention largely focused on the nearby past until after the Civil War, the nationalizing effect of which again encouraged a new and different way of looking at a preceding era.

Much nineteenth-century historical writing came from wealthy gentlemen for whom history was an absorbing pastime. Bancroft and the other patrician historians were romantics who also wrote poetry and prose, regarded history as literature, and preferred descriptive narrative to abstract analysis. They focused on heroic individuals and colorful episodes that served to extol the virtues and progress of Anglo-American democracy. Toward the end of the nineteenth century, these locally oriented patricians were joined by the commercial historians described in chapter 4, who for their own reasons produced volume after volume of uncritical, relentlessly cheerful local history. Both types focused on long-established leading citizens and community successes, ignoring lower-class groups (especially those racially, culturally, or religiously different) and community conflict, intolerance, or failure. However much a part of the local past, such matters were not part of the story they wished to remember or sell.

In the 1870s and 1880s a new type of historian began to appear: the professional scholar, trained in German-style graduate school seminars and committed to the belief that systematic, critical analysis of historical records could lead to an accurate, indeed scientific, and objective understanding of the past. History courses in college curricula increased rapidly, leading universities began awarding the Ph.D. in history, and in 1884 a group of these new professionals formed the American Historical Association (AHA). At first, nonacademic historians were encouraged to participate in the AHA. The academic historians, however, were committed to a belief in the importance of specialized research leading to a cooperatively produced overview. They also held to the notion that they were serving society and culture by concentrating on national history. This affected even those who began with a local interest, such as Frederick Jackson Turner, who wrote a doctoral dissertation on his Wisconsin hometown but soon began using his research to generalize in essays of grand sweep such as "The Influence of the Frontier on American History" that had a profound impact on American historical thought. Many academics, though not Turner, came to scorn nonprofessionals, whose approaches and interests differed from their own, and they tended to dismiss local history as lacking in sophisticated research and objectivity, which indeed was often the case, and possessing no importance, which was very shortsighted.

For their part, many local historians had little interest in matters outside the immediate realm of family and community, and they soon abandoned the AHA to the academics. The gulf between academic, nationally oriented history, and nonacademic, locally oriented history grew deeper and deeper during the first half of the twentieth century. Few historians outside the universities embraced the methods or analytical approaches of the professionals, while academics generally ignored the subject matter of local history.

Until the 1960s, only a handful of academic historians devoted serious attention to local history, and they often examined the local scene only for examples of national developments. The history of cities provided something of an exception. Arthur M. Schlesinger, Sr., argued that cities had transformed America and demanded the attention of scholars. Schlesinger offered an impressionistic national overview of American urban history in *The Rise of the* City (New York: Macmillan, 1933). His lead was followed by Carl Bridenbaugh, *Cities in the Wilderness: The First Century of Urban Life in America, 1625–1742* (New York: Ronald Press, 1938), and *Cities in Revolt: Urban Life in America, 1743–1776* (New York: Knopf, 1955); studies of particular cities such as Harold C. Syrett, *The City of Brooklyn, 1865–1898* (New York: Columbia University Press, 1944), and Bayrd Still, *Milwaukee* (Madison: State Historical Society of Wisconsin, 1948); and multivolume compendia by Bessie Pierce, *A History of Chicago,* 3 vols. (New York: Knopf, 1937–57), Blake McKelvey, *Rochester,* 4 vols. (vols. 1–3, Cambridge: Harvard University Press, 1945–56; vol. 4, Rochester: Christopher, 1961), and Constance M. Green, *Washington,* 2 vols. (Princeton: Princeton University Press, 1962–63). A rare and noteworthy specialized study of an aspect of a community's past was Oscar Handlin, *Boston's Immigrants, 1790–1880: A Study in Acculturation* (Cambridge: Harvard University Press, 1941).

Smaller communities received attention mostly from a few historians interested in testing Turner's view that the frontier stimulated democracy. Lewis Atherton, *Main Street on the Middle Border* (Bloomington: Indiana University Press, 1954), an examination of town life through an analysis of the institutions found along the typical main street, was an innovative effort to summarize the nature of Midwestern towns. Interesting generalizations also emerged from the brief examination of five Ohio Valley cities in Richard C. Wade, *The Urban Frontier: The Rise of Western Cities, 1790–1830* (Cambridge: Harvard University Press, 1959). Merle Curti,

The Making of an American Community: A Case Study of Democracy in a Frontier Community (Palo Alto: Stanford University Press, 1959), was both an impressive use of local records, census and property lists, newspapers, and letters to write a sophisticated community history of Trempeleau County, Wisconsin, and a pioneering attempt by an academic historian to base analytical generalizations upon a careful study of one locality's history. Atherton, Wade, and Curti all found support for Turner's ideas in their studies of frontier towns.

The history of the family received even less notice. A sociologist's impressionistic survey, Arthur W. Calhoun, *A Social History of the American Family from Colonial Times to the Present,* 3 vols. (Cleveland: A. H. Clark, 1917–19), and Edmund S. Morgan's outstanding colonial studies, *The Puritan Family* (1944; rev. ed., New York: Harper and Row, 1966) and *Virginians at Home* (Williamsburg: Colonial Williamsburg, 1952), stood practically alone. Utopian communities, business enterprises, schools, and churches attracted some attention, but generally for their distinctiveness rather than for their connection with the nearby area.

THE NEW SOCIAL HISTORY

The 1960s represented a turning point in the attitude of academic historians toward family and community history. Increasing numbers began to realize that concentration on national history and emphasis on progress, shared experience, and democratic values had taken no account of major elements in the American past. Social protest movements of the time made many historians conscious that their picture of the American past had not even included, much less accurately portrayed, blacks and other ethnic minorities, poor people, opponents of wars, or women. Recognition that the experience of ordinary people was as vital to historical understanding as knowledge of federal policy regarding such persons produced calls for "history from the bottom up."

Aware that the techniques employed to study leadership groups could not be used to study those who did not engage in the same types of activities or leave the same sorts of records, academic historians began to consider different approaches. The value of family and community history almost instantly became apparent. The individual experiences of ordinary people were most accessible through the study of their immediate social institutions, families, and communities; these in turn could serve as case studies for understanding national patterns. The advent of computers brought the possibility of handling vast amounts of information about large numbers of obscure people contained in census and other compiled records. By the 1970s, research activity in graduate schools and other academic centers had shifted perceptibly toward studies of ordinary people, workers, slaves, immigrants, families, and nonelite communities, often with statistical patterns replacing the named individuals of more traditional history.

Academic historians pursuing the new social history remained interested in general patterns of development, not just the isolated experience of one community, one institution, or one family. They found the descriptive narrative on which the strictly local historian had usually focused to be useful but not sufficient. Instead they concentrated on questions that facilitated the analysis and comparison of local situations in a search for universals. Their questions nevertheless deserve the attention of those concerned only with a particular place, for they suggest lines of inquiry that can enrich any effort to understand a nearby past.

Among the many questions that new social historians began asking about communities and their components, those dealing with patterns of structure and growth were especially prominent. Questions of community or family size, organization, and change over time were basic. It often proved to be surprisingly difficult to determine conclusively the size and makeup of a population, much less comprehend the factors influencing change. Related issues that provoked considerable inquiry involved migration, assimilation of outsiders, and physical, social, and economic mobility. The rate of individual and group movement from place to place and within a social pyramid came to be seen as a principal factor in family or community change. Questions of tension and conflict attracted attention because of what they could reveal about values and interests, divisions, authority, and the decision-making process within a household or larger institution.

A host of questions arose around the effects of modernization: the rise of urban, industrial mass society sensitive to the efficient use of time and oriented to the concept of progress; the alteration of the physical environment, the creation of bureaucratic structures to perform various functions, and the increase of individual autonomy and anonymity, what one historian labeled "privatism," within the community. Associated questions included the division of labor and authority within families, between sexes, and between family and community as well as the treatment of childhood, adolescence, and aging. As answers began to emerge, further questions arose regarding the persistence of rural communities, the gradual differentiation of urban space, and, in particular, the rise of suburbs. Ironically, the nature and behavior of social elites came to be examined once again, although in a very different light, as a result of the insights of the new social history. The nature, extent, and quality of changes produced by modernization were among the most important addressed by academic social historians.

EARLY AMERICAN COMMUNITIES

Historians of colonial America were among the first to embrace the new social history, concentrating on questions of community and family structure and evolution. This focus developed naturally from the great interest in American Puritanism and the much observed shift from religious solidarity and intensity to secularism and individuality. Intellectual historians had scrutinized Puritan sermons and analyzed Puritan thought but often had not made the connections to behavior despite the obvious relevance of community study to that of a congregational religious system. Among the first to do so was Sumner Chilton Powell, *Puritan Village: The Formation of a New England Town* (Middletown, CT: Wesleyan University Press, 1963). He used church and town records for an innovative examination of how Puritan settlers adapted English town patterns in establishing Sudbury, Massachusetts, in the 1640s as well as how power and property were initially distributed within the community. A more complex analysis focusing on the first two decades of Massachusetts Bay's principal settlement appeared in Darrett B. Rutman, *Winthrop's Boston: A Portrait of a Puritan Town, 1630–1649* (Chapel Hill: University of North Carolina Press, 1965). Through church records, private papers, and government records, Rutman traced the link between the religious ideas of Boston's founders and the nature of community governance, the evolution of commerce and land distribution, the general outlines of social activity, and the gradual decline of church dominance.

A trio of books, published in 1970 though foreshadowed for a half decade in their authors' articles, provided a more detailed and quantitative look at seventeenth-century New England family and community structure and growth. John Demos, *A Little Commonwealth: Family Life in Plymouth Colony* (New York: Oxford University Press), looked specifically at the cramped physical environment, close family relationships, and social responsibilities that tied the seventeenth-century community and family so closely together. A more extended analysis of another community, Philip J. Greven, Jr., *Four Generations: Population, Land, and Family in Colonial Andover, Massachusetts* (Ithaca: Cornell University Press), used vital, town, probate, and deed records to determine family characteristics and land ownership patterns. Greven found that as the community grew and land became more scarce, many fathers could no longer provide each son with a farm, ties between generations loosened, the tendency to delay marriage while awaiting inheritance declined, and instead more people married earlier and moved away. A similar pattern of development was seen by Kenneth A. Lockridge, *A New England Town: The First Hundred Years: Dedham, Massachusetts, 1636–1736* (New York: Norton), though his focus was less on family than on community evolution. With the close connection of purposeful church and civil leadership as well as the high degree of economic equality, Lockridge saw early Dedham as a utopian commune. Community growth, leading to land scarcity, social and economic division, and conflicts, transformed Dedham from a cooperative Puritan commonwealth into an individualistic, secular town.

A simultaneous book, *Peaceable Kingdoms: New England Towns in the Eighteenth Century* (New York: Knopf, 1970) was based on an examination of records from fifteen towns. Its author, Michael Zuckerman, contended that even as the influence of Puritanism ebbed, community solidarity and consensus remained strong. This was contrary to Lockridge's view and to that of Richard L. Bushman, *From Puritan to Yankee: Character and the Social Order in Connecticut,*

1690–1765 (Cambridge: Harvard University Press, 1967). The issue of whether communities from the seventeenth century to the twentieth remained cohesive or disintegrated would continue to intrigue and divide historians.

Other colonial community studies broadened the base of inquiry with efforts to illuminate a locale's *mentalité* (a French term popular with new social historians to refer to an overall climate of belief, thought, and emotion). Paul Boyer and Stephen Nissenbaum, *Salem Possessed: The Social Origins of Witchcraft* (Cambridge: Harvard University Press, 1974), used a study of land holding, social structure, and authority within the community as the basis for an impressive analysis of the deep-seated causes of the conflict that produced the famous Salem witchcraft trials of 1692. In *Divisions through the Whole: Politics and Society in Hampshire County, Massachusetts, 1740–1775* (New York: Cambridge University Press, 1983), Gregory H. Nobles sought to understand the religious passions of an eighteenth-century community during and after the Great Awakening in order to determine their social and political consequences.

Southern colonial development received comparable attention more slowly, in part because the widespread destruction of records during the Civil War made historical reconstruction more difficult. When studies did appear, however, they proved impressive in the use of available evidence to create a rich picture of community life. Darrett B. Rutman and Anita H. Rutman, *A Place in Time: Middlesex County, Virginia, 1650–1750*, 2 vols. (New York: Norton, 1984), provided a vivid and engaging description and a second volume explaining the evidence on which the text was based. Equally impressive were James Russell Perry, *The Formation of a Society on Virginia's Eastern Shore, 1615–1655* (Chapel Hill: University of North Carolina Press, 1990), and Lois Green, Russell R. Menard, and Lorena S. Walsh, *Robert Cole's World: Agriculture and Society in Early Maryland* (Chapel Hill: University of North Carolina Press, 1991).

Eighteenth-century Southern communities apart from the culture of plantations also received attention. Rhys Isaac, *The Transformation of Virginia, 1740–1790* (Chapel Hill: University of North Carolina Press, 1982) focused on the society of plain folks. So too did Richard R. Beeman, *The Evolution of the Southern Backcountry: A Study of Lunenburg County, Virginia, 1746–1832* (Philadelphia: University of Pennsylvania Press, 1984).

Community investigations even proved capable of yielding new insights on such a major event as the American Revolution. Using records from seventy-four New England towns, by far the largest sample to date, Edward M. Cook, Jr., analyzed the economic, family, and church background of men who became community political leaders in the Revolution. In *The Fathers of the Towns: Leadership and Community Structure in Eighteenth-Century New England* (Baltimore: Johns Hopkins University Press, 1976), Cook concluded that in political matters, citizens deferred to those of high social-economic status who were already proven community leaders. Robert A. Gross provided an outstanding study of the nature of community life and solidarity during the revolutionary crisis in Concord, Massachusetts, in *The Minutemen and Their World* (New York: Hill and Wang, 1976).

Not surprisingly, community historians focusing on the early national period carried forward the examination of some of the same issues raised by scholars of the colonial and revolutionary period. The process of community formation and development remained a central interest. James S. Young, *The Washington Community, 1800—1828* (New York: Columbia University Press, 1966), examined the physical setting and growth as well as the social structure of the new national capital, shedding light on how the local environment both mirrored and influenced early federal political conflict. Midwestern frontier community development received sophisticated treatment from Don Harrison Doyle, *The Social Order of a Frontier Community, Jacksonville, Illinois, 1825–70* (Urbana: University of Illinois Press, 1978). Doyle looked closely at voluntary association within an evolving town. These varied membership organizations, he concluded, both defined and limited strife, contributing to stability and cohesion within a dynamic, growing community.

Communities studies offered up new insights as well on the Civil War, to many historians the pivotal political event in American history. Ernest McKay examined the northern experience in *The Civil War and New York City* (Syracuse: Syracuse University Press, 1990). The nature of community life on the other side of the battle lines received the attention of Wayne K. Durrill, *War of Another Kind: A Southern Community in the Great Rebellion* (New York: Oxford University Press, 1990); and Steven Tripp, *Yankee Town, Southern City: Race and Class Relations in Civil War Lynchburg* (New York: New York University Press, 1997).

An impressive social-economic-political comparison of the rise of five Kansas communities, Robert R. Dykstra, *The Cattle Towns* (New York: Knopf, 1968), found that conflict between farmers and businessmen and among various groups of townspeople was as normal as cooperation, and that both helped shape the course of mid-nineteenth-century community growth. Dykstra uncovered little evidence of the placid consensus that Michael Zuckerman thought characterized the eighteenth-century New England town. Instead, he perceived that internal conflict was a central factor in community evolution and blamed town boosters, local historians, and academics alike for suppressing views of divisiveness on the questionable assumption that progress only resulted from harmony.

MODERN COMMUNITIES

Much of the academic study of nineteenth- and twentieth-century American community history has centered on the issue of modernization. As it is generally used by historians, the term "modernization" connotes a radical change in the basic character of life, a shift from a preindustrial society that anticipated a repetitive cycle of seasons and a continuation of traditional practices and organizations to an industrial society predicated on a faith in the possibility of progress, attuned to a search for efficiency through education, science, and technological advancement, and inclined to urbanization and the growth of bureaucracy. Some observers now suggest that America has already entered a "postmodern" era of diminishing faith in technological and bureaucratic solutions, skepticism about the values of life in huge organizations and urban settings, and doubts as to whether further social progress is possible. Whether or not they believe that the "modern" age is over, its analysts regard it as fundamentally different from the era preceding it.

Modernization is a complex concept and a social process without easily datable beginnings or limits. Some historians regard the modernization process as having begun in the eighteenth or early nineteenth century. Others argue that America was "born modern," exhibiting an interest in innovation and efficiency and a faith in progress from the time of settlement onward. Early stages of modernization received sensitive treatment in Michael H. Frisch, *Town into City: Springfield, Massachusetts, and the Meaning of Community, 1840–1880* (Cambridge: Harvard University Press, 1972); and Stuart M. Blumin, *The Urban Threshold: Growth and Change in a Nineteenth-Century American Community* [Kingston, NY] (Chicago: University of Chicago Press, 1976). Frisch and Blumin identified a change in the very idea of community as a village became a thriving city. Growth and the development of divisions carried the community beyond the reach of personal association but produced among residents a sense of interdependence.

The post–Civil War modernization process received the greatest attention. Robert H. Wiebe, *The Search for Order, 1877–1920* (New York: Hill and Wang, 1967), a very influential broad view of modernization (though he never uses the term), suggested that at the end of the Civil War, American communities generally remained islands unto themselves, but thereafter the impact of railroads, telegraphs, and other new technologies helped to bind the nation together, end local isolation, and standardize taste and behavior. The rush to industrialize, urbanize, and absorb large numbers of immigrants created momentary confusion but eventually produced a new social order. Large bureaucracies evolved to manage both government and business, and new types of communities of middle-class professionals arose, organizations based on shared expertise and interest rather than geographical proximity. In a modern urban setting, according to Wiebe, individuals found greater independence and anonymity but lost the sense of shared values and practices that characterized older, smaller communities.

Perhaps the most thoughtful overall exploration of the impact of modernization on a single community was Sam Bass Warner, Jr., *The Private City: Philadelphia in Three Periods of Its Growth* (Philadelphia: University of Pennsylvania Press, 1968). He considered the town of 1770–1780, the big city of 1830–1860, and the industrial metropolis of 1920–1930 and perceived a persistent pattern of "privatism," a preoccupation with personal happiness and the pursuit of wealth. Community growth and change, prosperity, and physical form resulted from individual ambition and choice, accounting for income-segregated residential patterns, narrow-purpose government, unresolved social problems, and poor city planning. Warner considered the Philadelphia example typical of modern American cities. His assessment of the results of modernization was notably more pessimistic than generalizations drawn by Thomas Bender, *Community and Social Thought in America* (New Brunswick, NJ: Rutgers University Press, 1978), and Robert Wiebe in their overviews of American community development.

SOCIAL MOBILITY AND ASSIMILATION

An early and continuing concern of academic historians investigating modernizing communities has been the matter of population mobility: changes in social-economic status, geographical movement, and assimilation of new arrivals into a society. Stephan Thernstrom's pioneering work, *Poverty and Progress: Social Mobility in a Nineteenth Century City* (Cambridge: Harvard University Press, 1964), used census data on Newburyport, Massachusetts, from 1850 to 1880 to test the long-popular notion of rapid social-economic advancement by the working class, the American "land of opportunity," or rags to riches, image. Thernstrom concluded instead that of those who remained in the community, most individuals within their lifetimes and families from one generation to the next climbed the social-economic ladder slowly and by small steps. Most strikingly, fewer than half the workers in the community at the time of one census remained ten years later; movement into and out of Newburyport in search of satisfactory circumstances was rapid.

Thernstrom's work inspired a host of similar mobility studies that confirmed patterns of high geographical and modest social working-class mobility. Among such works were Peter R. Knights, *The Plain People of Boston, 1830–1860: A Study of City Growth* (New York: Oxford University Press, 1971); Howard P. Chudacoff, *Mobile Americans: Residential and Social Mobility in Omaha, 1880–1920* (New York: Oxford University Press, 1972); Gordon W. Kirk, Jr., *The Promise of American Life: Social Mobility in a Nineteenth-Century Immigrant Community, Holland, Michigan, 1847–1894* (Philadelphia: American Philosophical Society, 1978); Peter R. Decker, *Fortunes and Failures: White-Collar Mobility in Nineteenth Century San Francisco* (Cambridge, MA: Harvard University Press, 1978); and Thernstrom's own *The Other Bostonians: Poverty and Progress in the American Metropolis, 1880–1970* (Cambridge: Harvard University Press, 1973). The similar Canadian experience was treated in Michael B. Katz, *The People of Hamilton, Canada West: Family and Class in a Mid-Nineteenth Century City* (Cambridge: Harvard University Press, 1975). Evidence of substantial mobility has many implications, not the least of which is the importance to communities of institutions and forces that promote stability and cohesion in the face of population turnover.

> *Although more of the new social history community studies seem to have focused on Massachusetts than on any other place, nearby historians elsewhere will usually find that some academic historians have studied their locality as well. If the community itself has not been examined, statewide or regional studies will often prove helpful. Indeed the less urbanized South, West, and Midwest have been dealt with more often at the state than at the local level. For instance, Iowa, a middle-sized state in the middle of the country, has not yet generated much community-level academic study, but it has been the subject of a number of excellent state or regional studies, which include:* Leland L. Sage, A History of Iowa *(Ames: Iowa State University Press, 1974);* Joseph F. Wall, Iowa: A Bicentennial History *(New York: Norton, 1978);* Allan G. Bogue, From Prairie to Corn Belt: Farming on the Illinois and Iowa Prairies in the Nineteenth Century *(Chicago: University of Chicago Press, 1963);* Robert Swierenga, Pioneers and Profits: Land Speculation on the Iowa Frontier *(Ames: Iowa State University Press, 1968) and* Acres for Cents: Delinquent Tax Auctions in Frontier Iowa *(Westport, CT: Greenwood, 1976);* Donald L. Winters, Farmers without Farms: Agricultural Tenancy in Nineteenth-Century Iowa *(Westport, CT: Greenwood, 1970);* Don S. Kirschner, City and Country: Rural Responses to Urbanization in the 1920s *(Westport, CT: Greenwood, 1970);* Richard J. Jensen, The Winning of the Midwest: Social and Political Conflict, 1888–1896 *(Chicago: University of Chicago Press, 1971);* Clarence A. Andrews, A Literal History of Iowa *(Iowa City: University of Iowa Press, 1972);* Morton M. Rosenberg, Iowa on the Eve of the Civil War—A Decade of Frontier Politics *(Norman: University of Oklahoma Press, 1972); and* Glenda Riley, Frontierswomen: The Iowa Experience *(Ames: Iowa State University Press, 1981). The local history and the state historical society can be very helpful in determining what has been published on your state.*

Assimilation of new groups into a modernizing community is closely tied to the process of social and geographic mobility but also raises issues of ethnic differences and their impact. Not only did communities have a great influence on newcomers, but the immigrants often had a shaping effect on the place where they settled. This influence was first recognized in sophisticated political histories of communities: J. Joseph Huthmacher, *Massachusetts People and Politics, 1919–1933* (Cambridge: Harvard University Press, 1959); Frederick C. Luebke, *Immigrants and Politics: The Germans of Nebraska, 1880–1900* (Lincoln: University of Nebraska Press, 1969); and John M. Allswang, *A House for All Peoples: Ethnic Politics in Chicago, 1890–1936* (Lexington: University of Kentucky Press, 1971).

A considerable variation became evident when the family patterns and social experiences of different ethnic groups were compared. This was done by Josef J. Barton, *Peasants and Strangers: Italians, Rumanians, and Slovaks in an American City* [Cleveland], *1890–1950* (Cambridge: Harvard University Press, 1975); Thomas Kessner, *The Golden Door: Italian and Jewish Immigrant Mobility in New York City, 1880–1915* (New York: Oxford University Press, 1977); Jon Gjerde, *From Peasants to Farmers: The Migration from Balstrand, Norway, to the*

Upper Middle West (New York: Cambridge University Press, 1985); and Gary R. Mormino and George E. Pozzetta, *The Immigrant World of Ybor City: Italians and Their Latin Neighbors in Tampa, 1885–1985* (Urbana: University of Illinois Press, 1987). Tensions among ethnic groups became the focus of Ronald H. Bayor, *Neighbors in Conflict: The Irish, Germans, Jews, and Italians of New York City, 1929–41* (Baltimore: Johns Hopkins University Press, 1978); Richard J. Oestreicher, *Solidarity and Fragmentation: Working People and Class Consciousness in Detroit, 1875–1900* (Urbana: University of Illinois Press, 1986); Olivier Zunz, *The Changing Face of Inequality: Urbanization, Industrial Development, and Immigration in Detroit, 1880–1920* (Chicago: University of Chicago Press, 1982); and Roger Waldinger, *Still the Promised City: African Americans and New Immigrants in Postindustrial New York* (Cambridge: Harvard University Press, 1996).

The singular experiences of Jewish communities have attracted the interest of a number of historians. Two of the most interesting studies to result are Jeffrey S. Gurock, *When Harlem Was Jewish, 1870–1930* (New York: Columbia University Press, 1979); and Walter Ehrlich, *Zion in the Valley: The Jewish Community of St. Louis*, Vol. 1: *1807–1907* (Columbia: University of Missouri Press, 1997).

Hispanics, another distinctive ethnic group, have also begun to receive attention. The peculiar circumstances of a community on an international border was considered in Oscar J. Martinez, *Border Boom Town: Ciudad Juárez since 1848* (Austin: University of Texas Press, 1978). A larger Chicano community was examined in Richard Griswold del Costillo, *The Los Angeles Barrio, 1850–1890: A Social History* (Berkeley: University of California Press 1980). More complex issues were addressed in Sara Deutsch, *No Separate Refuge: Culture, Class, and Gender on an Anglo-Hispanic Frontier in the American Southwest, 1880–1940* (New York: Oxford University Press, 1987).

The special circumstances of black people in the United States and the evolution of black ghettos within modern cities began to be investigated in Gilbert Osofsky, *Harlem: The Making of a Ghetto, Negro New York, 1890–1930* (New York: Harper and Row, 1966); and Allan H. Spear, *Black Chicago: The Making of a Negro Ghetto, 1890–1920* (Chicago: University of Chicago Press, 1967). These models were applied, tested, and refined in David M. Katzman, *Before the Ghetto: Black Detroit in the Nineteenth Century* (Urbana: University of Illinois Press, 1973); Kenneth L. Kusmer, *A Ghetto Takes Shape: Black Cleveland, 1870–1930* (Urbana: University of Illinois Press, 1976); James Borchert, *Alley Life in Washington: Family, Community, Religion, and Folklife in the City, 1850–1970* (Urbana: University of Illinois Press, 1980); Joe W. Trotter, Jr., *Black Milwaukee: The Making of an Industrial Proletariat* (Urbana: University of Illinois Press, 1985); and Cheryl Lynn Greenberg, *Or Does It Explode: Black Harlem in the Great Depression* (New York: Oxford University Press, 1991). The migration from the rural South that was a crucial aspect of the growth of northern black communities received particular attention in Peter Gottlieb, *Making Their Own Way: Southern Blacks' Migration to Pittsburgh, 1916–1930* (Urbana:

University of Illinois Press, 1987); and James R. Grossman, *Land of Hope: Chicago, Black Southerners, and the Great Migration* (Chicago: University of Chicago Press, 1989).

The impact of mid-twentieth-century developments on race relations within a community became the focus of Arnold Hirsch, *Making the Second Ghetto: Race and Housing in Chicago, 1940–1960* (New York: Cambridge University Press, 1983); Quintard Taylor, *The Forging of a Black Community: Seattle's Central District from 1870 through the Civil Rights Era* (Seattle: University of Washington Press, 1994); and Thomas J. Sugrue, *The Origins of the Urban Crisis: Race and Inequality in Postwar Detroit* (Princeton: Princeton University Press, 1996). Most recently, attention began shifting to black communities in segregated, and eventually desegregating cities of the South. This development was led by Earl Lewis, *In Their Own Interests: Race, Class, and Power in Twentieth-Century Norfolk Virginia* (Berkeley: University of California Press, 1991); and Ronald Bayor, *Race and the Shaping of Modern Atlanta* (Chapel Hill: University of North Carolina Press, 1996).

INSTITUTION BUILDING

The creation of durable institutions within communities characterized by changing populations interested social historians, especially after initial questions of community formation and population mobility began to be addressed. Initially, education, health care, and government drew the most attention. Questions about other matters inevitably followed.

Schools have been among the first institutions established by communities since the earliest days of settlement in North America. Especially useful studies of local schools have included Stanley K. Schultz, *The Culture Factory: Boston's Public Schools, 1789–1860* (New York: Oxford University Press, 1973); Selwyn Troen, *The Public and the Schools: Shaping the St. Louis School System, 1838–1920* (Columbia: University of Missouri Press, 1975); Vincent P. Franklin, *The Education of Black Philadelphia: The Social and Educational History of a Minority Community, 1900–1950* (Philadelphia: University of Pennsylvania Press, 1979); and Michael Homel, *Down From Equality: Black Chicagoans and the Public Schools, 1929–1941* (Urbana: University of Illinois Press, 1984).

The creation of a system of health care proved a revealing feature of community growth in many instances. Pioneering work on this topic was done by Morris J. Vogel, *The Invention of the Modern Hospital: Boston, 1870–1930* (Chicago: University of Chicago Press, 1980); Judith Walzer Leavitt, *The Healthiest City: Milwaukee and the Politics of Health Reform* (Princeton: Princeton University Press, 1982); and David Rosner, *A Once Charitable Enterprise: Hospitals and Health Care in Brooklyn and New York* (New York: Cambridge University Press, 1982). Virginia G. Drachman carried the investigation into new areas in *Hospital with a Heart: Women Doctors and the Paradox of Separation at the New England Hospital, 1862–1967* (Ithaca: Cornell University Press, 1984).

The development of local government has been an integral part of many community studies, but rarely the sole focus. The set of problems involving crime and the maintenance of public order is one aspect of government that has attracted special attention. Model studies include James F. Richardson, *The New York Police* (New York: Oxford University Press, 1970); Eric Monkkonen, *The Dangerous Class: Crime and Poverty in Columbus, Ohio, 1860–1885* (Cambridge: Harvard University Press, 1979); Roger Lane, *Violent Death in the City: Suicide, Accident, and Murder in Nineteenth Century Philadelphia* (Cambridge: Harvard University Press, 1979); and Lawrence M. Friedman and Robert V. Percival, *The Roots of Justice: Crime and Punishment in Alameda County, California, 1870–1910* (Chapel Hill: University of North Carolina Press, 1981). A noteworthy study of the early rise in the slave culture of the ante bellum South, of what is usually thought of as a modern feature of local government, is Dennis C. Rousey, *Policing the Southern City: New Orleans, 1805–1998* (Baton Rouge: Louisiana State University Press, 1997), an effective reminder that a community's or region's experience may depart from the common national pattern.

Interest in the development of working-class communities and labor organizations has drawn a number of historians to community studies. Among those that have produced significant insights into local circumstances as well as broader patterns have been Peter Friedlander, *The Emergence of a UAW Local, 1936–1939: A Study in Class and Culture* (Pittsburgh: University of Pittsburgh Press, 1975); Alan Dawley, *Class and Community: The Industrial Revolution in Lynn* (Cambridge: Harvard University Press, 1976); Daniel Walkowitz, *Worker City, Company Town: Iron and Cotton-Worker Protest in Troy and Cohoes, New York, 1855–1884* (Urbana: University of Illinois Press, 1978); August Meier and Elliott Rudwick, *Black Detroit and the Rise of the UAW* (New York: Oxford University Press, 1979); Robert A. Slayton, *Back of the Yards: The Making of a Local Democracy* (Chicago: University of Chicago Press, 1986); and Daniel Nelson, *American Rubber Workers & Organized Labor, 1900–1941* (Princeton: Princeton University Press, 1988). Lizabeth Cohen produced a study of unusual richness in *Making a New Deal: Industrial Workers in Chicago, 1919–1939* (New York: Cambridge University Press, 1990).

Social historians eventually came to reexamine the other end of the social spectrum as well, though in less laudatory and more analytical terms than had earlier been the case. The complicated role of elites as providers or withholders of leadership and philanthropy became the focus of attention. E. Digby Baltzell led the way with *Puritan Boston and Quaker Philadelphia: Two Protestant Ethics and the Spirit of Class Authority and Leadership* (New York: Free Press, 1979). Baltzell's pioneering work was soon followed by Frederic Cople Jaher, *The Urban Establishment: Upper Strata in Boston, New York, Charleston, Chicago, and Los Angeles* (Urbana: University of Illinois Press, 1982). A narrower but especially useful study was Kathleen D. McCarthy, *Noblesse Oblige: Charity and Cultural Philanthropy in Chicago, 1849–1929* (Chicago: University of Chicago Press, 1982).

POSTMODERNIZATION

While historical attention tended to focus on community growth as a result of modernization, variations in the picture did gain notice. Most common were investigations of urban expansion and differentiation as the result of modernization. One of the earliest and still most useful community modernization studies was Sam Bass Warner, Jr., *Streetcar Suburbs: The Process of Growth in Boston, 1870–1900* (Cambridge: Harvard University Press, 1962). Warner analyzed the influence of electric street railways and the extension of public utilities on the expansion and shaping of an industrial city. Infrastructure development permitted the middle classes to withdraw to new suburban settlements and leave the central city to immigrants and the poor, fragmenting the community.

Warner's pioneering study of the rise of suburbs around Boston was followed by several historians who began exploring in detail the nature of suburbanization. Kenneth T. Jackson provided an insightful overview in *The Crabgrass Frontier: The Suburbanization of the United States* (New York: Oxford University Press, 1985). Meanwhile Henry Binford reexamined the phenomenon in the same place but the period before Warner addressed it in *The First Suburbs: Residential Communities on the Boston Periphery, 1815–1860* (Chicago: University of Chicago Press, 1984). Thereafter, two detailed studies of Chicago, Michael H. Ebner, *Creating Chicago's North Shore: A Suburban History* (Chicago: University of Chicago Press, 1988); and Ann Durkin Keating, *Building Chicago: Suburban Development and the Creation of a Divided Metropolis* (Columbus: Ohio State University Press, 1989), offered alternative worthwhile approaches to the question. Margaret Marsh moved beyond the study of the physical creation of suburbs to the nature of their distinctive societies in *Suburban Lives* (New Brunswick: Rutgers University Press, 1990).

Similarities and distinctions in suburban development began receiving attention as more local studies were completed. Different suburbs of the same metropolis revealed dramatically divergent individual histories in Barbara M. Kelly, *Expanding the American Dream: Building and Rebuilding Levittown* (Albany: State University of New York Press, 1993); and Michael J. Birkner, *A Country Place No More: The Transformation of Birgenfield, New Jersey, 1894–1994* (Rutherford: Fairleigh Dickinson University Press, 1994). As he looked at local governance in Suffolk and Nassau Counties, New York; Oakland County, Michigan; DuPage County, Illinois; St. Louis County, Missouri; and Orange County, California; Jon C. Teaford found both patterns and variations in *Post-Suburbia: Government and Politics in the Edge City* (Baltimore: Johns Hopkins University Press, 1996).

Rural and small town communities unattached to metropolitan areas received less notice. Don Martindale and R. Galen Hanson, *Small Town* [Benson, Minnesota] *and the Nation: The Conflict of Local and Translocal Forces* (Westport, CT: Greenwood, 1969) was an early analysis. More recently outstanding studies have included Jane Adams, *The Transformation of Rural Life: Southern Illinois, 1890–1990* (Chapel Hill: University of North Carolina Press, 1994); and Paula M. Nelson, *The Prairie Winnows Out Its Own: The West River Country of South Dakota in the Years of Depression and Dust* (Iowa City: University of Iowa Press, 1996).

Community stagnation and decay require attention if modernization is to be fully examined. Instances of decline were investigated by Herman R. Lantz, *A Community in Search of Itself: A Case History of Cairo, Illinois* (Carbondale: Southern Illinois University Press, 1972); Joe R. Feagin, *Free Enterprise City: Houston in Political and Economic Perspective* (New Brunswick: Rutgers University Press, 1988); John T. Cumbler, *A Social History of Economic Decline: Business, Politics, and Work in Trenton* (New Brunswick: Rutgers University Press, 1989); and Andrew Hurley, *Environmental Inequalities: Class, Race, and Industrial Pollution in Gary, Indiana, 1945–1980* (Chapel Hill: University of North Carolina Press, 1995).

FAMILIES

Discussions of privatism call attention to the importance of the elements within the community to an understanding of its overall character. Histories of businesses, churches, social agencies, and voluntary associations have generated a rich literature of general works and specific studies. Many of the works already cited have paid particular attention to the history of the family and related matters.

Several scholars have provided insight into various aspects of family life. Child rearing has been examined in Bernard Wishy, *The Child and the Republic: The Dawn of Modern American Child-Nurture* (Philadelphia: University of Pennsylvania Press, 1968). The complex transition from childhood to adulthood received attention from Joseph F. Kett, *Rites of Passage: Adolescence in America, 1790 to the Present* (New York: Basic, 1977); Paula S. Fass, *The Damned and the Beautiful: American Youth in the 1920s* (New York: Oxford University Press, 1977); Beth Bailey, *From Front Porch to Back Seat: Courtship in Twentieth Century American* (Baltimore: Johns Hopkins University Press, 1988); and John Modell, *Into One's Own: From Youth to Adulthood in the United States, 1920–1975* (Berkeley: University of California Press, 1989). The other end of the family life cycle was the focus of David Hackett Fischer, *Growing Old in America* (New York: Oxford University Press, 1977); and W. Andrew Achenbaum, *Old Age in the New Land: The American Experience since 1790* (Baltimore: Johns Hopkins University Press, 1978).

12.3 Uncovering the history of daily life in ordinary families remains a challenge for nearby historians. The lives of women and children have generally been less well documented than adult males. What might be found in the interior of this modest home? What was the work day like for this young mother? What was childhood like for these two little girls, and what would be the nature of their adolescence experience in a few years? (Photo courtesy of the Library of Congress.)

Aspirations for the family as well as disappointed expectations and marital breakdown received considerable attention in Elaine Tyler May, *Great Expectations: Marriage and Divorce in Post-Victorian America* (Chicago: University of Chicago Press, 1980); and Glenda Riley, *Divorce: An American Tradition* (New York: Oxford University Press, 1991). Families outside the conventional mold began receiving historical attention in Linda Gordon, *Pitied But Not Entitled: Single Mothers and the History of Welfare, 1890–1935* (New York: Free Press, 1994). The distinctive circumstances of black families were treated in John Blassingame, *The Slave Community* (New York: Oxford University Press, 1972); and Herbert Gutman, *The Black Family in Slavery and Freedom, 1750–1925* (New York: Pantheon, 1976). Steven Mintz and Susan Kellogg attempted to synthesize scholarship on the family in *Domestic Revolutions: A Social History of American Family Life* (New York: Free Press, 1988).

As the new social history took hold, women finally began receiving considerable attention from historians, both as important persons in their own right and as central figures in the family. Within the steadily expanding library of women's history are several general studies that help clarify women's role within the family and community. They include: Lyle Koehler, *A Search for Power: The "Weaker Sex" in Seventeenth-Century New England* (Urbana: University of Illinois Press, 1980); Mary Beth Norton, *Founding Mothers and Fathers: Gendered Power and the Forming of American Society* (New York: Knopf, 1996); Nancy F. Cott, *The Bonds of Womanhood: 'Woman's Sphere' in New England, 1780–1835* (New Haven: Yale University Press, 1977); Anne Firor Scott, *The Southern Lady: From Pedestal to Politics, 1830–1930* (Chicago: University Chicago Press, 1970); Julie Roy Jeffrey, *Frontier Women: The Trans-Mississippi West, 1840–1880* (New York: Hill and Wang, 1979); and Karen J. Blair, *The Torchbearers: Women and Their Amateur Arts Associations in America, 1890–1930* (Bloomington: Indiana University Press, 1994).

The details of women's daily lives received attention in Elizabeth Fox-Genovese, *Within the Plantation Household: Black and White Women of the Old South* (Chapel Hill: University of North Carolina Press, 1988); David M. Katzman, *Seven Days a Week: Women and Domestic Service in Industrializing America* (New York: Oxford University Press, 1978); Susan Estabrook Kennedy, *If All We Did Was to Weep at Home: A History of White Working-Class Women in America* (Bloomington: Indiana University Press, 1979); Winifred Wandersee, *Women's Work and Family Values, 1920–1940* (Cambridge: Harvard University Press, 1981); Alice Kessler-Harris, *Out to Work: A History of Wage-Earning Women in the United States* (New York: Oxford University Press, 1982); Ruth Schwartz Cohen, *More Work for Mother: The Ironies of Household Technology from the Open Hearth to the Microwave* (New York: Basic Books, 1983); and Suellen Hoy, *Chasing Dirt: The American Pursuit of Cleanliness* (New York: Oxford University Press, 1995).

Insightful works that explore women's place within a specific community but have wider implications include Laurel Thatcher Ulrich, *Good Wives: Image and Reality in the Lives of Women in Northern New England, 1650–1750* (New York: Knopf, 1982); and *A Midwife's Tale: The Life of Martha Ballard, Based on Her Diary* (New York: Knopf, 1990); Joan Jensen, *Loosening the Bonds: Mid-Atlantic Farm Women, 1750–1850* (New Haven: Yale University Press, 1986); Suzanne Lebsock, *The Free Women of Petersburg; Status and Culture in a Southern Town, 1784–1860* (New York: Norton, 1984); Christine Stansell, *City of Women: Sex and Class in New York, 1789–1860* (New York: Knopf, 1986); Mary Ryan, *Cradle of the Middle Class: The Family in Oneida County, New York, 1790–1865* (New York: Cambridge University Press, 1981); Nancy A. Hewitt, *Women's Activism and Social Change: Rochester, New York, 1822–1872* (Ithaca: Cornell University Press, 1983); Dolores Janiewski, *Sisterhood Denied: Race, Gender, and Class in a New South Community* (Philadelphia: Temple University Press, 1985); and Paula Petrik, *No Step Backward: Women and Family in ton the Rocky Mountain Mining Frontier, Helena, Montana, 1865–1900* (Helena: Montana Historical Society Press, 1987).

The most up-to-date overviews of the topic are Sara Evans, *Born for Liberty: A History of Women in America* (New York: Free Press, 1989); and Rosalind Rosenberg, *Divided Lives: American Women in the Twentieth Century* (New York: Hill and Wang, 1992), while a more narrowly focused but nevertheless important survey is John D'Emilio and Estelle Freedman, *Intimate Matters: A History of Sexuality in America* (New York: Harper and Row, 1988).

Family life also involves men of course. While men's role in the family has received less notice, it requires attention for a balanced picture. Useful starting points include Mark C. Carnes and Clyde Griffen, eds., *Meanings for Manhood: Construction of Masculinity in Victorian America* (Chicago: University of Chicago Press, 1990); and E. Anthony Rotundo, *American Manhood: Transformations in Masculinity from the Revolution to the Modern Era* (New York: Basic, 1993).

THE NEW CULTURAL HISTORY

As the methodology of the new social history became more familiar, some historians became aware that it did not encompass a sufficient range of factors bearing upon the human condition in time past. Like early academics or 1960s' historians raised to concentrate on national government, economics, and foreign relations, these historians recognized that other issues existed besides those currently being addressed. Art, literature, and theater; commerce and advertising; film, music, sport, and other forms of popular entertainment; and thought, religion, and superstition were all aspects of culture shaping people's lives and nearby world. A "new cultural history" linking both sophisticated elite culture and popular mass culture to social, economic, and political developments began emerging in the 1980s and 1990s.

While studies of individual cultural institutions—orchestras, libraries, museums, theaters, and the like, such as Richard K. Lieberman, *Steinway and Sons* (New Haven: Yale University Press, 1995), and Lynn Boyd Hinds, *Broadcasting the Local News: The Early Years of Pittsburgh's KDKA-TV* (University Park: Pennsylvania State University Press, 1995), and have frequently appeared, integrated studies of a particular community's culture have been rare. An exception focused on high culture was provided by Robert C. Vitz, *The Queen and the Arts: Cultural Life in Nineteenth Century Cincinnati* (Kent: Kent State University Press, 1989). The somewhat less elevated but equally important culture of community festivals, parades, and celebrations attracted the notice of April R. Schultz, who focused on Minneapolis in *Ethnicity on Parade: Inventing the Norwegian American Through Celebration* (Amherst: University of Massachusetts Press, 1994).

The popular culture of communities has garnered more notice. Noteworthy studies have included Perry Duis, *The Saloon: Public Drinking in Chicago and Boston, 1880–1920* (Urbana: University of Illinois Press, 1983); Roy Rosen-

12.4–12.5   Historians have moved beyond questions about the physical development of cities to questions about the human activity that took place within them. Gaining a sense of urban life, especially the activities people engaged in outside of earning a living and managing the basic necessities of daily existence, can help historians understand why millions of people were drawn to cities and others wanted to keep their distance.

(Photo courtesy of the Library of Congress.)

(Photo courtesy of the Library of Congress.)

zweig, *Eight Hours for What We Will: Workers and Leisure in an Industrial City, 1870–1920* (New York: Cambridge University Press, 1983); Kathy Peiss, *Cheap Amusement: Working Women and Leisure in Turn-of-the-Century New York* (Philadelphia : Temple University Press, 1986); and Scott Martin, *Killing Time: Leisure and Culture in Southwestern Pennsylvania, 1800–1850* (Pittsburgh: University of Pittsburgh Press, 1995).

The notable role of sports as an element of a community's culture has deserved and received particular notice. Works that go beyond enthusiastic descriptions of individual and team sporting triumphs to portray the recreational culture of a community are relatively rare, however. Exceptions include Melvin Adelman, *A Sporting Time: New York City and the Rise of Modern Athletics, 1820–70* (Urbana: University of Illinois Press, 1986); Neil J. Sullivan, *The Dodgers Move West* (New York: Oxford University Press, 1987); and Bruce Kuklick, *To Every Thing a Season: Shibe Park and Urban Philadelphia, 1900–1976* (Princeton: Princeton University Press, 1991). An exemplary effort to explore a community's nonprofessional sporting culture is Rob Buck, *Sandlot Seasons: Sport in Black Pittsburgh* (Urbana: University of Illinois Press, 1993).

A variety of cultural elements and perspectives have increasingly been incorporated into histories of individual communities. Among those that did so effectively were Jacquelyn Dowd Hall, James Leloudis, Robert Korstad, Mary Murphy, LuAnn Jones, and Christopher B. Daly, *Like a Family: The Making of a Southern Cotton Mill World* (Chapel Hill: University of North Carolina Press, 1987); Philip J. Ethington, *The Public City: The Political Construction of Urban Life in San Francisco, 1850–1900* (New York: Cambridge University Press, 1994); and a particularly rich comparison of three small towns in Idaho, Oregon, and Utah, Dean L. May, *Three Frontiers: Family. Land, and Society in the American West, 1850–1900* (New York: Cambridge University Press, 1994). A very different sort of study that argues for the influence of external cultural factors on the development of a community is William Cronon, *Nature's Metropolis: Chicago and the Great West* (New York: Norton, 1991).

An effective application of the new cultural history as well as one of the most complex and imaginative community histories to date was produced by Alan Taylor. In *William Cooper's Town: Power and Persuasion on the Frontier of the Early American Republic* (New York: Knopf, 1995), Taylor examined the settlement and early development of a central New York community. He considered how the literary skill and effectiveness of a great novelist, James Fenimore Cooper, could reshape the image and historical memory of a community that his father had established and controlled for a time.

Taylor and other thoughtful scholars have come to appreciate that history itself is a reflection of culture. They acknowledge that history is not scientific and objective truth but rather an evolving understanding of the beliefs, perceptions, and available evidence as well as the most vivid and lasting memories, myths, and misperceptions of people at a particular moment. While this concept has yet to be effectively translated into many works of nearby history, it is worth consideration by all who do such work.

Several thoughtful considerations of history as a manifestation of culture have appeared. Peter Novick, *That Noble Dream: The "Objectivity Question" and the American Historical Profession* (New York: Cambridge University Press, 1988) initiated a discussion that was carried further by David Glassberg, *American Historical Pageantry: The Uses of Tradition in the Early Twentieth Century* (Chapel Hill: University of North Carolina Press, 1990); and John Bodnar, *Remaking America: Public Memory, Commemoration, and Patriotism in the Twentieth Century* (Princeton: Princeton University Press, 1992). Michael Kammen advanced the discussion with *Mystic Chords of Memory: The Transformation of Tradition in American Culture* (New York: Knopf, 1991); and *In the Past Lane: Historical Perspectives on American Culture* (New York: Oxford University Press, 1997).

12.6 *The faces in this photograph taken of people watching the Cincinnati Sesquicentennial Parade in 1938 radiate the intense interest generated in some, though not all, residents by a celebration of a community's past. (Photo courtesy of the Library of Congress.)*

CONCLUSION

The great outpouring of scholarly nearby history studies of disparate nature, which shows no signs of subsiding, suggests that academic interest in community and family history is likely to remain strong. This trend will be valuable for all historians of the nearby world. Observing the methods that other historians use to probe the past can often point the way to the answer to one's own questions. Even more important, the histories of other people, institutions, and communities enrich the understanding of one's own nearby history, the ways in which it parallels the experience of others, and the respects in which it is unique.

Much obviously remains to be learned about the past, and the past of communities in particular. "Community" was once defined as an interactive population in a specific location, but in modern society physical proximity may lead to relationships or experiences shared to only a very limited extent, while strong attachment to a group may not depend on geographic closeness but upon an Internet connection, a telephone, or an annual meeting. Modern cities may contain a great many semiautonomous communities with ethnic, class, geographical, occupational, cultural, or other attachments, each of which has internal ties much stronger than links to the larger community. Likewise, an individual may feel a strong bond with a group that is geographically dispersed but defines acceptable group behavior, provides support, and offers a sense of belonging, functions that are associated with membership in a community. Disgust with existing communities may lead to efforts to form new types of communities or to movement from one location to another but seldom to abandonment of all social contact or rejection of the quest for community. The attempt of most people to form a new family of some sort after death, divorce, or departure has disrupted the old family reflects the same human desire for social attachment. As long as communities continue to be a vital part of human experience, each new generation will need to reestablish their meaning and sort out their realities from misperceptions and myths that have arisen about them. The value of nearby history for understanding one's self and circumstance will remain as constant and fresh as the need for satisfying human relationships.

NOTES AND FURTHER READING

Since academic historians discovered the value of community and family studies, a flood of books has appeared in addition to those discussed in this chapter. A great many master's theses and doctoral dissertations have also been written, and many extremely worthwhile articles, far too numerous to mention here, have been published. New research and insights often appear first as articles and only much later, if ever, in books. The journals that regularly publish community and family history articles as well as review new books in the field include *American Quarterly, Historical Methods Newsletter, Journal of American*

History, Journal of the Early Republic, Journal of Family History, Journal of Interdisciplinary History, Journal of Social History, Journal of Urban History, Journal of Women's History, William and Mary Quarterly, and the many local, state, and regional historical journals.

Several edited collections of shorter essays have brought together valuable insights and examples of research methods. See Stephan Thernstrom and Richard Sennett, eds., *Nineteenth-Century Cities: Essays in the New Urban History* (New Haven: Yale University Press, 1969); Kenneth Jackson and Stanley K. Schultz, eds., *Cities in American History* (New York: Knopf, 1972); and Raymond A. Mohl and James F. Richardson, eds., *The Urban Experience: Themes in American History* (Belmont, CA: Wadsworth, 1973). A great deal of useful information has been gathered in Stephan Thernstrom, ed., *Harvard Encyclopedia of American Ethnic Groups* (Cambridge: Harvard University Press, 1980) and parallel state-level works on Minnesota and Indiana.

Specific cities have become the focus of a number of collaborative efforts by groups of historians. See, for instance, Allen F. Davis and Mark H. Haller, eds. *The People of Philadelphia: A History of Ethnic Groups and Lower-Class Life, 1790–1940* (Philadelphia: Temple University Press, 1973); and Irwin Yellowitz, ed., *Essays in the History of New York City* (Port Washington, NY: Kennikat, 1978).

A growing phenomenon is the urban encyclopedia in which scores of historians contribute to a rich reference on one metropolis. David D. Van Tassel and John J. Grabowski provided a model in *The Encyclopedia of Cleveland History* (Bloomington: Indiana University Press, 1987). Appearing subsequently have been David J. Bodenhamer and Robert G. Barrows, eds., *The Encyclopedia of Indianapolis* (Bloomington: Indiana University Press, 1994); Kenneth Jackson, ed., *The Encyclopedia of New York City* (New Haven: Yale University Press, 1995); and Leonard Pitt and Dale Pitt, eds., *Los Angeles A to Z: An Encyclopedia of the City and County* (Berkeley: University of California Press, 1997). A number of other urban encyclopedias are currently in preparation or being planned. Their appearance should further stimulate the growth of historical study of nearby communities.

Appendices

Appendix A

Forms to Request Information from Federal Agencies

These forms are inaccessible via the World Wide Web, or may be difficult to download.

1. Application for Search of Census Records
   U.S. Dept of Commerce, Bureau of the Census, Personal Census Search Unit, Jeffersonville, IN 47131. 812-218-3046. (See pages 245-248 for explanatory information and a sample form.)
2. Ordering Copies of Census Records
   The National Archives can provide copies of specifically identified pages of federal population census schedules, ordered by mail. For information, write to: General Reference Branch (NNRG), National Archives and Records Administration, 7th and Pennsylvania Avenue NW, Washington, DC 20408. (See pages 249-251 for a sample order form and partial instructions for completing it.)
3. Ship Passenger Arrival Records
   Old Military and Civil Records (NWCTB), Textual Archives Services Division, National Archives and Records Administration, 700 Pennsylvania Avenue NW, Washington, DC 20408. (See the sample form on pages 252-253.)
4. Veterans' Records
   Military Service Records (NNCC), National Archives, GSA, Washington, DC 20408. The form provides fourteen different addresses for acquiring military records. (See the sample form on pages 254-256.)
5. Land Entry Files
   Textual Reference Branch-Land (NMDT4), National Archives and Records Administration, 7th and Pennsylvania Avenue NW, Washington, DC 20408. (See the sample form on pages 257-258.)
6. Social Security Statement (also known as the Earnings and Benefit Estimate Statement, Form SSA-7004). Social Security Administration, Wilkes Barre

Data Operations Center, P.O. Box 7004, Wilkes Barre, PA 18767-7004, 1-800-772-1213. Available online at: <www.ssa.gov/online/forms.html>, a site that leads to many sources of information on Social Security. (See the sample form on page 259.) [Note: Responding to a congressional mandate, in October 1999 the Social Security Administration began sending annual reports to more than 125 million workers age 25 and older who are not receiving Social Security benefits. The statements are to arrive about three months before each recipient's birthday.]

APPLICATION FOR SEARCH OF CENSUS RECORDS

IMPORTANT INFORMATION

PLEASE READ AND FOLLOW CAREFULLY

This application is for use in requesting a search of census records.*
Copies of these census records often are accepted as evidence of age,
citizenship, and place of birth for employment, social security benefits,
insurance, and other purposes.

If the applicant is located, an official transcript will be provided
including the following information:

Personal Census Information	Available for census year(s)
• Census year	1910–1990
• County where taken	1910–1980
• State where taken	1910–1990
• Name	1910–1990
• Relationship to head of household	1910–1990
• Name of person in whose household you were counted	1910–1990
• Age at the time of the census	1910–1950, 1970–1990
• Date of birth	
Year and quarter	1960
Month and year	1970–1980
Year	1990
• Place of birth	1910–1950
• Citizenship if requested or if foreign born	1910–1950
• Occupation (if requested)	1910–1950

The Census Bureau's records with **INDIVIDUAL NAMES ARE NOT
ON A COMPUTER.** They are on microfilm, arranged according to the
address at the time of the census. Censuses are taken primarily for
statistical, not legal, purposes. Attention is called to the possibility that
the information shown in the census record may not agree with that
given in your application. **The record must be copied exactly as it
appears on the census form.** The Census Bureau CANNOT make
changes even though it realizes that enumerators may have been
misinformed or made mistakes in writing down the data they collected.
Those agencies that accept census transcripts as evidence of age,
relationship, or place of birth usually overlook minor spelling
differences but would be reluctant to consider a record that was
changed years later at an applicant's request.

If you authorize the Bureau of the Census to send your record to
someone other than yourself, you must provide the name and address,
including ZIP Code, of the other person/agency.

Birth certificates, including delayed birth certificates, are **not issued** by
the Bureau of the Census. You can obtain the birth certificate from the
Health Department or the Department of Vital Statistics of the state in
which the applicant was born.

The average time it should take you to fill out the BC-600, "Application for Search of Census
Records", including the time spent reading instructions is 12 minutes.

If you have any questions regarding these estimates or any other aspect of this form, please
call or write the Associate Director for Administration/Comptroller, Paperwork Reduction
Project 0607-0117, Room 3104, FB 3, Bureau of the Census, Washington, D.C. 20233.

Respondents are not required to respond to any information collection unless it displays a
valid approval number from the Office of Management and Budget. This 8-digit number
appears in the top right corner of page 3 of this form.

* Information from 1920 and earlier censuses is public information and is available from the National Archives.

**The completed application should be mailed to the Bureau of the Census, P.O. Box 1545, Jeffersonville, IN 47131, together with a
money order or check payable to "Commerce-Census."**

Figure A1.1

INSTRUCTIONS FOR COMPLETING THIS FORM
PRINT OR TYPE INFORMATION EXCEPT SIGNATURE
PLEASE FOLLOW NUMBERED INSTRUCTIONS

1. **Purpose**

The purpose for which the information is desired must be shown so that a determination may be made under 13 U.S.C. 8(a) that the record is required for proper use. For proof of age, most agencies require documents closest to date of birth; therefore we suggest you complete information for the EARLIEST CENSUS AFTER DATE OF BIRTH.

2. **Signature**

Each application requires a signature. The signature should be the same as that shown on the line captioned "full name of person whose census record is requested." When the application is for a census record concerning another person, the requester must sign the application, and the authority of the requester must be furnished as stated in instruction 3 below. If signed by marking (X), please indicate the name of the person whose mark it is and have witnesses sign as instructed. IF SIGNATURE IS PRINTED, please indicate that is the usual signature.

3. **Confidential information given to other than person to whom it relates**

(a) Census information is confidential and ordinarily will not be furnished to another person unless the person to whom it relates authorizes this in the space provided or if there is other proper authorization as indicated in 3(b), 3(c), and 3(d).

(b) Minor children – Information regarding a child who has at this time not reached the legal age of 18 may be obtained upon the written request of either parent or guardian.

(c) Mentally incompetent persons – Information regarding persons who are mentally incompetent may be obtained upon the written request of the legal representative, supported by a certified copy of the court order naming such legal representative.

(d) **Deceased persons – If the record requested relates to a deceased person, the application MUST be signed by (1) a blood relative in the immediate family (parent, brother, sister, or child), (2) the surviving wife or husband, (3) the administrator or executor of the estate, or (4) a beneficiary by will, or insurance. IN ALL CASES INVOLVING DECEASED PERSONS, a certified copy of the death certificate MUST be furnished, and the relationship to the deceased MUST be stated on the application. Legal representatives MUST also furnish a certified copy of the court order naming such legal representatives; and beneficiaries MUST furnish legal evidence of such beneficiary interest.**

4. **Fee required**

The $40.00 fee is for a search of one census for one person only. The time required to complete a search depends upon the number of cases on hand at the particular time and the difficulty encountered

in searching a particular case. The normal processing time requires 4 to 6 weeks. Since the fee covers return postage, do not send a stamped self-addressed envelope with the application.

No more than one census will be searched and the results furnished for one fee. Should it be necessary to search more than one census to find the record, you will be notified to send another fee before another search is made. Tax monies are not available to furnish the information. **If a search has been made, the fee cannot be returned even if the information is not found.**

5. **Full schedules (For Genealogy)**

The full schedule is the complete one-line entry of personal data recorded for that individual ONLY. The names of other persons will not be listed. If the applicant specifies "full schedule," the Census Bureau will furnish, in addition to the regular transcript, whatever other information appears on the named person's record in the original schedule, but only for THAT PERSON. In this case the information is typed on a facsimile of the original census schedule and verified as a true copy. There is an additional charge of $10.00 for EACH full schedule requested.

The Census Bureau also will provide "full schedule" information for those other members of the same household for whom authorizations are furnished. (See Instruction 3 for authorization requirements). A fee of $10.00 is required for each person listed on the full schedule.

LIMITATIONS — Certain information, such as place of birth, citizenship, and occupation, is available only for census years 1910 through 1950. Full schedule information is not available for census years 1970, 1980, and 1990.

6. **Census years 1910–1920–1930–1940– 1950– 1960–1970–1980–1990**

The potential of finding an individual's census record is increased when the respondent provides thorough and accurate address information FOR THE DAY THESE CENSUSES WERE TAKEN. If residing in a city AT THE TIME THESE CENSUSES WERE TAKEN, it is necessary to furnish the house number, the name of the street, city, county, state, and the name of the parent or other head of household with whom residing at the time of the census. If residing in a rural area, it is VERY IMPORTANT to furnish the township, district, precinct or beat, AND the direction and number of miles from the nearest town.

1990 Request — It is VERY IMPORTANT to provide a house number and street name or rural route and box number. Always include a ZIP Code.

7. **Locator Map (optional)**

Box 7 is provided for a sketch of the area where the applicant lived at the time of the requested census.

IF YOU NEED HELP FILLING OUT THIS APPLICATION,
PLEASE CALL ~~812-285-5314~~, MONDAY THROUGH FRIDAY
7:00 A.M. THROUGH 4:30 P.M. EASTERN TIME
812-218-3046

FORM BC-600 (3-14-97)

Figure A1.2

FORM **BC-600**
(3-14-97)

U.S. DEPARTMENT OF COMMERCE
BUREAU OF THE CENSUS

OMB No. 0607-0117: Approval Expires 09/30/98

APPLICATION FOR SEARCH OF CENSUS RECORDS

RETURN TO: Bureau of the Census, P.O. Box 1545, Jeffersonville, IN 47131

NAME OF APPLICANT

1. Purpose for which record is to be used (*See Instruction 1*)

☐ Passport _____ (date required)
☐ Proof of age
☐ Genealogy
☐ Other – *Please specify*

I certify that information furnished about anyone other than the applicant will not be used to the detriment of such person or persons by me or by anyone else with my permission.

2. Signature – Do not print (*Read instruction 2 carefully before signing*)

PRESENT MAILING ADDRESS

Number and street

City | State | ZIP Code

Telephone number (Include area code)

IF SIGNED BY MARK (X), TWO WITNESSES MUST SIGN HERE

Signature _____ Signature _____

NOTICE – Intentionally falsifying this application may result in a fine of $10,000 or 5 years of imprisonment, or both (title 18, U.S. Code, section 1001).

DO NOT USE THIS SPACE – OFFICIAL USE ONLY

$ _____ (Fee)   Case number _____

☐ Money Order
☐ Check
☐ Other

Papers received (itemize) | Returned

Received by | Date | Returned by | Date

---

3. If the census information is to be sent to someone other than the person whose record is requested, give the name and address, including ZIP Code, of the other person or agency.

This authorizes the Bureau of the Census to send the record to: (*See instruction 3*)

_____
_____
_____

4. FEE REQUIRED: (*See instructions 4 and 5*) A check or money order (**DO NOT SEND CASH**) payable to "Commerce – Census" must be sent with the application. This fee covers the cost of a search of no more than one census year for one person only.

5. Fee required . . . . **$ 40.00**

____ extra copies @ $2.00 $ _____

____ full schedules @ $10.00 $ _____
(for genealogy)

TOTAL amount enclosed $ _____

FULL NAME OF PERSON WHOSE CENSUS RECORD IS REQUESTED

First name | Middle name | Maiden name (*If any*) | Present last name | Nicknames

Date of birth (*If unknown, estimate*) | Place of birth (*City, county, State*) | Race | Sex

Full name of father (*Stepfather, guardian, etc.*) | Nicknames

Full maiden name of mother (*Stepmother, etc.*) | Nicknames

First marriage (*Name of husband or wife*) | Year married (*Approximate*) | Second marriage (*Name of husband or wife*) | Year married (*Approximate*)

Names of brothers and sisters

Name and relationship of all other persons living in household (*Aunts, uncles, grandparents, lodgers, etc.*)

PLEASE COMPLETE REVERSE SIDE

Figure A1.3

GIVE PLACE OF RESIDENCE FOR APPROPRIATE CENSUS DATE (SEE INSTRUCTIONS 1 AND 6)					
Census date	Number and street (Read instruction 6 first)	City, town, township (Read instruction 6 first)	County and State	Name of person with whom living (Head of household)	Relationship of head of household
April 15, 1910 (See instruction 6)					
Jan. 1, 1920 (See instruction 6)					
April 1, 1930 (See instruction 6)					
April 1, 1940 (See instruction 6)					
April 1, 1950 (See instruction 6)					
April 1, 1960 (See instruction 6)					
April 1, 1970 (See instruction 6)					
April 1, 1980 (See instruction 6)					
April 1, 1990 (See instruction 6)		ZIP Code			

FORM BC-600 (3-14-97)

7. LOCATOR MAP (Optional)
PLEASE DRAW A MAP OF WHERE THE APPLICANT LIVED, SHOWING ANY PHYSICAL FEATURES, LANDMARKS, INTERSECTING ROADS, CLOSEST TOWNS, ETC., THAT MAY AID IN LOCATING THE APPLICANT FOR THE CENSUS YEAR REQUESTED.

HAVE YOU SIGNED THE APPLICATION AND ENCLOSED THE CORRECT FEES?

*U.S. GPO: 1998-438-970/79188

Figure A1.4

ORDER FOR COPIES OF CENSUS RECORDS

Dear Researcher,

Before completing the form, please read this page for ordering instructions and general information about the types of records that can be ordered with this form. For more information, please write to: *General Reference Branch (NNRG), National Archives and Records Administration, 7th and Pennsylvania Avenue NW., Washington, DC 20408.*

IMPORTANT INFORMATION ABOUT YOUR ORDER

What We Can Provide: The National Archives can provide copies of specifically identified pages of Federal population census schedules, ordered by mail. To receive this photocopying service, you must provide the name of the individual listed, page number, census year, State, and county; for the 1880 through 1920 censuses, also include the enumeration district. Frequently it is possible to use a census index to locate this information. In recent years, many private firms have produced statewide indexes to census records for specific years. These are available throughout the country in libraries that have genealogical collections. In addition to the printed indexes, there are microfilm indexes to the 1900 and 1920 censuses and partial indexes to the 1880 and 1910 censuses. From these printed and microfilm indexes, you can determine the exact page on which a family was enumerated and then place your order.

The National Archives does not search census indexes, nor do we provide census research service by mail.

Alternative Approaches: Federal population census records, 1790-1920, are available to you for research at the National Archives Building in Washington, DC, and in regional archives located in various parts of the United States (see the back of this page for addresses). Furthermore, many public and private libraries and other research institutions have purchased microfilm copies of Federal censuses. Your local library, genealogical, or other research institution may be able to advise you about the availability of census records in your area.

Microfilm copies of Federal censuses, 1790-1920, and indexes to the 1880 and 1900-1920 censuses can be rented through a program operating in local libraries and historical or genealogical societies. This is a program established by the National Archives with a private contractor. For more information, please contact your local library.

Microfilm copies of census records are available for purchase. An entire county or enumeration district for a given State or census year may be on one or more rolls of microfilm. For information about the cost of microfilm, write to: *Publication Services Staff (NEPS), National Archives and Records Administration, 7th and Pennsylvania Avenue NW., Washington, DC 20408.* Include in your inquiry the census year, the State, and the county or enumeration district.

INSTRUCTIONS FOR COMPLETING THIS FORM

Use a separate NATF Form 82 for each file that you request. Remove this instruction sheet. You must complete blocks 1-6 (and 7, when applicable) or we cannot search for the file. Print your name (last, first, middle) and address in the box provided at the bottom of the form, which is your mailing label. The information must be legible on all copies. Keep the PINK copy of the form for your records. Mail the remaining three pages of the form to: *General Reference Branch (NNRG), National Archives and Records Administration, 7th and Pennsylvania Avenue NW., Washington, DC 20408.* Please allow 8 to 10 weeks for processing your order. **DO NOT SEND PAYMENT WITH YOUR INITIAL REQUEST.** When we search your order, we will make photocopies of records that relate to your request. For credit card orders, we will mail the copies immediately. For other types of orders, we will invoice you for the cost of these copies and hold them up to 45 days pending receipt of your payment.

NATIONAL ARCHIVES TRUST FUND BOARD | INSTRUCTIONS | NATF Form 82 (rev. 4-92)

Figure A2.1

THE NATIONAL ARCHIVES REGIONAL ARCHIVES SYSTEM

You may visit one of the regional archives listed below to research Federal population census records, 1790-1920. We suggest that you call for current hours of operation. Please note: The mail order photo-copying service by using this form is available **ONLY** from **General Reference Branch (NNRG), National Archives and Records Administration, 7th and Pennsylvania Avenue NW., Washington, DC 20408.**

National Archives - New England Region
380 Trapelo Road
Waltham, MA 02154
Phone: 617-647-8100
Areas served: Connecticut, Maine, Massachusetts, New Hampshire, Rhode Island, and Vermont

National Archives - Mid-Atlantic Region
9th & Market Streets, Room 1350
Philadelphia, PA 19107
Phone: 215-597-3000
Areas served: Delaware, Pennsylvania, Maryland, Virginia, and West Virginia

National Archives - Great Lakes Region
7358 South Pulaski Road
Chicago, IL 60629
Phone: 312-581-7816
Areas served: Illinois, Indiana, Michigan, Minnesota, Ohio, and Wisconsin

National Archives - Southwest Region
501 West Felix Street
Fort Worth, TX 76115
Phone: 817-334-5525
Areas served: Arkansas, Louisiana, New Mexico, Oklahoma, and Texas

National Archives - Pacific Southwest Region
24000 Avila Road
Laguna Niguel, CA 92656
Phone: 714-643-4241
Areas served: Arizona; southern California counties of Imperial, Inyo, Kern, Los Angeles, Orange, Riverside, San Bernardino, San Diego, San Luis Obispo, Santa Barbara, and Ventura; and Clark County, Nevada

National Archives - Pacific Northwest Region
6125 Sand Point Way
Seattle, WA 98115
Phone: 206-526-6507
Areas served: Idaho, Oregon, and Washington

National Archives - Northeast Region
201 Varick Street
New York, NY 10014
Phone: 212-337-1300
Areas served: New Jersey, New York, Puerto Rico, and the Virgin Islands

National Archives - Southeast Region
1557 St. Joseph Avenue
East Point, GA 30344
Phone: 404-763-7477
Areas served: Alabama, Georgia, Florida, Kentucky, Mississippi, North Carolina, South Carolina, and Tennessee

National Archives - Central Plains Region
2312 East Bannister Road
Kansas City, MO 64131
Phone: 816-926-6272
Areas served: Iowa, Kansas, Missouri, and Nebraska

National Archives - Rocky Mountain Region
Building 48, Denver Federal Center
Denver, CO 80225
Phone: 303-236-0817
Areas served: Colorado, Montana, North Dakota, South Dakota, Utah, and Wyoming

National Archives - Pacific Sierra Region
1000 Commodore Drive
San Bruno, CA 94066
Phone: 415-876-9009
Areas served: Northern California, Hawaii, Nevada (except Clark County), and the Pacific Ocean area

National Archives - Alaska Region
654 West 3rd Avenue
Anchorage, AK 99501
Phone: 907-271-2441
Area served: Alaska

NATIONAL ARCHIVES TRUST FUND BOARD   NATF Form 82 (rev. 4-92)

Figure A2.2

ORDER FOR COPIES OF CENSUS RECORDS
(See Instructions page before completing this form)

DATE RECEIVED IN NNRG

INDICATE BELOW THE METHOD OF PAYMENT PREFERRED.

☐ **CREDIT CARD** *(VISA or MasterCard)* for IMMEDIATE SHIPMENT of copies
Account Number:

Exp. Date: Signature   Daytime Phone:

☐ **BILL ME**
(No credit card)

REQUIRED MINIMUM IDENTIFICATION OF ENTRY - MUST BE COMPLETED OR YOUR ORDER CANNOT BE SERVICED

1. CENSUS YEAR	2. STATE OR TERRITORY	3. COUNTY
4. TOWNSHIP OR OTHER SUBDIVISION	5. NAME OF HEAD OF HOUSEHOLD	6. PAGE NO. 7. ENUMERATION DISTRICT (for 1880, 1900, 1910, and 1920 only)

PLEASE PROVIDE THE FOLLOWING ADDITIONAL INFORMATION, IF KNOWN

	NAME	AGE	SEX	NAME	AGE	SEX
8. MEMBERS OF HOUSEHOLD						

NATIONAL ARCHIVES TRUST FUND BOARD   NATF Form 82 (rev. 4-92)

DO NOT WRITE BELOW - SPACE IS FOR OUR REPLY TO YOU

☐ **NO--We were unable to locate the entry you requested above. No payment is required.**

SEARCHER	DATE SEARCHED

☐ REQUIRED MINIMUM IDENTIFICATION OF ENTRY WAS NOT PROVIDED. Please complete blocks 1, 2, 3, 4, 5, 6, and 7 and resubmit your order.

☐ Due to the poor quality of the microfilm, the pages you requested cannot be reproduced clearly on our equipment.

☐ The microfilm roll for the State and county for which you requested copies is missing and will take 1 to 2 months to replace.

☐ OTHER:

☐ **YES--We located the entry you requested above. We have made copies of the entry for you. The cost for these copies is $6.**

CENSUS YEAR	STATE OR TERRITORY
COUNTY	
MICROFILM PUBLICATION	ROLL PAGE NO.
SEARCHER	DATE SEARCHED

Make your check or money order payable to NATIONAL ARCHIVES TRUST FUND. Do not send cash. Return this form and your payment in the enclosed envelope to:

NATIONAL ARCHIVES TRUST FUND
P.O. BOX 100221
ATLANTA, GA 30384-0221

PLEASE NOTE: We will hold these copies awaiting receipt of payment for only 45 days from the date completed, which is stamped below. After that time, you must submit another form to obtain photocopies of the record.

THIS IS YOUR MAILING LABEL. PRESS FIRMLY.

NAME (Last, First, MI)	
STREET	
CITY, STATE	ZIP CODE

C188643

INVOICE/REPLY COPY - DO NOT DETACH

Figure A2.3

OMB Control No. 3095-0027 Expires 10-31-01

NATIONAL ARCHIVES ORDER FOR COPIES OF SHIP PASSENGER ARRIVAL RECORDS

Dear Researcher,

Before completing the form, please read this page for ordering instructions and general information about the records that can be ordered with this form. Mail order photocopying service using this form is available ONLY from *Old Military and Civil Records (NWCTB), Textual Archives Services Division, National Archives and Records Administration, 700 Pennsylvania Avenue NW., Washington, DC 20408*. For more information, please write to us at the address above.

IMPORTANT INFORMATION

WHAT WE HAVE: The National Archives has inbound Federal ship passenger arrival records dating back to 1820 for most east coast and gulf coast ports and a few lists dating back to 1800 for Philadelphia. Ship passenger lists in our custody are not complete. Fire, dampness, or other causes destroyed many records in the 19th century before the creating agencies transferred them to the National Archives. During the 19th century, no law required passenger arrival records to be kept for persons entering the United States by land from Canada or Mexico. No law required the keeping of outbound passenger lists.

WHAT WE CAN SEARCH: *Passenger Indexes:* We can search indexes if you supply the following information: full name of the passenger, port of entry, and approximate date of arrival. The following major indexes exist: Baltimore (1820-1952), Boston (1848-91 and 1902-20), New Orleans (1853-1952), New York (1820-46 and 1897-1948), Philadelphia (1800-1948), and minor ports (1820-74 and 1890-1924). *Unindexed Passenger Lists:* We cannot search these lists without more specific information than we require for index searches. To search unindexed passenger lists through 1892, you must supply port of entry, the name of the vessel, approximate date of arrival, and the full name of the passenger. For those lists, we can also make a search with port of embarkation, exact date of arrival, port of entry, and the full name of the passenger. To search unindexed lists after 1892, we need the port of entry, the name of the vessel, the exact date of arrival, the full name of the passenger, and the names and ages of accompanying passengers, if any. PLEASE NOTE: *There is no index for New York for the period 1847 through 1896 or for the period 1949 through the present.*

ADDITIONAL INFORMATION: You may order copies of an entire passenger list by making a specific request. Write to Old Military and Civil Records at the address above. We will notify you of the cost. In addition, you or your representatives may search records that are too voluminous for the National Archives staff to search. We do not maintain a list of persons who do research for a fee. However, many researchers advertise their services in genealogical periodicals, usually available in libraries. *Naturalization (Citizenship) Records:* Naturalization records are separate from passenger arrival lists. The National Archives has copies of naturalization papers (1798-1906) for Massachusetts, New Hampshire, Rhode Island, and Maine and original records (1802-1926) for the District of Columbia. For information about citizenship granted elsewhere through September 26, 1906, write to the Federal, State, or municipal court that issued the naturalization. The Immigration and Naturalization Service, Washington, DC 20536 can furnish information on naturalizations that occurred after September 26, 1906.

INSTRUCTIONS FOR COMPLETING THIS FORM

Use a separate NATF Form 81 for each passenger arrival record. Remove this instruction sheet. Print your name (last, first, middle) and address in the block provided at the bottom of the form, which is your mailing label. Because of the volume of requests we receive, we are not able to write names and addresses on the form for you. We will return forms without return addresses when we are able. If the form is separated from the envelope, we will be forced to destroy requests without return addresses. The information must be legible on all copies. Keep the PINK copy of the form for your records. Mail the remaining three pages of the form to: *Old Military and Civil Records (NWCTB), Textual Archives Services Division, National Archives and Records Administration, 700 Pennsylvania Avenue NW., Washington, DC 20408.* Please allow 8 to 10 weeks for processing your order. **DO NOT SEND PAYMENT WITH THIS FORM.** When we search your order, we will make photocopies of records that relate to your request. For credit card orders, we will mail the copies immediately. We accept MasterCard, VISA, American Express, and NOVUS (Discover, Bravo, Private Issue) credit cards. For other types of orders, we will invoice you for the cost of these copies and hold them up to 45 days pending receipt of your payment.

**PRIVACY ACT STATEMENT AND PAPERWORK REDUCTION ACT PUBLIC BURDEN STATEMENT
APPEAR ON THE REVERSE OF THE PINK CUSTOMER COPY.**

NATIONAL ARCHIVES TRUST FUND BOARD   INSTRUCTIONS   NATF Form 81 (rev. 5-98)

Figure A3.1

NATIONAL ARCHIVES TRUST FUND BOARD   NATF Form 81 (rev. 5-98)   OMB Control No. 3095-0027 Expires 10-31-01

NATIONAL ARCHIVES ORDER FOR COPIES OF SHIP PASSENGER ARRIVAL RECORDS
(See Instructions page before completing this form)

IDENTIFICATION OF ENTRY

		AGE	SEX
DATE OF ARRIVAL	FULL NAME OF PASSENGER *(Give last, first, and middle names)*		
PORT OF ENTRY			
WHERE NATURALIZED *(if known)*	NAMES OF MEMBERS OF IMMIGRANT FAMILY		
SHIP NAME *(or Carrier Line)* *A 3-2*			
PASSENGER'S COUNTRY OF ORIGIN			

DO NOT WRITE BELOW - SPACE IS FOR OUR REPLY TO YOU

☐ **NO--We were unable to locate the record you requested above. No payment is required.**

MICROFILM PUBLICATION	ROLL	PAGE
RECORDS SEARCHED		SEARCHER
		DATE SEARCHED

☐ A SEARCH WAS NOT MADE because the records you requested are not documented in our ship passenger arrival list records. Please see the reverse of this form. Also, please see the enclosed pamphlet for further information about our holdings.

☐ A SEARCH WAS NOT MADE because insufficient information was supplied. Please see the reverse of this form.

☐ A SEARCH WAS MADE BUT THE RECORD YOU REQUESTED ABOVE WAS NOT FOUND. Please see the reverse of this form.

☐ A SEARCH WAS MADE BUT THE EXACT RECORD YOU REQUESTED ABOVE WAS NOT FOUND. We found a record that may be the one you seek. Please see the reverse of this form.

☐ **YES--We located the record you requested above. We have copied the record for you. The cost for these copies is $10.**

MICROFILM PUBLICATION	ROLL	PAGE
SEARCHER		DATE SEARCHED
ARRIVAL DATE		
PORT		
SHIP		

Make your check or money order payable to NATIONAL ARCHIVES TRUST FUND. Do not send cash. Return this form and your payment in the enclosed envelope to:

NATIONAL ARCHIVES TRUST FUND
P.O. BOX 100221
ATLANTA, GA   30384-0221

PLEASE NOTE: We will hold these copies awaiting receipt of payment for only 45 days from the date completed, which is stamped below. After that time, you must submit another form to obtain photocopies of the record.

INDICATE BELOW THE METHOD OF PAYMENT PREFERRED.

☐ **CREDIT CARD for IMMEDIATE SHIPMENT** of copies *(see Instructions for credit cards we can accept).*   Exp. Date: Signature   Daytime Phone:

☐ **BILL ME** *(No credit card)*

THIS IS YOUR MAILING LABEL.	NAME (Last, First, MI)	
PRESS FIRMLY.	STREET	
	CITY, STATE	ZIP CODE

B596682

INVOICE/REPLY COPY - DO NOT DETACH

Figure A3.2

OMB Control No. 3095-0032 Expires 9-30-98

NATIONAL ARCHIVES ORDER FOR COPIES OF VETERANS RECORDS

Dear Researcher,

Before completing the form, please read both sides of this page for ordering instructions and general information about the types of records that can be ordered with this form. Mail order photocopying service by using this form is available ONLY from *Textual Reference Branch (NWDT1), National Archives and Records Administration, 7th and Pennsylvania Avenue NW., Washington, DC 20408.* For more information, please write to us at the address above.

IMPORTANT INFORMATION ABOUT YOUR ORDER

The success of our search depends on the completeness and accuracy of the information you provide in blocks 3-18 on this form. Please note that each NATF Form 80 is handled separately. When you send more than one form at a time, you may not receive all of your replies at the same time.

Military service records rarely contain family information. Pension application files generally are most useful to those who are doing genealogical research and contain the most complete information regarding a man's military career. We suggest that you first request copies of a man's pension file. You should request copies of a bounty-land warrant file or a military record only when no pension file exists. If the veteran's service was during the Revolutionary War, bounty-land warrant applications have been consolidated with pension application papers. You can obtain both files by requesting the pension file only.

We will copy complete compiled military service and bounty-land application files. When we are unable to provide copies of all pension documents because of the size of a pension application file, we will send copies of the documents we think will be most useful to you for genealogical purposes. Many of the documents in these files are repetitive or administrative in nature. You may order copies of all remaining documents in a file by making a specific request. We will notify you of the cost of the additional copies.

Do NOT use this form to request photocopies of records relating to service in World War I or II, or subsequent service. Write to: *National Personnel Records Center (Military Records), NARA, 9700 Page Boulevard, St. Louis, MO 63132.*

INSTRUCTIONS FOR COMPLETING THIS FORM

Use a separate NATF Form 80 for each file that you request. Remove this instruction sheet. You must complete blocks 3-7 or we cannot search for the file. Print your name (last, first, middle) and address in the block provided at the bottom of the form, which is your mailing label. The information must be legible on all copies. Keep the PINK copy of the form for your records. Mail the remaining three pages of the form to: *Textual Reference Branch (NWDT1), National Archives and Records Administration, 7th and Pennsylvania Avenue NW., Washington, DC 20408.* DO NOT SEND PAYMENT WITH THIS FORM. When we search your order, we will make photocopies of records that relate to your request. For credit card orders, we will mail the copies immediately. We accept MasterCard, VISA, American Express, and NOVUS (Discover, Bravo, Private Issue) credit cards. For other types of orders, we will invoice you for the cost of these copies and hold them until we receive your payment.

SEE THE REVERSE OF THIS PAGE FOR DESCRIPTIONS OF
THE TYPES OF RECORDS THAT CAN BE ORDERED WITH THIS FORM.

PRIVACY ACT STATEMENT AND PAPERWORK REDUCTION ACT PUBLIC BURDEN STATEMENT ON REVERSE OF THIS PAGE.

NATIONAL ARCHIVES TRUST FUND BOARD   INSTRUCTIONS   NATF Form 80 (rev. 8-97)

Figure A4.1

TYPES OF RECORDS THAT CAN BE ORDERED WITH THIS FORM

PENSION APPLICATION FILES

Pension application files, based on Federal (not State) service before World War I, usually include an official statement of the veteran's military service, as well as information of a personal nature. Pensions based on military service for the Confederate States of America were authorized by some Southern States but not by the Federal Government until 1959. Inquiries about State pensions should be addressed to the State archives or equivalent agency at the capital of the veteran's State of residence after the war.

BOUNTY-LAND WARRANT APPLICATION FILES

Bounty-land warrant application files are based on Federal (not State) service before 1856. Documents in a bounty-land warrant application file are similar to those in a pension application file. In addition, these files usually give the veteran's age and place of residence at the time the application was made.

MILITARY SERVICE RECORDS

Military service records are based on service in the UNITED STATES ARMY (officers who served before June 30, 1917, and enlisted men who served before October 31, 1912); NAVY (officers who served before 1903 and enlisted men who served before 1886); MARINE CORPS (officers who served before 1896 and enlisted men who served before 1905); and CONFEDERATE ARMED FORCES (officers and enlisted men, 1861-65). In addition to persons who served in regular forces raised by the Federal Government, volunteers fought in various wars chiefly in the Federal Government's interest from the Revolutionary War through the Philippine Insurrection, 1775-1902.

Compilations of information concerning most military service performed by individuals in volunteer organizations during the 19th and early 20th centuries are available, but such records were not compiled for Regular Army officers who served before 1863 and for Regular Army enlisted men and Navy and Marine Corps personnel who served during most of the 19th century. Records pertaining to such service are scattered among many files and generally contain few details concerning a man's service. We cannot undertake the research necessary to locate all such documents. If you request a military service record, we will copy the documents that best summarize the veteran's service.

The record of an individual's service in any one organization is entirely separate from his record of service in another organization. We are unable to establish accurately the identity of individuals of the same name who served in different organizations. If you know that an individual served in more than one organization and you desire copies of all of the military service records, submit a separate form for the service record in each organization.

Discharge certificates are not usually included as a part of a compiled military service record. Before 1944, Army regulations allowed the preparation of an original discharge certificate only, which was given to the soldier. Confederate soldiers in service at the time of surrender did not receive discharge certificates. They were given paroles, and these paroles became the property of the soldier.

PRIVACY ACT STATEMENT
Collection of this information is authorized by 44 U.S.C. 2108. Disclosure of the information is voluntary; however, we will be unable to respond to your request if you do not furnish your name and address and the minimum required information about the records. The information is used by NARA employees to search for the record; to respond to you; to maintain control over information requests received and answered; and to facilitate preparation of internal statistical reports. If you provide credit card information, that information is used to bill you for copies.

PAPERWORK REDUCTION ACT PUBLIC BURDEN STATEMENT
Public burden reporting for this collection of information is estimated to be 10 minutes per response. Send comments regarding the burden estimate or any other aspect of the information collection, including suggestions for reducing this burden, to National Archives and Records Administration (NHP), 8601 Adelphi Road, College Park MD 20740. DO NOT SEND COMPLETED FORMS TO THIS ADDRESS. SEND COMPLETED FORMS TO THE ADDRESS INDICATED ON THE FORM ITSELF.

NATIONAL ARCHIVES TRUST FUND BOARD   NATF Form 80 (rev. 8-97)

Figure A4.2

OMB Control No. 3095-0032 Expires 9-30-98

NATIONAL ARCHIVES
ORDER FOR COPIES OF VETERANS RECORDS
(See Instructions page before completing this form)

DATE RECEIVED IN NWDT1

INDICATE BELOW THE TYPE OF FILE DESIRED AND THE METHOD OF PAYMENT PREFERRED.

1. FILE TO BE SEARCHED (Check one box only)
☐ PENSION
☐ BOUNTY-LAND WARRANT APPLICATION (Service before 1856 only)
☐ MILITARY

2. PAYMENT METHOD (Check one box only)
☐ **CREDIT CARD** for IMMEDIATE SHIPMENT of copies (see Instructions for credit cards we can accept) .
Exp. Date:
Signature:
Daytime Phone:
☐ **BILL ME** (No Credit Card)

REQUIRED MINIMUM IDENTIFICATION OF VETERAN - MUST BE COMPLETED OR YOUR ORDER CANNOT BE SERVICED

3. VETERAN (Give last, first, and middle names)

4. BRANCH OF SERVICE IN WHICH HE SERVED
☐ ARMY   ☐ NAVY   ☐ MARINE CORPS

5. STATE FROM WHICH HE SERVED

6. WAR IN WHICH, OR DATES BETWEEN WHICH, HE SERVED

7. IF SERVICE WAS CIVIL WAR,
☐ UNION   ☐ CONFEDERATE

PLEASE PROVIDE THE FOLLOWING ADDITIONAL INFORMATION, IF KNOWN

8. UNIT IN WHICH HE SERVED (Name of regiment or number, company, etc, name of ship)

9. IF SERVICE WAS ARMY, ARM IN WHICH HE SERVED
☐ INFANTRY   ☐ CAVALRY   ☐ ARTILLERY
If other, specify:

Rank
☐ OFFICER   ☐ ENLISTED

10. KIND OF SERVICE
☐ VOLUNTEERS   ☐ REGULARS

11. PENSION/BOUNTY-LAND FILE NO.

12. IF VETERAN LIVED IN A HOME FOR SOLDIERS, GIVE LOCATION (City and State)

13. PLACE(S) VETERAN LIVED AFTER SERVICE

14. DATE OF BIRTH

15. PLACE OF BIRTH (City, County, State, etc.)

18. NAME OF WIDOW OR OTHER CLAIMANT

16. DATE OF DEATH

17. PLACE OF DEATH (City, County, State, etc.)

NATIONAL ARCHIVES TRUST FUND BOARD   NATF Form 80 (rev. 8-97)

DO NOT WRITE BELOW - SPACE IS FOR OUR REPLY TO YOU

☐ **NO—We were unable to locate the file you requested above. No payment is required.**

DATE SEARCHED   SEARCHER

☐ REQUIRED MINIMUM IDENTIFICATION OF VETERAN WAS NOT PROVIDED. Please complete blocks 3 (give full name), 4, 5, 6, and 7 and resubmit your order.

☐ A SEARCH WAS MADE BUT THE FILE YOU REQUESTED ABOVE WAS NOT FOUND. When we do not find a record for a veteran, this does not mean that he did not serve. You may be able to obtain information about him from the archives of the State from which he served.

☐ See attached forms, leaflets, or information sheets.

☐ **YES—We located the file you requested above. We have made copies from the file for you. The cost for these copies is $10.**

DATE SEARCHED   SEARCHER

FILE DESIGNATION

Make your check or money order payable to NATIONAL ARCHIVES TRUST FUND. Do not send cash. Return this form and your payment in the enclosed envelope to:

NATIONAL ARCHIVES TRUST FUND
P.O. BOX 100221
ATLANTA, GA   30384-0221

PLEASE NOTE: We will hold these copies awaiting receipt of payment for only 45 days from the date completed, which is stamped below. After that time, you must submit another form to obtain photocopies of the file.

SEND TO:
THIS IS YOUR MAILING LABEL.
PRESS FIRMLY.

NAME (Last, First, MI)
STREET
CITY, STATE   ZIP CODE

A347389

INVOICE/REPLY COPY - DO NOT DETACH

Figure A4.3

OMB Control No. 3095-0033 Expires 02-28-2000

NATIONAL ARCHIVES ORDER FOR COPIES OF LAND ENTRY FILES

Dear Researcher,

Before completing the form, please read both sides of this page for ordering instructions and general information about the types of records that can be ordered with this form. Mail order photocopying service by using this form is available ONLY from *Textual Reference Branch-Land (NWDT1), National Archives and Records Administration, 7th and Pennsylvania Avenue NW., Washington, DC 20408.* For more information or additional copies of this form, please write to us at the address above.

IMPORTANT INFORMATION ABOUT YOUR ORDER

You may use this form to order copies of land entry files (such as credit, cash, homestead, and mineral) or surrendered military bounty land warrants files (Acts of 1788, 1812, 1847, 1850, 1852, 1855). **You may request one land entry file per form.**

The National Archives has custody of the land entry files for all Federal public domain states. There are Federal land records for all states **except** the thirteen original states, Vermont, Kentucky, Tennessee, Maine, West Virginia, Texas, and Hawaii. These states were never part of the Federal public domain. Some of the original colonies and eastern states also sold land and awarded military bounty land warrants on their own. Researchers interested in such records should contact the appropriate state archives or historical society. **Please note:** Federal land records document only the **FIRST** transfer of title to land, from the United States to another party. Records of later transfers should be found in county records.

The success of our search depends on the completeness and accuracy of the information you provide in blocks 1-13 on this form. The National Archives has custody of more than ten million individual land entry files. Depending on the time period and state for the land entry file you request, we may need different information from you to find it. Please see the reverse of this page for specific information requirements for different land entry files.

INSTRUCTIONS FOR COMPLETING THIS FORM

Use a separate NATF Form 84 for each file that you request. Remove this instruction sheet. You must complete blocks 3-5 or we cannot search for the file. In addition, you must provide the information required for the type of land entry file you request, as identified on the reverse of this page. Print your name (last, first, middle) and address in the block provided at the bottom of the form, which is your mailing label. The information must be legible on all copies. Keep the PINK copy of the form for your records. Mail the remaining three pages of the form to: *Textual Reference Branch-Land (NWDT1), National Archives and Records Administration, 7th and Pennsylvania Avenue NW, Washington, DC 20408.* **DO NOT SEND PAYMENT WITH THIS FORM.** When we search your order, we will make photocopies of the complete file we locate. For credit card orders, we will mail the copies immediately. We accept MasterCard, VISA, American Express, and NOVUS (Discover, Bravo, Private Issue) credit cards. For other types of orders, we will invoice you for the cost of these copies and hold them until we receive your payment.

SEE THE REVERSE OF THIS PAGE FOR LAND ENTRY FILE
INFORMATION REQUIREMENTS.

PRIVACY ACT STATEMENT AND PAPERWORK REDUCTION ACT PUBLIC BURDEN STATEMENT ON REVERSE OF THIS PAGE.

NATIONAL ARCHIVES TRUST FUND BOARD

INSTRUCTIONS

NATF Form 84 (8-97)

Figure A5.1

National Archives Trust Fund Board   NATF Form 84 (8-97)   OMB Control No. 3095-0033 Expires 02-28-2000

NATIONAL ARCHIVES
ORDER FOR COPIES OF LAND ENTRY FILES
(See Instructions page before completing this form)

| | DATE RECEIVED IN NWDT1 |

INDICATE BELOW THE TYPE OF FILE DESIRED AND THE METHOD OF PAYMENT PREFERRED.

1. FILE TO BE SEARCHED
(Check one box only)

☐ GENERAL LAND ENTRY FILES

☐ BOUNTY-LAND WARRANT FILES

Please refer to Instructions for descriptions of these types of land entry files.

2. PAYMENT METHOD *(Check one box only)*

☐ **CREDIT CARD** for *IMMEDIATE SHIPMENT* of copies
(see Instructions for credit cards we can accept).

Exp. Date:

Signature:

Daytime Phone:

☐ **BILL ME**
(No Credit Card)

REQUIRED MINIMUM IDENTIFICATION OF LAND FILE - MUST BE COMPLETED OR YOUR ORDER CANNOT BE SERVICED

| 3. NAME OF ENTRYMAN *(Give last, first, and middle names)* | 4. LAND LOCATED IN STATE OF | 5. APPROXIMATE DATE OF ENTRY *(Exact date, if known)* |

PLEASE PROVIDE THE FOLLOWING ADDITIONAL INFORMATION FOR GENERAL LAND ENTRY FILES

| PRE-1908 GENERAL LAND ENTRY FILES | POST-1908 GENERAL LAND ENTRY FILES |

6. LEGAL DESCRIPTION OF LAND

| SECTION NUMBER | TOWNSHIP NUMBER | RANGE NUMBER |

10. SERIAL PATENT NUMBER

7. TYPE OF GENERAL LAND ENTRY *(Check one)*   *If other, specify:*

☐ CREDIT   ☐ CASH   ☐ HOMESTEAD ACT

| 8. PATENT, FINAL CERTIFICATE, OR DOCUMENT NUMBER | 9. NAME OF LAND OFFICE |

PLEASE PROVIDE THE FOLLOWING ADDITIONAL INFORMATION FOR MILITARY BOUNTY LAND WARRANTS

| 11. YEAR OF ACT AUTHORIZING WARRANT | 12. NUMBER OF ACRES | 13. WARRANT NUMBER |

If available, please attach one copy of the original land patent, tract book pages,
or Bureau of Land Management GLOARS listing for this land entry.

DO NOT WRITE BELOW - SPACE IS FOR OUR REPLY TO YOU

☐ **NO--We were unable to locate the file you requested above. No payment is required.**

| DATE SEARCHED | SEARCHER |

☐ REQUIRED MINIMUM IDENTIFICATION OF LAND FILE WAS NOT PROVIDED. Please complete blocks 3 (give full name), 4, and 5 and resubmit your order.

☐ A SEARCH WAS MADE BUT THE FILE YOU REQUESTED ABOVE WAS NOT FOUND.

☐ See attached forms, leaflets, or information sheets.

☐ **YES--We located the file you requested above. We have made copies from the file for you. The cost for these copies is $10.**

| DATE SEARCHED | SEARCHER |
| FILE DESIGNATION | |

Make your check or money order payable to NATIONAL ARCHIVES TRUST FUND. Do not send cash. Return this form and your payment in the enclosed envelope to:

NATIONAL ARCHIVES TRUST FUND
P.O. BOX 100221
ATLANTA, GA 30384-0221

PLEASE NOTE: We will hold these copies awaiting receipt of payment for only 45 days from the date completed, which is stamped below. After that time, you must submit another form to obtain photocopies of the file.

THIS IS YOUR MAILING LABEL.

PRESS FIRMLY.

NAME *(Last, First, MI)*	
STREET	
CITY, STATE	ZIP CODE

E181828

INVOICE/REPLY COPY - DO NOT DETACH

Figure A5.2

Request for Earnings and Benefit Estimate Statement

☐ Please check this box if you want to get your statement in Spanish instead of English.

Please print or type your answers. When you have completed the form, fold it and mail it to us. (If you prefer to send your request using the Internet, contact us at http://www.ssa.gov)

1. Name shown on your Social Security card:

First Name _____ Middle Initial _____

Last Name Only _____

2. Your Social Security number as shown on your card:

☐☐☐–☐☐–☐☐☐☐

3. Your date of birth (Mo.-Day-Yr.)

☐☐–☐☐–☐☐☐☐

4. Other Social Security numbers you have used:

☐☐☐–☐☐–☐☐☐☐

☐☐☐–☐☐–☐☐☐☐

5. Your Sex: ☐ Male ☐ Female

For items 6 and 8 show only earnings covered by Social Security. Do NOT include wages from State, local or Federal Government employment that are NOT covered for Social Security or that are covered ONLY by Medicare.

6. Show your actual earnings (wages and/or net self-employment income) for last year and your estimated earnings for this year.

A. Last year's actual earnings: *(Dollars Only)*

$ ☐☐☐,☐☐☐.☐0☐0

B. This year's estimated earnings: *(Dollars Only)*

$ ☐☐☐,☐☐☐.☐0☐0

7. Show the age at which you plan to stop working.

☐☐ *(Show only one age)*

8. Below, show the average yearly amount (not your total future lifetime earnings) that you think you will earn between now and when you plan to stop working. Include performance or scheduled pay increases or bonuses, but not cost-of-living increases.

If you expect to earn significantly more or less in the future due to promotions, job changes, part-time work, or an absence from the work force, enter the amount that most closely reflects your future average yearly earnings.

If you don't expect any significant changes, show the same amount you are earning now (the amount in 6B).

Future average yearly earnings: *(Dollars Only)*

$ ☐☐☐,☐☐☐.☐0☐0

9. Do you want us to send the statement:
   • To you? Enter your name and mailing address.
   • To someone else (your accountant, pension plan, etc.)? Enter your name with "c/o" and the name and address of that person or organization.

Name _____

Street Address (Include Apt. No., P.O. Box, or Rural Route)
_____

City _____ State _____ Zip Code _____

NOTICE:
I am asking for information about my own Social Security record or the record of a person I am authorized to represent. I understand that if I deliberately request information under false pretenses, I may be guilty of a Federal crime and could be fined and/or imprisoned. I authorize you to use a contractor to send the statement of earnings and benefit estimates to the person named in item 9.

▲

Please sign your name (Do Not Print)

_____

Date _____ (Area Code) Daytime Telephone No. _____

Figure A6.1

GENEALOGY FAQ

1. Where are Census Data for Genealogical and/or Historical Research?
    The Census Bureau does not provide genealogical information.
    For archival purposes, information collected from individuals becomes available to the public after 72 years. For businesses the information becomes available after 30 years.
    Copies of decennial census forms from 1790 through 1920 are available, usually on microfilm, for research at the United States National Archives in Washington, D.C. (www.nara.gov/), at Archives regional centers, and at select depository libraries throughout the United States, and the Library of Congress. Ask the reference librarian in your local library about its own holdings and about borrowing film through the National Archives' census microfilm rental program (1-800-788-6282). The records can also be borrowed from the Church of Jesus Christ of Latter Day Saints (LDS) (Mormon) Library in Salt Lake City through any LDS Family History Center. (NOTE: microfilm is analog data, *not* digital . . . it is copies of the original handwritten records.)
    The kind of data requested by genealogists about individuals is not currently available on the Internet.

2. Where Can I Find Information on Immigration or Emigration?
    Immigration records for major U.S. ports have been kept on a regular basis since 1820. These include: Boston, New York, Philadelphia, Baltimore, and New Orleans. Others, such as Mobile and Galveston began keeping records later in the nineteenth century, while western ports (San Francisco and Seattle) began in the last years of the 19th century.
    These records have been microfilmed and are in the custody of the National Archives and LDS. These passenger arrival records include the name of every passenger on the ship, including those who were born or who died during the voyage. Generally, the lists include the full name, age, sex, place of origin, and destination.
    Emigration (departure) lists do exist for some European ports, but not all, and not even every major one (for example, no comprehensive departure lists are known for the British Isles). Among the ports for which emigration lists are available are Stockholm, Oslo, Copenhagen, and Hamburg (but *not* Bremen).
    Microfilm copies of these lists are available at the same places as the immigration lists.

3. What about Naturalization Records?
    By law, a person can be naturalized in any "regular" court. The Immigration and Naturalization Service does have records for the entire country beginning in 1906, but before this time, the procedure will only be located in the records of the court where it took place.

Many of these court records are in the custody of the government which administrates the court. That is to say, a municipal court's records would be in the custody of the city, a county court's records in the custody of the county, etc.

Although court records are routinely indexed, these indexes do not always include the name of each person naturalized. And in fact, during periods of our country's history, only the head of a household would have to be naturalized for the whole family to gain citizenship.

A further caveat: Not everyone who immigrated was naturalized. And although the person being naturalized had to renounce his allegiance to his former state, the records only rarely give the exact place of his birth or previous residence.

4. What about Vital Records (Birth/Marriage/Divorce/Death)?

Generally the states have all vital records, beginning about 1900 (this varies in each state). However, counties will usually have marriage records, beginning at the date the county was organized. For these records write to: Vital Records, P.O. Box 309, Madison, WI 53701, 608-266-1371, fee $12. Like the court records, many of these have been microfilmed and are also available at LDS.

5. Censuses Taken by States or Local Governments

Many local and state governments have taken censuses at different times. Others have not done so. Again, many are available on microfilm at LDS or in the archives of the city/county/state that took the census.

Source: U.S. Census Bureau

Appendix B

Sample Gift Agreements

B-1. FAMILY HISTORY DEPOSIT AGREEMENT

I hereby donate this family history, entitled _____
and dated _____, along with all literary and administrative rights thereto, to _____.

In accepting this family history, the above named institution obtains the right to make the document available for use by all researchers whom it deems qualified, provided the researcher agrees that no names or other personal characteristics obtained from the document which would identify living persons discussed therein are published or otherwise publicly uttered without my permission and, if I so stipulate at the time of the request, the permission of any person so identified.

Signed _____

Date _____

B-2. HISTORICAL MATERIALS GIFT AGREEMENT

I hereby donate to _____
hereinafter referred to as the Repository, the following materials:

_____

_____

_____

Title to the materials shall pass to the Repository upon their delivery to its authorized representative.

The Repository shall administer, care for, and exhibit the materials according to accepted professional standards and practices. The Repository may loan the materials for exhibit elsewhere if in the Repository's judgment reasonable care of the materials can be provided.

When not on public exhibit or loan, the materials shall be made available for examination by the Donor or for research by qualified persons, as determined by the Repository.

Should any or all of the materials be deemed by the Repository to be inappropriate for retention, these may be disposed of, provided that they are first offered to:

_____

_____

_____

Signed: _____ Date: _____

This gift is accepted on behalf of the Repository, subject to the terms set forth.

Signed: _____ Date: _____

B-3. HISTORICAL RECORDS GIFT AGREEMENT

I hereby donate to _____
hereinafter referred to as the Repository, the following materials;

_____

_____

_____

Title to the materials shall pass to the Repository upon their delivery to its authorized representative. Such literary property rights as the Donor possesses in these materials and any others in the custody of the Repository are hereby dedicated to the public.

The Repository shall administer and care for the materials according to accepted professional standards. An inventory of the materials shall be prepared and a copy provided to the Donor. The Donor and persons designated by the Donor shall have access to the materials during the Repository's regular hours of service.

The materials shall be made available for research by qualified persons as determined by the Repository, commencing _____.

Thereafter, the materials may, with the Repository's permission, be copied, reproduced, and/or published.

Should part or all of the materials be deemed by the Repository to be inappropriate for retention, these may be disposed of, provided that the are first offered to

_____.

Signed: _____ Date: _____

This gift is accepted on behalf of the Repository, subject to the terms set forth.

Signed: _____ Date: _____

B-4. ORAL HISTORY GIFT AGREEMENT

I hereby donate the tape recording of this interview, constituting an oral history, recorded on _____, to the archives of _____. I also donate the transcription of the recording. These donations are made with the understanding that when it accepts the deposit of this tape and the accompanying transcript, the archives will obtain all copyright and all other rights, title, and interest that might exist, or that I might have in the tape and transcript being donated.

By virtue of this donation, _____ will have the right to use the work for any research, educational, or other purpose that it may deem appropriate. In addition, this work will also be available to me for my own personal use and to my heirs for their personal use.

The information disclosed by me will be made available to researchers without restriction after _____ (date), except for the passages restricted as follows (attach the pages with the restrictions). Passages so marked will not be made available until _____ (date), after which they will be made available without reservation.

The granting of this permission accords to researchers the right to use information from this oral history in scholarly publications or public utterances, to identify me by name or other personal characteristics, and to identify living persons discussed therein, with the understanding that they will use utmost discretion in so doing.

Other provisions:

_____

_____

_____

_____

_____

INTERVIEWEE   INTERVIEWER

_____   _____
(Signature)   (Signature)

_____   _____
(Typed or printed name)

_____   _____
(Date)   (Date)

Appendix C

Sources of Archival Storage Products and Information

This list of vendors of archival storage products does not represent an endorsement of those included, nor is the list exhaustive. By requesting information from a number of these and other vendors, or by visiting their Web pages, prospective buyers can make comparisons among vendors concerning the quality, availability, and cost of products needed for their specific purposes.

Archival Products
P.O. Box 1413
Des Moines, IA 50305-1413
(800) 247-5323; (515) 262-3191
FAX (515) 262-1535
<www.archival.com>

Gaylord Bros.
Box 4901
Syracuse, NY 13321-4901
(800) 428-3631—help line, Thurs. & Fri.
(800) 448-6160—ordering
FAX (800) 272-3412
e-mail: orders@gaylord.com
<www.gaylord.com>

Archivart
7 Caesar Place
Moonachie, NJ 07074
(201) 804-8986
FAX (201) 935-5964
e-mail: archivart@aol.com
<www.archivart.com>

Hollinger Corp.
P.O. Box 8360
Fredericksburg, VA 22404
(800) 634-0491
FAX (800) 947-8814
e-mail: Hollingercorp@erols.com
<www.hollingercorp.com>

Conservation Resources International
8000-H Forbes Place
Springfield, VA 22151
(800) 634-6932; (703) 321-7730
FAX (703) 321-0629
<www.conservationresources.com>

Light Impressions
P.O. Box 940
Rochester, NY 14603
(800) 828-6216; (716) 271-8960
FAX (800) 828-5539

Conservators' Emporium
100 Standing Rock Circle
Reno, NV 89511
(702) 852-0404
FAX (702) 852-3737
e-mail: consemp@aol.com
<www.consemp.com>

University Products
P.O. Box 101
Holyoke, MA 01041
(800) 762-1165; (800) 628-1912
FAX (800) 532-9281
<www.universityproducts.com>

For a more comprehensive list of vendors, see the Web site of Solinet Preservation Services: <palimpsest.stanford.edu/solinet/consuppl.htm>.

The nonprofit Northeast Document Conservation Center provides detailed information about preservation in Sherelyn Ogden, ed., *Preservation of Library and Archival Materials: A Manual*, 3rd edition, revised and expanded, 1999. This is available on-line at <www.nedcc.org/pubs.htm> or in printed form; write or call the NEDCC at: 100 Brickstone Square, Andover, MA 01810-1494. Telephone: (978) 470-1010. FAX: (978) 475-6021.

The NEDCC Web site also includes a variety of preservation-related Technical Leaflets (available also in print), including one with links to suppliers and services in these areas: appraisals; archival supplies and equipment; bookbinding supplies and equipment; consultants; emergency supplies and equipment; environmental engineering and design; environmental monitors; exhibit materials, design, and construction; housekeeping; indoor air quality; lighting; pest control; reformatting; scientific supplies and equipment; storage equipment, furnishings, and supplies; storage facilities; time capsules; and transport companies.

The NEDCC's mission is "to improve the preservation programs of libraries, archives, museums, and other historical and cultural organizations; to provide the highest quality services to institutions that cannot afford in-house conservation facilities or that require specialized expertise; and to provide leadership to the preservation field."

Appendix D

Using the World Wide Web (WWW)
in Nearby History

The text of this book contains repeated references to the World Wide Web and identifies sites that are particularly useful, even essential, for engaging in research in nearby history. This appendix presents a brief introduction to the World Wide Web and identifies addresses relevant to such research.

Be mindful, however, that the Web changes daily. As it takes on new features and as addresses change and new ones are added, readers will have to bring the information provided here up to date. That will be done best by exploring the Web itself, not through printed sources.

Knowing the meaning of a few terms and codes is helpful to Web users. The *Internet* is a global network that offers a variety of services, including transmission of electronic mail, known as *e-mail,* and access to the *World Wide Web,* the source of vast amounts of information. Users connect with the Web through an institutional or commercial *Internet service provider.* They locate Web information through *browsers,* such as *Netscape* and Microsoft *Internet Explorer.* This is done by entering specific addresses (known as *uniform resource locators,* or *URLs)* or through *search tools* that navigate the Web and display graphics and formatted pages with links to the source or subject being sought. Nine popular search tools, each with distinctive features, are:

Altavista <www.altavista.com>
Excite <www.excite.com>
Google <www.google.com>
Hotbot <www.hotbot.com>
Infoseek <infoseek.go.com>
Lycos <www.lycos.com>
Metacrawler <www.metacrawler.com>
Northern Light <www.northernlight.com>
Yahoo! <www.yahoo.com>.

Note that the addresses are enclosed between angle brackets, which are not part of the addresses. Entering http:// before an Internet address is usually unnecessary; this "hypertext transfer protocol" is necessary for moving documents across the Web, but some computers will enter it automatically.

If you believe that having a glossary of terms and codes used in World Wide Web addresses and understanding how it all works would make you a more effective user, a number of sponsors of Web addresses stand ready to help, including:

Wired magazine: <www.hotwired.com/hardwired/wiredstyle>.

MacintoshOS.com: <www.macintoshos.com/internet.connectivity/internet.glossary.html>.

St. Martin's Press: <www.bedfordstmartins.com/online/>. This site is based on a book titled *Online!: A Reference Guide to Using Internet Resources,* by Andrew Harnack and Eugene Kleppinger (New York: St. Martin's Press, 1998). Several of the chapters appear in their entirety, and for all there are links to other sites.

As noted above, the World Wide Web changes constantly and rapidly. The addresses in this book were verified before it went to press, and even though we have included only those that seem at this time to be among the most stable, they may be different, or possibly even defunct, by the time you attempt to use them. If you encounter one that does not work, try locating it by deleting the last syllable in the address; this may lead you to links that will produce the results you are looking for. If that fails, delete another syllable, and so on, until you come to the *domain name* (which most commonly ends with *.com* for commercial sites; *.edu* for college and university sites; *.gov* or *.us* for federal government sites; *.mil* for military sites; *.net* for network type organizations; *.org* for sites of organizations, many of them nonprofit, but this is becoming something of a catchall domain name). If results still elude you, try entering the name of the site on a search tool, enclosing the phrase in quotation marks so that the search tool will look for the whole phrase and not only individual words in it.

One more thing: The World Wide Web really *is* a web. The threads, or routes, in the web run in many directions and intersect repeatedly. The *homepage* of most Web sites, that is, the first "page" you see when you access a particular one, often displays *links* (technically *hypertext links* or *hyperlinks)* that show connections with other Web sites. Hyperlinks are also represented on the user's screen by highlighted icons or words in the text. By clicking on a highlighted icon or word, the user moves the screen to a new display.

The sections that follow include a directory of addresses likely to be most useful to historians of the nearby past. The addresses are correct as this book goes to press.

WORLD WIDE WEB ADDRESSES

Sites with State Directories

State Museum Associations. The National Conference of State Museum Associations: <www.io.com/~tam/smanet/directory.html>. Phone 512-328-6812 (Texas Association of Museums).

State Humanities Councils. National Endowment for the Humanities: <www.neh.gov/state/index.html>. Phone 800-634-1121 or 202-606-8400.

State Historical Societies. American Association for State and Local History: <www.aaslh.org>; this site also lists numerous other state, regional, and national resource links. Phone: 615-320-3203.

Heritage Preservation Services of the National Park Service lists all State Historic Preservation Officers: <grants.cr.nps.gov/shpos/shpo_search.cfm/>.

National Resources

Census Bureau: <www.census.gov>. Available through this site is the *Statistical Abstract of the United States,* which provides detailed statistics on a great variety of subjects of interest to local historians: <www.census.gov/prod/www/statistical-abstract-us.html>.

Library of Congress: <lcweb.loc.gov>.

National Archives and Records Administration provides information about the hours, locations, service policies, and accessibility of all the facilities it administers nationwide: <www.nara.gov/nara/gotonara.html>. For a directory of the NARA's regional records services see: <www.nara.gov/regional/nrmenu.html>.

National Park Service/National Center for Cultural Resource Stewardship and Partnership Programs. This is a good starting place for information and forms pertaining to historic preservation (but see also the sites identified in chapter 10): <www.cr.nps.gov/whatwedo.htm#HPS>.

Social Security Administration provides forms online (Adobe Acrobat is required for downloading; it is provided free at the site): <www.ssa.gov/online/forms.html>.

Genealogy Sites

AfriGeneas: African-Ancestored Genealogy. Provides databases, discussion groups, and other resources for African Americans: <www.afrigeneas.com>.

Ancestry.com. Has a large family history and genealogy database and links to a wide variety of resources: <www.ancestry.com/>. Some of the information is fee-based.

Census Bureau: <www.census.gov/genealogy/www/>. (As with the Social Security Administration site, Adobe Acrobat is required for downloading; it is provided free at the site).

Church of Jesus Christ of the Latter-day Saints. Has millions of family records: <www.familysearch.org/>.

Cyndi's List of Genealogy Sites: <www.cyndislist.com>. This is perhaps the most comprehensive genealogy site, with links to many others.

JewishGen: The Home of Jewish Genealogy: <www.jewishgen.org>.

My History Is America's History. A Millennium Project of the National Endowment for the Humanities: <www.myhistory.org>

National Archives and Records Administrations Genealogy Page: <www.nara.gov/genealogy/genindex.html>.

Rootsweb. This commercial site provides many resources, such as a large surname index and links to many more sites, including others listed here: <www.rootsweb.com/>.

USGenWeb Project: <www.usgenweb.com>. This expanding site includes genealogical information gathered in all states and many counties.

Organizations

American Association of Museums: <www.aam-us.org>.

American Historical Association: <www.theaha.org/>.

American Library Association: <www.ala.org>.

Association of Living History, Farm and Agricultural Museums. Provides links to hundreds of museum sites: <www.alhfam.org>.

Heritage Preservation. Programs and publications provide guidance on the proper care and maintenance of historic documents, books and archives, works of art, photographs, architecture, monuments, anthropological artifacts, historic objects and family heirlooms, and natural science specimens: <www.heritagepreservation.org>.

National Council on Public History: <www.iupui.edu/~ncph/home.html>.

National Trust for Historic Preservation: <www.nthp.org>.

Oral History Association: <omega.dickinson.edu/organizations/oha>.

Organization of American Historians provides links to many historical organizations and resources: <www.oah.org/announce/links.html>.

Teaching History, a journal published at Emporia State University. Provides links to many historical organizations and resources: <www.emporia.edu/socsci/journal/link_am.htm>.

Other

World Wide Web Virtual Library—History: Central Catalog (University of Kansas Virtual Library): <www.ukans.edu/history/VL/>. Provides access to a vast array of resources and is accompanied by searchable databases.

Index

Page numbers in italic refer to figures or tables.

About the Authors

David E. Kyvig, Presidential Research Professor and Professor of History at Northern Illinois University, is a former president of the National Council on Public History. His book *Explicit and Authentic Acts: Amending the U.S. Constitution, 1776–1995* won the 1997 Bancroft Prize and other awards.

Myron A. Marty is the Ann G. and Sigurd E. Anderson University Professor at Drake University. His publications include *Daily Life in the United States, 1960–1990: Decades of Discord* and (with Shirley Marty) *Frank Lloyd Wright's Taliesin Fellowship*.